Sheri Oz, MSc
Sarah-Jane Ogiers

Overcoming Childhood Sexual Trauma
A Guide to Breaking Through the Wall of Fear for Practitioners and Survivors

*Pre-publication
REVIEWS,
COMMENTARIES,
EVALUATIONS . . .*

"**A**n interesting collaborative effort between a trauma therapist and her ex-client providing hope to sexual abuse survivors regardless of where they may be on their healing journeys. The book shows that it is possible for a survivor to break through that 'Wall of Fear' and emerge a happier, healthier person, a person who is free to make choices based on her present and future, not her past."

Wanda Karriker, PhD
Retired Psychologist and Novelist

"**O**z's expertise and Ogiers' insights into the nature of child sexual abuse shine through the whole book. The authors, a therapist and a client, engage in a beautiful dance in their process to cross the 'Wall of Fear.' The book combines theory and practice enriched with techniques and journaling as well as questionnaires and exercises which make it an excellent tool for both therapists and survivors of trauma. Clinicians should give special attention to the chapter which deals with issues and dilemmas they face in their work with CSA survivors. It is highly recommended for CSA survivors, beginner therapists, and clinicians. A must for all health professionals!"

Andreas Orphanides, MSc
*Marriage and Family Therapist,
AAMFT Clinical Member*

More pre-publication
REVIEWS, COMMENTARIES, EVALUATIONS . . .

"Sheri Oz and Sara-Jane Ogiers have done an excellent job. They provide a very clear explanation of how children's minds react to childhood abuse and the effects of CSA on the developing child's cognitive, emotional, and interpersonal development are discussed in an accessible manner for both professional and lay persons alike. Ogiers provides a heartwarming, open, and honest depiction of the experience of traumatization from CSA and the trials and tribulations of recovery.

The authors also provide a clear and realistic description of the difficulties encountered during the therapeutic process for both client and therapist, as well as the benefits of persevering with the often difficult emotional process of recovery from CSA. This book can assist the most despairing of clients to have hope when they need it the most and to know that they are not alone in their experience. Oz's openness provides clinicians with the understanding that what they experience when treating survivors of CSA, including inevitable human error, is shared by other therapists as well. Therapists will also find the material in the Appendix to be of practical value."

Anne M. Dietrich, PhD
Registered Psychologist,
Vancouver General Hospital
Outpatient Psychiatry

"With a voice filled with compassion and professional expertise, Sheri Oz, a gifted clinician and an accomplished scholar, and Sarah-Jane Ogiers, a courageous and inspirational survivor, have completed one of the most powerful and moving books ever published on the subject of child sexual abuse. Together, they vividly describe the mechanisms by which the victims of child sexual abuse repress traumatic memories, shut off their feelings, and struggle to form intimate connections in their lives. They explain in rich detail the slow and painful yet hopeful and healing therapeutic process of helping people who have been sexually abused to move from the horror, shame, and fear of victimization to the self-understanding, self-acceptance, and optimism associated with survival.

Any practitioner who truly wants to know how to assist children and adults who have suffered the terror of childhood sexual abuse should read this deeply informative book. And any person who has been violated by a sexually abusive adult will find comfort, encouragement, and recovery that are chronicled in this captivating book. This is a masterpiece!"

Mark S. Kiselica, PhD, HSPP, NCC, LPC
Professor of Counselor Education,
The College of New Jersey;
Fellow, American Psychological Association

More pre-publication
REVIEWS, COMMENTARIES, EVALUATIONS . . .

"In this beautifully written book, Sheri Oz and Sarah-Jane Ogiers set out to create a useful resource for both therapists and clients. They have succeeded! This is a book that is both intelligent and compassionate. Oz exposes the reader to the current theory, practice, and research in the area of childhood sexual abuse which is grounded in the lived experiences of both authors. Ogiers invites us to walk alongside her as she courageously penetrates the wall of fear built by traumatic experience. This book moves us further in the direction of therapy and authorship as true collaboration. I recommend this book to my clients, colleagues, and students."

Sharon Mayne Devine, MSc
Couple and Family Therapist,
On Faculty in the Department of Family
Relations and Applied Nutrition,
The University of Guelph

"This is one of the very few successful combinations of a book as a clinical professional guide to the understanding, knowledge, and treatment of sexual abuse, as well as a deeply moving and well reflected self-report. It treads the fine line of being compassionate and professional without being confessional. The professional data guide and knowledge and the self-report enhance each other in a complementary and illuminating way, enhancing the understanding of the effects of sexual abuse and the complex position of the therapist in the therapeutic process. The book illustrates the huge impact of CSA and the courage a sexual abuse victim needs to go through in the process of healing.

What impressed me most was the courage of the two writers to reflect on experiences, and to challenge and examine traditional roles of therapists and therapeutic techniques, especially with the need in sexual abuse work to examine the use of the self of therapists involved in victim work. The unique dialogue between patient and therapist enhances the understanding of each other's position and the complex process as a whole. This aspect makes the book an invaluable contribution to clinicians and women and men who have experienced sexual abuse themselves."

Tilman Fürniss, MD, MPhil, FRCPsych,
Professor of Child and Adolescent Psychiatry,
University Hospital, Muenster, Germany

The Haworth Press
New York • London • Oxford

Overcoming Childhood Sexual Trauma

A Guide to Breaking Through the Wall of Fear for Practitioners and Survivors

The Haworth Press
Maltreatment, Trauma, and Interpersonal Aggression

Identifying Child Molesters: Preventing Child Sexual Abuse by Recognizing the Patterns of the Offenders by Carla van Dam

Patterns of Child Abuse: How Dysfunctional Transactions are Replicated in Individuals, Families, and the Child Welfare System by Michael Karson

Growing Free: A Manual for Survivors of Domestic Violence by Wendy Susan Deaton and Michael Hertica

We Are Not Alone: A Guidebook for Helping Professionals and Parents Supporting Adolescent Victims of Sexual Abuse by Jade Christine Angelica

We Are Not Alone: A Teenage Girl's Personal Account of Incest from Disclosure Through Prosecution and Treatment by Jade Christine Angelica

We Are Not Alone: A Teenage Boy's Personal Account of Child Sexual Abuse from Disclosure Through Prosecution and Treatment by Jade Christine Angelica

The Insiders: A Man's Recovery from Traumatic Childhood Abuse by Robert Blackburn Knight

Simple and Complex Post-Traumatic Stress Disorder: Strategies for Comprehensive Treatment in Clinical Practice edited by Mary Beth Williams and John F. Sommer Jr.

Child Maltreatment Risk Assessments: An Evaluation Guide by Sue Righthand, Bruce Kerr, and Kerry Drach

Mother-Daughter Incest: A Guide for Helping Professionals by Beverly A. Ogilvie

Munchausen by Proxy Maltreatment: Identification, Intervention, and Case Management by Louisa J. Lasher and Mary S. Sheridan

Effects of and Interventions for Childhood Trauma from Infancy Through Adolescence: Pain Unspeakable by Sandra B. Hutchison

The Socially Skilled Child Molester: Differentiating the Guilty from the Falsely Accused by Carla van Dam

Child Trauma Handbook: A Guide for Helping Trauma-Exposed Children and Adolescents by Ricky Greenwald

A Safe Place to Grow: A Group Treatment Manual for Children in Conflicted, Violent, and Separating Homes by Vivienne Roseby, Janet Johnston, Bettina Gentner, and Erin Moore.

Overcoming Child Sexual Trauma: A Guide to Breaking Through the Wall of Fear for Practitioners and Survivors by Sheri Oz and Sarah-Jane Ogiers

Overcoming Childhood Sexual Trauma

A Guide to Breaking Through the Wall of Fear for Practitioners and Survivors

Sheri Oz, MSc
Sarah-Jane Ogiers

The Haworth Press
New York • London • Oxford

For more information on this book or to order, visit
http://www.haworthpress.com/store/product.asp?sku=5668

or call 1-800-HAWORTH (800-429-6784) in the United States and Canada
or (607) 722-5857 outside the United States and Canada

or contact orders@HaworthPress.com

Published by

The Haworth Press, Inc., 10 Alice Street, Binghamton, NY 13904-1580.

PUBLISHERS NOTE
The development, preparation, and publication of this work has been undertaken with great care. However, the Publisher, employees, editors, and agents of The Haworth Press are not responsible for any errors contained herein or for consequences that may ensue from use of materials or information contained in this work. The Haworth Press is committed to the dissemination of ideas and information according to the highest standards of intellectual freedom and the free exchange of ideas. Statements made and opinions expressed in this publication do not necessarily reflect the views of the Publisher, Directors, management, or staff of The Haworth Press, Inc., or an endorsement by them.

Identities and circumstances of individuals discussed in this book have been changed to protect confidentiality.

Cover design by Lora Wiggins.

Library of Congress Cataloging-in-Publication Data

Oz, Sheri.
    Overcoming childhood sexual trauma : a guide to breaking through the wall of fear for practitioners and survivors / Sheri Oz, Sarah-Jane Ogiers.
      p. ; cm.
    Includes bibliographical references and index.
    ISBN-13: 978-0-7890-2979-9 (case : alk. paper)
    ISBN-10: 0-7890-2979-0 (case : alk. paper)
    ISBN-13: 978-0-7890-2980-5 (soft : alk. paper)
    ISBN-10: 0-7890-2980-4 (soft : alk. paper)
    1. Adult child sexual abuse victims—Case studies. I. Ogiers, Sarah-Jane. II. Title.
    [DNLM: 1. Child Abuse, Sexual—psychology—Case Reports. 2. Stress Disorders, Post-Traumatic—psychology—Case Reports. 3. Adult. 4. Child Abuse, Sexual—therapy—Case Reports. 5. Survivors—psychology—Case Reports. WM 170 O99t 2007]
RC569.5.A28O92 2007
616.85'83690651—dc22

                                          2006017058

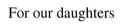

For our daughters

ABOUT THE AUTHORS

Sheri Oz, MSc, is founder and director of Machon Eitan, a private clinic for the treatment of sex trauma survivors and their families, located in Kiryat Motzkin in northern Israel. She is considered one of the country's top experts in the area of child sexual abuse. She writes and lectures on topics related to childhood sexual abuse and therapist sexual abuse, provides clinical training and supervision to therapists, and consults with public agencies regarding issues of mandated reporting and early intervention strategies when there is suspicion of child sexual abuse. She is one of the founding members of the newly formed Israel Association for the Treatment of Domestic Violence and Sexual Abuse and is on its ethics committee.

Sarah-Jane Ogiers is employed in the hi-tech industry and is a graduate student of English literature at Haifa University and a closet fiction and poetry writer. Her contributions to projects such as this book are intended to help others learn from her experiences and gain strength in their own struggles with recovery. She has served as a "buddy" for individual survivors who do not yet have a support network of their own. She has also been invited to speak in support group meetings to answer survivors' questions as one who has "been there."

CONTENTS

PART II: THE JOURNEY

PART III: COMPANIONS ON THE JOURNEY

Foreword

It is both a pleasure and an honor to write this foreword to *Overcoming Childhood Sexual Trauma* for this is an important addition to the literature, and it gets it right. This book offers both the therapist's and the survivor/client's perspectives on the process and aftermath of sexual abuse and what is required in the healing process. It admirably meets its goals of adding "another blow to the wall of denial surrounding the subject of childhood sexual abuse, creating yet another crack through which to view the horrible reality of sexual terrorism in a world that has been hesitant to accept its existence and insensitive to the needs of its many victims" and providing "a road map for victims and survivors against which they can measure their progress along the path toward healing."

Part I, "Living with the Trauma," offers one of the most compelling descriptions I've read of what it means to an individual to be sexually abused, especially when perpetrated by someone in a role that mandates protection and trust rather than exploitation. The authors' metaphors the "World of Trauma" and the "Wall of Fear" are apt descriptions of what the sexually abused child experiences. Many of the child's behaviors that may seem strange or hard to interpret by those unfamiliar with or uninformed about child abuse trauma are explained with great clarity, and from a position of empathy. The historical and contemporaneous diary entries and commentaries by co-author Sarah-Jane add first-person immediacy to the more academic description provided by therapist Sheri Oz. Their descriptions give a developmental overview of the impact of child sexual abuse and illustrate how the aftereffects can impact the victim's life in large and small ways across all life domains, ranging from the child's self-concept to her or his ability to choose a suitable partner and to adequately parent children. The material presented here is up-to-date theoretically;

Overcoming Childhood Sexual Trauma
Published by The Haworth Press, Inc., 2006, All rights reserved.
doi:10.1300/5668_a

however, the authors have taken great care not to just parrot the litera-ture but to challenge some of it from a victim-sensitive position. Too often the victims of sexual abuse have been misunderstood and blamed for the reactions caused by the abuse. This book challenges this viewpoint, replacing it with cogent and well-thought-out expla-nations for a wide variety of reactions and behaviors.

For survivors, healing from childhood sexual abuse is an act of courage. It is a daunting process that often lasts years and involves nothing short of rebuilding the self and developing trust in others. Survivors must be able to break the secrecy surrounding their abuse and, over time, learn to express their emotions about it. Only by iden-tifying the Wall of Fear and the various defensive strategies that they have developed can the formerly abused adult work through the World of Trauma. The story with its attendant emotions and cogni-tions must be processed to the point where they are no longer impedi-ments to the individual's freedom of body and mind. Resolution brings with it a lessening of the symptoms, defenses, and maladaptive behaviors, leaving the individual with more life options and choices that are less encumbered by the past.

The therapeutic relationship is crucial and is where many of the most salient issues are played out. It is both catalyst and context for the client's potential development and where he or she enacts rela-tional themes from the past. The therapist must first and foremost be aware of the various relational issues that will be presented by survi-vor clients (along with all of the other abuse-related reactions and their various manifestations). Therapists walk a number of fine lines in doing this work: They must strive to be both emotionally open and available while maintaining appropriate boundaries. They need to be disclosing of emotions "in the moment" and "in the real time" of the session but not be too self-revelatory in a way that encourages the cli-ent to breech boundaries and roles. Therapists must present them-selves as humans who make mistakes and who communicate to the point of repair when a rupture within the relationship occurs and not present themselves as unavailable "authorities on high" who have all of the answers. Finally, they must recognize and appreciate the strength and resilience of their clients and must encourage empower-ment and personal responsibility. Throughout the therapeutic en-deavor, they must operate from a position of empathy and compas-sion—qualities that are conveyed throughout this book. This book is a gift to survivor clients and therapists alike. It helps them understand the difficult terrain of healing from sexual abuse and guides them on the journey.

Christine A. Courtois, PhD
Psychologist, Independent practice, Washington, DC;
Clinical consultant, The CENTER:
Posttraumatic Disorders Program,
The Psychiatric Institute of Washington
Author: Recollections of Sexual Abuse: Treatment Principles *and* Guidelines Healing the Incest Wound: Adult Survivors in Therapy

Preface

Sheri

Sarah-Jane and I were a team long before we decided to combine our efforts in writing this book. Sarah-Jane came to me for therapy and asked me to be her partner in what turned out to be a most painful journey, backward in time, to the little girl who was hurt by her father and neglected by her mother. Sarah-Jane was a most remarkable client to have—resourceful, brave, intelligent, determined, stubborn, demanding of herself and of me, and more.

Sarah-Jane kept a diary during therapy. She would read me parts of it and I was impressed with the strength of her descriptions of her mental state as she passed from one crisis to the next, never believing an end to the nightmare would come. This window into her life outside our sessions was invaluable, and it helped me to refine my growing understanding of the stages of sexual abuse therapy as depicted in the model in this book. As I worked with more and more clients who suffered childhood sexual abuse, I was witness to the validity of this schema.

When clients understand the stages of therapy and recovery it helps them endure the process with a little more confidence. Therefore, I felt it was critical for clients and their therapists to know that when survivors describe feeling crazy they are usually experiencing emotions that they had previously buried. During an abuse event, as will be explained in this book, children generally cannot let themselves feel anything, as the emotions generated are more intense than their short life experience has equipped them to handle. This usually causes them to shut their feelings off altogether. Later, in situations having nothing to do with the abuse, any kind of feeling can be a source of fear rather than a normal part of being human. In therapy, the emotions that arise are so overwhelming that the client really feels he or she is going insane.

Overcoming Childhood Sexual Trauma
Published by The Haworth Press, Inc., 2006, All rights reserved.
doi:10.1300/5668_b

Sometimes therapists grow fearful as well of the seemingly uncontainable swell of fear, pain, and rage. My clients often groan when I repeat my mantra: What you're feeling now are *just feelings*. These emotions just give you information about yourself that you have not been able to accept until now. This fear, this pain, this rage—they are *just feelings*.

"But what do I do now?" my clients ask.

I answer: "Nothing. You do nothing. Now is the time to just be, not to do. Just to feel. Just to let the feelings be there. This *doing nothing* is the hardest thing you will ever have to do."

The meaning of this will become clear in this book as Sarah-Jane's diaries bring us into her world as an abused child and into her life during the most difficult moments of therapy. They show the way into and the way out of the nightmare her life had become. They show how she learned to just be, to just feel, to "live."

I deeply respect and appreciate the courage of those individuals who choose to break their silence and let me into their worlds, so that I can bear witness to the horrors they have endured. Some come to me still very much the victim, while most are definitely survivors who have decided to try to heal the wounds of terror inflicted so long ago.

The most difficult wound of all is that of shame. Regardless of how much society grows aware of the rampant sexual and emotional victimization perpetrated against children and youth in their own families, schools, and neighborhoods, the victim still feels shamed. Shamed by the initiation into acts far removed from the world of children growing up in healthy environments, and shamed by the uncontrollable responsiveness of their own bodies that makes it seem as if their victimizers were right when they told them they liked it. If this book succeeds at nothing else, let it succeed at placing the shame back where it belongs: in the hands of the victimizer and in the hands of a society that refuses to take a more active part in breaking the chains of secrecy and silence.

In this book, in addition to Sarah-Jane, other survivors will speak for themselves. All voices here are those of clients I have worked with. However, their stories are combined and demographic details changed slightly to protect their identities. They, themselves, will probably not be able to recognize any one story as being wholly their own but will find parts here and there that fit them. This highlights that their experiences of victimization and survival are more similar than they are different, even though they come from many kinds of families and all parts of the globe. Among them are Jews, Muslims, and Christians. Some of their families have long roots in Israel; others are the sabra children of immigrants from Europe, Asia, Africa, and the Americas. Some immigrated to Israel as children, and others as young adults, from Argentina, England, India, Morocco, South Africa, Spain, and the United States.

Some are the oldest and some the youngest in families with many children, while others are the only child in a family. Some are raised in intact nuclear families with large or small extended families, and some are raised with divorced, and sometimes remarried, parents. Some have been removed from their parents' home (not always because of disclosure of sexual abuse) and grow up in boarding schools or with foster families.

Regardless of the differences, the clients have all grown up troubled, bearing a phenomenally powerful secret that those around them chose not to see. They lived secret lives of trauma in parallel with the apparently normal facades they presented to the world. They screamed silent screams underneath a mask that protected not them but both their victimizers and others around them who wanted life to run smoothly. This book seeks to add another blow to the wall of denial surrounding the subject of childhood sexual abuse, creating yet another crack through which to view the horrible reality of sexual terrorism in a world that has been hesitant to accept its existence and insensitive to the needs of its many victims.

Sarah-Jane

July 9, 1994

I owe it to myself to record this trip back into my childhood. And maybe I even owe it to other survivors. Perhaps one day I'll meet a woman like me who doesn't understand what the hell she's going through and I can show her that she's not alone.

I thought it pertinent to open my introduction with my thoughts and feelings on childhood sexual abuse in general, but each time I started to write I found that everything I wrote had already been said. Then I realized that I was using other people's words because I did not have my own. And I did not have my own because I could not relate to "childhood sexual abuse in general." Well, how could I? There is nothing general about it—to me it is undoubtedly specific. It happened to me, I can't talk about it objectively, it's personal. In this book, you will read about my personal experience with childhood sexual abuse. So what is left to say? Just this. . .

Nothing that has ever been said or written about childhood sexual abuse can capture the horror and pain—physical and/or emotional—of a child who is being used to satisfy the distorted sexual needs of an adult he or she loves. Nothing can express the emptiness and desolation a child feels at the betrayal of his or her trust. No words can describe the legacy of shame that these children carry with them into adulthood: A man whose memories of the abuse he suffered surface during lovemaking with his partner; a woman whose string of unsuitable partners use her for sex and then walk away, while she moves on to the next in line, to a place so familiar to her that she cannot resist its magnetic pull. Many of these casualties—children and adults—spend their lives trying to hold on to their sanity.

When I decided that "holding on to my sanity" was no longer enough, I took a deep breath and began my journey, hoping to reach a place of peace with myself. I had no idea it would take so long, and even though much of it was almost unbearable, I would not take back a minute.

I was lucky to find Sheri as one of the guides for my journey, and I am grateful for her inexhaustible well of love and nurturing. I also feel privileged to have known her as a person, not just a therapist. For although she is not the only good soul helping people recover from childhood sexual abuse, the energy and unflagging determination she invests in her "mission" is something to see.

Several years after I ended therapy with Sheri I decided I wanted to give something back. In spite of all the anguish I went through, I felt blessed, blessed with good, kind, patient people who stood by my side, by no means passively, while I struggled to face a childhood that had warped my perception of reality and crushed my self-esteem. They held my hand while I healed—prodding me when I stalled, embracing me when I needed comfort, waiting when I needed space. Despite my rotten start in life and my uncertainty about the existence of a God who does not stop children from being abused, it does rather look as though someone has been looking out for me. And I am thankful for that.

The best way I could think of to repay this "debt" was to try and help other survivors of childhood sexual abuse. Despite the feminine gender of the survivor I refer to in my opening journal entry, I would be very pleased if I could help male survivors too. So, I started writing this book with Sheri, hoping that telling my story might make a difference to men and women whose souls were battered and bruised, hearts broken and futures snatched away from them in one fell swoop, when they were at their most vulnerable. I want my story to show them that they can nurse their souls back to health, heal their hearts, and take their lives back. They won't be as good as new; they'll be better. For when facing the ghosts of the past that have haunted them ever since they were first betrayed they will see that there *is* a dinosaur in the living room and realize that the only way to make it go away is to find out why it is there. Even if they sometimes fear that facing the truth will kill them, they *will* live to tell the tale.

Sheri and Sarah-Jane

This book provides a road map for victims and survivors against which they can measure their progress along the path toward healing. All too often, those attempting to find relief from the ravages of abuse—within therapy and without—have no means to assess the distance they have gone at any given point, nor do they have any clear indication of what still lies ahead. They feel lost in an unfamiliar swamp with no sight of dry land on the horizon. It is not enough, for many of them, to know that the therapist they trust and depend on is familiar with the territory; they want to be able to orient themselves. Although the therapist holds the compass, it does not mean that the client cannot see the map. So here is the map as we know it to be. We hope it helps.

Acknowledgments

Sheri

Participants in lectures and workshops I have conducted in Israel and elsewhere raised the idea that I put my thoughts and clinical experience into print. I thank them for giving me the impetus to embark upon this project. I am very grateful for the support and encouragement I have received from friends and colleagues without whom the book would not have been carried through to fruition. I am especially indebted to Sarah-Jane and the many individuals, couples, and families who have sought out my help. Through their trust and courage they have taught me so much about trauma, resilience, hope, and patience.

A number of friends and colleagues have read this book, in part or in full. Their comments and suggestions have contributed to making this a sounder presentation of my ideas and of Sarah-Jane's experience. I list them here in alphabetic order: Haim Aharonson, for his authenticity, openness, and attention to detail; Bob Buckwald, who inspired me to write, and his wife, Sue, who lifts my spirits; Amy Cohen, for her open heart; Ruti Gavish, for her enthusiasm, her sharp mind and her caring; Annita Jones, a warm and enthusiastic teacher; Wanda Karriker, who is an inspiration and whose sensitivity and strength come out loud and clear in the written word; Mark Kiselika, a virtual colleague who has been so warm and supportive; Ivy Medeiros, an indefatigable, amazing woman whose laugh stays with me across time and the ocean; Esti Neeman, with whom I can struggle over difficult issues and ideas, both personal and professional; Yael Reiner, cheerfully supportive; Adriane Schuster, whose upbeat enthusiasm is so catchy and her husband, Richard, my good, serious, funny friend for so many years; Bonnie Simone, a true friend and unique individual; Yvonne Tauber, who supports me and challenges me; Rivka Yahav, who nudges me along persistently and makes me

Overcoming Childhood Sexual Trauma
Published by The Haworth Press, Inc., 2006, All rights reserved.
doi:10.1300/5668_c   *xxi*

laugh. Thanks also to Shimshon Rubin and Pam Farkas for their supportive comments.

In today's world of the Internet, individuals I have never met, too numerous to name here, sent me references and ideas for literature searches. Others agreed to read particular chapters and give me feedback. Thank you Kymbra Clayton and Clark Peters. I have had the rare privilege of corresponding with well-known professionals in the field and feel honored that they were willing to take the time to exchange e-mails and help me iron out some ideas for this book: Christine Courtois, Laura Davis, Julie Exline, Steven Jay Lynn, Jeremy Safran, Alan Schore, Jan C.M. Willems, and Ofer Zur.

A special word of thanks to Yazeed Karyanni, who encouraged me to look deeper into the subject of religion and healing and to Reverend Thomas Ball, Judge Mohammed Abu Obied, Rabbi Dr. Eli Kahn, Father Dr. George Khoury and Dr. Hani Jahshan who helped me in this venture. I will pick up this ball and continue this line of exploration. It is fascinating.

My appreciation is also extended to friends and colleagues who have not read this work prepublication, but who have, in different ways, contributed to my professional development: Khawla Abu-Baker, Gafnit Agassi, Vered Arbit, Dorit Balshan-Radai, Shlomit Bar, Ahuva Beny, Gerald French, Rachel Gezler-Yosef, Claude Guldner and the staff at the Guelph University Family Therapy Unit, Liz Halevi and the Haifa Rape Crisis Center, Rivka Mosari, Orit Nave, Ruth Ragulant-Levy, Ilana Sobol, Rali Taus. A big special thank-you hug to Danny Brom, who gives me boundless support and makes me laugh when I least expect to.

I would like to thank my mother, Evelyn Weinrib, for reading the manuscript from cover to cover in spite of its difficult subject matter and for sharing her thoughts about it with me.

And, of course, my two daughters. I thank both of you for putting up with my lack of time and attention as I focused on this project. You have your mother back now.

Sarah-Jane

When I told people that I was writing, together with Sheri, a book about recovering from childhood sexual abuse, I was moved by their reaction. Not one of them, regardless of how well they knew me, had anything but support and empathy to offer. Many thanks to all those who encouraged me.

I would also like to thank the following people:

Laura Cane and Liat Slann for giving me the benefit of their writing skills and advice on organizing the material, not to mention soothing my writing anxiety and making me laugh on more than one occasion.

Jonathan Beimel for never letting me forget that I wanted to write a book, and for being a good friend even though he thinks I'm weird.

The Dahans and the Vincents, who, at different times in my life, provided me with a family when I most needed it and who gave me the hope and faith I needed to build a family of my own.

Anna Handelzalts and Tal Horowitz, who with their compassion and sense of humor made my days at work bearable and safe during the difficult moments of my healing process.

Maggy Burrowes, my dear friend of thirty-seven years, for her gift of love, which cuts across time and space, and for lighting up my life—childhood, adolescence, and adulthood—with her honesty and devotion.

Mazi Elkayam, my soul mate, for holding my hand during this long and often painful journey. Her faith in me, together with her love, patience, obstinate refusal to freak out, and ability to make me laugh, nurtured me and made it possible to reach the milestones.

Sheri Oz and Sary Shell, my favorite therapists, for helping me face the truth, guiding me toward the light, and showing me a way to reclaim my life, but most of all for believing I could do it.

My ex-husband for giving me the space to write this book, and for feeding me while I wrote it, without grumbling too much.

My two beautiful daughters for being so brave and understanding while I wrote this book. It's so easy to love you.

PART I:
LIVING WITH THE TRAUMA

Chapter 1

Why Is Childhood Sexual Abuse
So Traumatic?

Sheri Oz

I am not afraid of storms, for I am learning how to sail my ship.

Louisa May Alcott

It is night. Thursday night. Another workweek is almost over. Somewhere in the distance I can hear a rock song playing. Maybe a high school student is studying late for an exam. A neighbor's dog barks and mine synchronizes a howl together with him. As I lay in bed drifting in the twilight zone between waking and sleeping I think of those for whom this world between worlds is a daily terror. Then I see in my mind's eye a six-year-old girl who will not let herself fall asleep before she knows for sure that her father has gone to bed in his own room, and another one who cries out in her heart, silently begging her stepfather to stop as he enters her body from behind. Yet another little girl prays to Jesus on the cross above her bed to save her from the ripping pain and the humiliation brought upon her by an uncle. I see the little boy of eight whose father is teaching him how to masturbate in the shower, and the teenager in the boarding school whose bigger roommate sodomizes him. At another boarding school in another part of the country a group of older girls molest a younger boy during lunch break. Somewhere else a brother fondles his little sister gently, partly out of curiosity but mostly as a respite from a loveless and lonely home, and she enjoys the warmth of his closeness but is wracked with guilt. Another older brother in another town is not so gentle and inflicts a great deal of shame. In a children's house in a

Overcoming Childhood Sexual Trauma
Published by The Haworth Press, Inc., 2006, All rights reserved.
doi:10.1300/5668_01

kibbutz a dark shadow hovers over a little girl who is pretending to be asleep—he makes her body feel funny and then he's gone. A community bomb shelter in a small town becomes a torture chamber for a four-year-old girl who is repeatedly abused there by six teenage boys for more than a year and a half. And on and on and on. Each of these children are the secret victims of someone else's war—someone who was also badly hurt in some way (not necessarily sexually) but did not fight his or her own demons.

As can be seen, many different behaviors fall under the heading of childhood sexual abuse (CSA), but what makes CSA so traumatic? This chapter will address this question by (1) defining CSA, looking at issues concerning gender and age of victim and perpetrator, children's natural needs for love and protection, informed consent, the abuse of power, and secrecy, and by (2) describing the child's experience of the sexual abuse event.

DEFINING CSA

Among professionals in the field, no absolute agreement exists regarding what exactly constitutes CSA (Haugaard, 2000). In some studies, only those behaviors that include some kind of physical contact with the sex organs are considered sexually abusive (Finklehor, 1984; Fleming, 1997). Most workers in the field, however, are of the opinion that sexual abuse includes a wide range of behaviors along a continuum from milder to more severe: inappropriate sexual remarks made to a minor by an adult; ogling of a child or teenager by an adult; an adult's exposure of his or her sexual organs in view of a minor; peeping at a child or teen who is dressing, using the toilet, in the bath, etc.; kissing; fondling; mutual masturbation; and penetration (Sgroi et al., 1982; Halperin et al., 1996).

The extent of the resulting harm is not merely a factor of where the offending behavior is on the continuum, but is a combination of the sexual inappropriateness and other aspects of family relationships (DiLillo, 2001; Nelson et al., 2000). In fact, my clinical experience shows that serious consequences can occur from a single abuse event when the family environment is toxic and unsupportive. On the other hand, the potential serious negative impact of ongoing abuse can, in some cases, be mitigated by an appropriate response to a child's disclosure of abuse, leaving the victim relatively unaffected in the long term.

Furthermore, some professionals contend that abuse without any form of touching is not necessarily less damaging than abuse that includes penetration (Courtois, 1988; Dolan, 1991; Halperin et al., 1996). Survivors' experiences, such as those of Ronit and Benny described in the following case study, support this contention.

Ronit's father considered himself to be a modern, open person. He always used to say he wanted his children to receive a liberal sex education. For this reason, he forbade members of the family to close the doors to their rooms when changing their clothes. He allowed them to shut the bathroom door, but not to lock it. Ronit remembers how she expended a great deal of energy trying to avoid the piercing eyes of her father and brothers. In addition, her father would walk around the house in underpants that were too loose and that did not cover his genitals. He would make a point, it seemed to her, of calling her to bring him something he "forgot" to take into the shower with him. She would often find him masturbating when she opened the curtain to give him what he had requested. At age thirteen, Ronit tried to get her mother to support her in her need for privacy, but her mother stood by the wishes of her father.

When she married, Ronit was unable to undress in front of her husband. She was overcome with apparently inexplicable rage when he changed clothes beside her. The couple developed an elaborate ritual around undressing and going to bed at night so that Ronit did not have to be exposed to her husband's naked body. Furthermore, she found the motherly tasks that involved contact with her children's bodies to be particularly distasteful and today feels guilty about any negative messages she may have imparted to them over the years. With time, the issues of sexuality with her husband became so complex and burdened with guilt that she became totally unresponsive sexually to avoid the pain and confusion she felt.

As opposed to Ronit, who felt emotionally isolated from both her parents, Benny was particularly close to his mother. His father was absent from home much of the time and Benny became his mother's companion, giving her advice with regard to his younger siblings and also providing emotional support when she was depressed. During their evening talks, after the younger children had gone to bed, she would sit opposite him with her legs slightly apart, just enough for Benny to be able to see her underwear. Occasionally, she would leave her housecoat unbuttoned. She would always ask him to fasten her bra or zip up a dress or skirt. At the age of sixteen, Benny began to distance himself from his mother in order to avoid situations such as these.

Approaching adulthood, Benny was plagued by memories of his mother's seductive behavior toward him: while masturbating and even after he had become sexually involved with women he was troubled by the erotic fantasies that included images of his mother. Both his marriages were troubled by sexual difficulties.

The subtle form of abuse, illustrated in the two examples, can be particularly confusing for the victims who often do not recognize the abusiveness of their parents' behaviors. Furthermore, any attempt by the child to comment on his or her discomfort is often dismissed by the parent who may ridicule the child for being too sensitive. In many cases, however, what starts out with "merely" exposure or peeping may gradually progress to more and more invasive behaviors. These subtle forms of abuse are not restricted to individual perpetrators; they can be seen all around us.

Our Oversexualized Media

When teaching sex education and running workshops on the prevention of sexual coercion for pupils in grades six to eight I am confronted with the possibility that young people today are subjected to what could be referred to as media-based and societally sanctioned sexual abuse. Pornographic material readily available on the Internet is probably more damaging to the young than pornographic photos in the magazines father hid in the back of a drawer, once the only form of pornography brought into the home. Music video clips can show explicit sex scenes that are sometimes quite violent and television advertisements can be overtly erotic. Furthermore, movies with sex scenes that would once have been restricted to adult viewers are now available on video and DVDs and are shown on television at all hours of the day. In fact, in contrast with family entertainment television of the previous decades, parents and children today often feel uncomfortable watching the same movie together. One parent may go to the kitchen to prepare refreshments, while the other parent suddenly "remembers" something that cannot wait, and the children are left to watch the sex scenes alone.

A general contention holds that women's bodies are exploited in television and magazine advertisements for the purposes of promoting sales. In one class I taught, the boys came to the conclusion that *their* bodies are being exploited by erotic advertising no less than women's bodies because their natural sexual response, generated by the ads, presumably leads men (those with more financial resources) to purchase the products advertised. The boys found this constant bombardment of sexual stimuli unwanted and disturbing.

The research is not conclusive, but it appears that sexually explicit materials can traumatize some young people, lead to hypersexualization, or desensitize them regarding coercive sexual practices (Hayez, 2002; Rogala and Tyden, 2003). Studies conducted before the advent of the Internet pointed to a possibility that sexually explicit movies lead youth to have unreasonable expectations regarding sexual activities, and thus they were subsequently less satisfied with their own sexuality (Strasburger, 1989). Children and adolescents have been, and continue to be, exposed to sex in the media to a degree that may be detrimental to the healthy development of their sexuality at their own pace; it may, in fact, be considered abusive.

Children's need for protection from this overexposure stands in conflict with adults' desires for free uncensored access to all forms of media, yet adults are expected to define the boundaries within which minors can safely and gradually experience their surroundings and to make decisions affecting children with the children's best interests in mind. Although this might not always be convenient, when adults accept responsibility for taking care of children as our society claims they do, the needs of children are primary. For example, a baby crying at night when parents are asleep is a significant inconvenience for the parents; however, the child may need comforting, may be ill or wet, or may have some other need that requires attention, and it is the parents' duty to get up and see to the child even though this conflicts with their need for sleep. Similarly, censorship is an infringement on adults' rights that they should be willing to consider for the children's sake.

The societal-level abuse inherent in overexposure to erotic stimuli in the media and to pornography on the Internet has some characteristics in common with sexual abuse experienced by children at a personal level (to be discussed in the following sections). It has even been implicated in the sexual crimes of young offenders (Gail Ryan, cited in Bross, 2005). Although it is beyond the scope of this book to explore this issue further, professionals and the community should seriously consider the potential links between the media and sexual abuse.

A Matter of Age?

Sexual abuse perpetrators can be of any age. According to many professionals, what is significant is the difference in ages between abusers and victims such that the abusers are able to initiate the victims into a level of sexuality that is cognitively and emotionally beyond them. According to accepted views, sex play among children of the same age serves to satisfy curiosity about their bodies and is not harmful. In the past, researchers claimed that sexual behaviors are considered abusive when an age difference of five years or more exists between the individuals when children are involved, and ten years or more with teenagers (Wyatt and Peters, 1986). In contrast with this, a later study shows that sex play, even among same-age children, can occur under duress and force and, therefore, can be abusive and damaging (Lamb and Coakley, 1993). Two examples of such a situation are described in the following case studies:

When Miriam was nine, her eleven-year-old brother invited her to play doctor with him. This is well beyond the age when children play such games. At the beginning, she enjoyed their secret alliance. However, after some time, Miriam wanted to stop playing. Her brother did not want the activities to end and threatened to tell their mother that Miriam started the games. Miriam was sure that her mother would believe him and not her because she was convinced that he was her favorite. Her brother expanded the repertoire of their sexual games, showing her pornographic movies that he had discovered in a drawer in their parents' bedroom, and had her reenact with him some of the things the actors did in the films.

Mike was in sixth grade when he finally told his teacher that some boys from another class in his grade were bullying him. The teacher observed the pupils during breaks over the next few days and did not see any bullying, so she assumed Mike was just trying to get attention and told him what she had concluded. What she did not see was how the other boys found ways during school hours, or on the way to and from school, to isolate Mike from the other children, pull down his pants, and fondle him. After his unsuccessful attempt to get help, he just gave up and became listless and apathetic. His grades went down in school and he became sickly, having frequent headaches and stomachaches and low-grade fevers that kept him home from school more and more often. Mike's parents, busy professionals, were not attentive to his needs and, in fact, he was expected to take care of his younger sister much of the time. They were more irritated than concerned by Mike's changes. The abuse continued until another boy reported having seen what was going on.

Although not definitively proven by research, it seems that any young child or teenager who initiates sexual activities with another child, beyond what can be considered normal curiosity-motivated sex play, may be suspected as having been a victim of another abuser (Cavanaugh-Johnson, 1988; Murphy et al., 2001). Such abuse may not necessarily have been sexual, since severe physical and emotional forms of maltreatment can also be precursors of later sexual abuse perpetration (Cavanaugh-Johnson, 1988; Wood, 2000).

Adolescent Boy and Adult Woman

A prevailing myth in many societies suggests that, for a teenage boy, having sexual relations with an older woman is a dream come true. The older woman can teach the adolescent boy to be a good lover in a way no teenage girl ever could. Generally, such a situation is not considered to be abusive, and in some cases it may not be. Rob also thought at one time that he had been lucky.

At fifteen, Rob was quite grown-up for his age. He was good at sports and his body was muscular. His neighbor, a good-looking thirty-year-old woman, married but childless, asked him to help her with some heavy work in her apartment. At the end of the day, she seduced him, and they ended up in bed but did not have full sexual relations. Rob was proud that this woman was attracted to him and excited by their sexual activities. Over time, the neighbor gently introduced him to sexual intercourse. He fell in love with her, and over the next few months he was happy with the occasional sexual encounter. She also confided in him, which made him feel very important and grown-up. Even though she claimed to love Rob, she made him promise not to tell a single soul about their relationship. At some point, Rob began to realize that everything in their relationship always went according to her whims. His needs or desires were never taken into account. All attempts to discuss this with her were unsatisfactory. Rob began to understand that she was using him. He felt deceived and was ashamed.

Later, when he began to date girls his own age, he was afraid to get close to them. Girls liked him—he was charming and a sensitive and gentle lover—but he never let himself lose control of his feelings. Within the first year of his own marriage he began to carry on affairs. He claimed that he loved women and could see no reason to deny himself when a sexual encounter presented itself. His wife insisted that they either begin marital therapy or divorce. While exploring issues of communication, commitment, sexuality, and closeness, he recognized the link between his mistreatment at the hands of his neighbor and his fear of intimacy, which to him meant weakness and vulnerability.

POWER AND EXPLOITATION

Inherent in sexual abuse is the perpetrator achieving some sort of gain at the expense of the abused. This gain most often comprises feeling powerful and having control through sexual domination. Therefore, we can consider sexually abusive behavior as violence via the sexual organs (even when touch is not involved, because sexual excitement on the part of the abuser and/or the victim is usually present).

The abuser's exploitation of power can be understood by exploring the following four factors:

1. The perpetrator takes advantage of the child's needs to satisfy his or her own sexual and/or emotional needs
2. The minor does not possess the cognitive or emotional maturity to give informed consent to the sexual activity
3. The perpetrator misuses his or her authority or power over the child to obtain the child's passive, and sometimes active, participation in the sexual situation
4. The activities occur within the bounds of secrecy

Each of these points will be examined in turn.

Satisfaction of Needs

Children have specific needs that must be satisfied in order to grow and develop healthily, among them being shelter, love, food, education. They are totally dependent on the adults in their environment who are supposed to answer these needs. When children suffer sexual abuse, shelter is ultimately denied them. Shelter—home—is supposed to be a safe nurturing place, a place to run to when the demands of the external environment become too great. At home most children can find relief and support, which equip them to venture out beyond the walls of their immediate environment. Children who experience sexual abuse at the hands of their mother, father, or older sibling can never feel safe in their home. They cannot run home to the security of a door that locks out danger and fear. Loren describes how this very situation felt:

> I used to see other children run to their mothers when they came to pick them up from day care. I was jealous of them. I didn't want the day

to end. I didn't want to be taken home. I was angry a lot and would hit the other kids. The teacher yelled at me all the time, but that was better than what waited for me at home. It was better than the things she did to me in the bath. I just hated coming home and being alone with my mother.

In some cases, the child's abuser does not live in the same house with the child's family. The perpetrator can be a babysitter, a grandparent, an uncle, aunt, cousin, or friend of the family. Yet somehow this person finds a way to get to the child in his or her own home, as shown in the following case study:

Dora used to wait all week for Friday when her grandparents would come to eat with her family. They always stayed late, until it was time for her to go to sleep. When Dora was about eight years old, her grandfather wanted to be the one to tuck her in. She was really happy about this because he was funny and liked to tell stories. The first few times it was great. But once, when he kissed her good night, he suddenly stuck his tongue in her mouth. Dora froze:

"It was disgusting," she explained. "After that, I didn't want him to put me to bed anymore. But my mother got angry, saying I mustn't hurt his feelings. When he began to touch me under my pajamas I couldn't stand it anymore. It didn't matter how much my mother screamed at me, I refused to go to bed before my grandparents went home."

Sometimes the abuse occurs outside the family home: in a building's bomb shelter, in a deserted building, in a field, at school, or at a relative's or friend's home. If the victim cannot come home and tell what happened, or worse, is punished for behavior that is symptomatic of the abusive situation, then the home is no more a safe place for this child than it is for the child who suffers abuse in the home itself. This is what happened to Galit:

I went to the butcher for my mother, and the owner was in the store alone. He asked me to help him with something in the back of the shop. I went in the back with him and he pulled his pants down almost immediately. I ran home and told my mother. She just got irritated with me and told me to stop telling disgusting lies about such a nice old man. When I started to cry, she said I probably watch too much television and that's what put such nonsense into my head. I went to bed early that night as punishment. After that I never told her anything important that happened in my life. I just stopped trusting her.

Galit's story is very different from the one told to me by Zarin, a participant in a course I taught one year. She related to the class how one day her nine-year-old daughter came home from buying groceries, telling a story very similar to the one Galit had told her mother. In contrast to Galit's mother, however, Zarin was enraged, not at her daughter, but at the grocer. She went immediately to the shop and, taking him aside, told him if he ever tried with anyone else what he tried with her daughter, she would make sure he was charged with molestation. Unlike Galit, Zarin's daughter was believed and supported. The trust in her mother reconfirmed, her home remained a safe haven.

The need for unconditional love is also damaged for the child who experiences sexual abuse. In fact, it is this basic need that is exploited in order to obtain the child's compliance. Nurit tells how she gladly accepted her uncle's advances:

> My mother and father were very busy people. I think they loved me but they didn't have much time for me. We didn't play games and they stopped reading me stories at night when I still wanted more. When my aunt and uncle took me for weekends it was great. I really loved my uncle. He was my father's brother and he had a farm in a farming community with lots of space around his house. They didn't have any children yet and it was like they were practicing at being parents with me. When I got to be six years old, my uncle began to hug me close and French-kiss me. He would tell me it was because he loved me. He said that's how people kiss when they love each other. At first, I would ask him for the "loving" but I soon became confused because I knew I couldn't go home and kiss my mother and father that way. I knew I loved him and I knew I loved them, but I was afraid to tell him I didn't want any more of those kisses because I didn't want him to stop loving me.

Itai describes what happened between him and his mother until he was conscripted into the army. His mother was widowed when he was four years old:

> We were always very close. Nobody will ever love me like my mother does. She also used to say so. We were always very open and told each other everything. When I didn't want to be alone, I would sleep in bed with her. We hugged and then I could fall asleep easily. My mother was so beautiful. She was slim and had a great body. I was proud of her. She also taught me everything about sex—how to masturbate, how a woman masturbates, everything! I can't tell you how much I loved her. And now I know how sick it was.

It is clear how, in Nurit and Itai's cases, a child's need for love was exploited. But what needs on the adults' part motivate such misuse of trust and love? This is a question that still preoccupies many who are attempting to understand the forces that can bring an adult to sexually abuse a child. First, we must understand that all sexual behavior, whether abusive or not, is based in part on needs that are not purely sexual: the desire to demonstrate love, wanting closeness, a need to prove femininity or masculinity, etc. (Finklehor, 1984). As long as the participants in the sexual activity are adults who can either consent, or refuse, to engage in such activities, sex can be an appropriate vehicle for the satisfaction of these other needs. However, in sexual abuse, love and the desire for closeness are confused.

Micha grew up in a home barren of warmth and affection—no hugs, no kisses, no words of love and caring, not even affectionate nicknames. At age thirteen, an older female cousin, in whose company he had always felt comfortable, initiated sexual relations with him. This relationship satisfied his need for closeness with someone he cared about. Later, after he married, he didn't understand that his teenage sister-in-law's hugs and kisses were merely expressions of affection. He saw them as a sign that she wanted to be close to him, that she wanted him sexually, and he acted on that false belief.

Informed Consent

Informed consent can be defined as the agreement to participate in something, or allow something to occur, after the individual is clear about the nature of what is about to happen, what risks and benefits are involved, and is knowledgeable about alternative choices. The term *informed consent* typically refers to medical procedures or to participation in research. The medical professional must tell the patient the reasons for any impending procedure, the anticipated results, the risks involved, and other options that may be attempted if the procedure is particularly noxious. Potential participants in a research project must be informed of the purposes of the research, the anticipated benefits to society from the study, the possible positive and/or negative effects of participating in the study, and that the participant can withdraw freely at any time.

Because children do not yet have the cognitive skills necessary for weighing facts and options, parents are responsible, on their behalf, for giving informed consent for medical interventions or participation in research projects. Children have to rely on the judgment of those responsible for their welfare, and only gradually take responsibility for themselves as they develop the capacity to do so. Furthermore, children rely on their caretakers to determine in which situations it is appropriate for them to make their own decisions.

Adults who sexually abuse children often claim that the child was a willing partner. However, to be considered a willing partner (giving informed consent), the child would have to comprehend what is being asked of them, and children do not understand the nature of sexual behavior. Adults, in fact, may not fully understand the nature of sexual drive, sexual desire, sexual response, orgasm, or the relationships between sexual behavior and caring relationships. In my clinical work and as a sexuality educator I have been struck by the gaps in understanding about sexuality in some intelligent, curious, and otherwise well-informed adults, whether or not they had been sexually traumatized at some point of their lives. Naturally children are even less comprehending.

Not only do children not understand the nature of the sexual activity into which they are being coerced, they are lied to about the "benefits." "This is for your own good," they may be told. "It is better for you to get your sex education from someone who cares about you and can teach you well." Or, they may be told that this is a natural result of love: "I love you and you love me and this is what people who love each other do."

Abused children are certainly not given a list of possible risks before their "consent" is obtained. They are not warned about the possibility of contracting a sexually transmitted disease, becoming pregnant, or impregnating an adult female abuser. They are not told that they will probably feel guilty for having participated in their own abuse, that they will feel shame and humiliation that could cripple their future friendships and couples relationships, nor are they informed of the other possible symptoms, such as depression, anxiety, post-traumatic stress disorder (PTSD), or dissociation, that may arise from the abuse. The only risk of which the abused child is informed is the risk of not going along with it. This carries the risk of the infliction of physical injury, arousal of the rage of the abuser, total rejection by the abuser, being called a liar if the child tries to disclose to a responsible adult, or the abuser leaving the current child and abusing a younger sibling toward whom the victim feels protective. No other options are available to the victim than to "agree" to their own abuse. This is not informed consent!

Misuse of Power and Authority

It is amazing to note that, regardless of class, race, religion, culture, geographic location, etc., all perpetrators use the same means to abuse children. It is as if they all follow a universal guide to the sexual victimization of children. Abusers begin by selecting a victim. If the potential victim is not a member of the family, then the process may be long and involved, because the abuser must ingratiate himself or herself with the victim and/or the victim's family, thereby gaining authority over the child. This is most easily accomplished with children who do not enjoy sufficient parental supervision. Such children are deficient in adult attention and will seek to satisfy this essential need wherever it is offered. Obvious candidates for the role of parent-compensator are teachers, sports coaches, youth group leaders, friends of the family, or neighbors.

If the intended victim is a member of the family, then the power and authority afforded to older members of the family are automatically in effect. In the absence of adults, older siblings or cousins have the authority normally reserved for the adults.

When adults sexually abuse children, they put their own needs ahead of the child's need for safety and caring. The natural authority and power of the adult over the child is exploited to gain the child's compliance with acts that are decidedly contrary to his or her healthy development, both physically and psychologically.

The Bounds of Secrecy

Like Harry Potter under his invisibility cloak, sexual abuse is often undetected in the very environment in which it exists; the abuse can be a "presence" that is felt but not seen. The secrecy of the abuse protects perpetrators and isolates the victims from other people in their world who may be able to help them escape.

The perpetrator uses a variety of means to ensure that the child victim does not tell anyone about the secret. He or she may threaten the child with harm to himself or herself or to someone the child cares about should he or she tell about the abuse. Alternatively, the abuser may lie to the child, telling him or her that he or she wanted the sexual activity, using the child's own natural orgasmic response to sexual touch as affirmation of this lie. Confused and shamed, the child feels guilty and will not tell.

Yet another means by which the secret is kept relies on dissociation. Dissociation is a result of two factors: the way in which the abuser manipulates the child's sense of reality, and the child's own psychological defenses for dealing with the overwhelming emotional impact of the abuse. This will be discussed in detail in the following section.

THE CHILD'S EXPERIENCE OF THE ABUSE EVENT

Now we have a good idea of what makes CSA so traumatic, yet in order to really understand the experience of the traumatized child we need to look at what happens during a single incident of abuse. Figure 1.1 graphically illustrates this experience. The Shared World in Figure 1.1 refers to the family interactions that are generally known to all members of a household and can be talked about openly. Even when family members are not together physically, a sense of togetherness or shared reality can exist; for example, a mother can look at her watch and realize it is ten o'clock and that her son is in the middle of taking a math exam, wondering how he is doing, fearing he did not study enough, or a husband can feel as if he is accompanying his wife

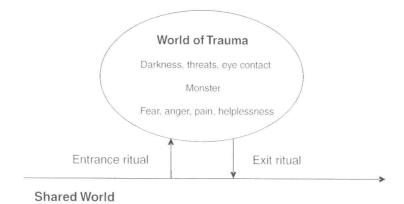

FIGURE 1.1. Nature of trauma. *Source:* Adapted from Furniss, 1991.

into a very important meeting she has that morning, hoping that by thinking about her he can bring her good luck.

When a husband or wife has an affair, for example, a secret is created that is not part of the family's shared reality. An investment in keeping the secret from other family members occurs in order to maintain the status quo. When the secret becomes known, the family is thrown into open crisis and the marital couple must make decisions that will determine the future of the family.

However, a far more dangerous secret exists when sexual abuse occurs and a child is removed from the family's shared reality and taken cruelly into a World of Trauma about which either no one in the family is aware, or, if aware, does not comment on. This leaves the child isolated and in constant psychological and/or physical danger. We will look at the ways in which children are taken into the World of Trauma and what they experience in that world, but first the means by which the perpetrator selects and "grooms" the victim will be briefly discussed.

The victim, as discussed, is someone over whom the abuser has authority and who is dependent on the abuser, or is someone with whom a relationship of dependence can be developed. At first, the abuser is considerate of the child, spending time with him or her, giving gifts, and/or offering help. The abuser is careful during this stage to hide sexual feelings he or she may have toward the child.

When the abuser is confident that the victim trusts him or her, and for family members this will be mostly automatic, he or she will let the sexual feelings seep into their interactions very insidiously. Adults are generally aware when another adult is sexually attracted to them; sexual energy can be felt in a handshake or a look. However, children do not have the experience necessary to differentiate between a neutral touch or look and a sexual touch or look. If the confusion this entails for the child does not, however, bring the child to pull away, then gradually, over time, more and more daring sexual behaviors will be instigated. During this process of grooming, the victim becomes indoctrinated to the abuser's signals. In time, these signals become triggers of a somewhat hypnotic state, forming the entrance ritual (Furniss, 1991) leading into the World of Trauma, as shown in Figure 1.1.

Debra (twelve) would lie awake in bed until she heard her father's footsteps on his way to sleep—if the steps went in the direction of her parents' bedroom, she would relax and fall asleep, knowing that, on that particular night, he was not going to abuse her. However, if the steps came in the direction of her bedroom, it meant she was likely to be abused by him. Knowing she could not escape the horror, she mentally prepared for it to happen. At the same time, she would freeze, not feeling anything.

Amnon (nine) was abused by his youth group leader, Tom (sixteen). Tom would tell the other children they could go home, adding, "Amnon will help me finish here." Amnon knew that Tom wanted to fool around with him and that if he did not stay, Tom would make something up that would get him expelled from the youth movement. So Amnon would say good-bye to his friends and sit on the battered sofa on which the abuse took place. He would sit with a vacant look on his face, waiting for Tom to come to him. Like Debra, he, too, would freeze and feel numb.

Perhaps the experience of being in the World of Trauma is similar to being in an episode of *The Twilight Zone*—going into another dimension parallel to our known reality, but inhabited only by the abuser and the victim. Momentarily, the victim ceases to live in the real world and even fears that he or she may not be able to return to reality.

The World of Trauma, then, is characterized by several features. The first of these is darkness (Furniss, 1991). Even if the abuse occurs in the light of day, it is as if a heavy cloud descends and covers the child's entire world, plunging him or her into darkness. Second, threats are made that ensure the child's obedience both during the abuse itself and even afterward by not telling anyone. The abuser may warn the child that if he or she tells, no one will believe it, and even if believed, the child will be blamed. This is a particularly effective threat, since, until recently, the child's story of abuse was often not believed. Alternatively, the child may be threatened with physical harm to himself or herself or those he or she loves.

When Dan was six years old his stepfather warned him that if he dared tell anyone about the abuse he would break his arms, and that if he had to go to jail and could not do it himself he would send someone else to carry out the threat.

When Dina was eight years old her uncle, who was often called in to babysit, said that if she told her mother about what was happening her mother would think she had flirted with him. "Then your mother will be furious at you and even have a heart attack and die," the uncle convinced Dina, "because your mother loves me more than anyone in the world."

Young children believe such threats. Before the age of six or seven, they have not yet developed the ability to distinguish between reality and fantasy, or reality and metaphor. Selma Fraiberg (1959) tells of a five-year-old child who developed symptoms of anxiety because his parents were going to fly to vacation in Europe over the summer, and because he had not yet learned to fly he would be left behind.

Threats of serious consequences need not always be verbalized because the child already feels guilty by having been led to believe that he or she wanted the abuse. Therefore, he or she deserves the worst punishment possible.

Another factor that increases the child's fear and reinforces verbal or nonverbal threats is the nature of the eye contact during the abuse. In healthy adult lovemaking, looking deeply into each others eyes' enhances the experience, adding another element to the communication of love for one's partner. However, sexual abuse is not love and it is not lovemaking—it is violence via the sex organs, so eye contact is not a sign of love, it is a mechanism for inspiring yet greater fear. The eye contact is a one-way street, from the abuser to the victim, and it can be described by the common phrase "He had murder in his eyes." Even if the abuser feels he or she is looking at the child lovingly, the sexuality of the look is confusing to the child and it does not register as loving. The effect of eye contact during abuse is to instill fear, ultimately the fear of death, into the child victim. After all, is that not what happens in child sexual abuse—the murder of the young innocent soul of a child?

In situations in which no eye contact occurs, it is as if even the abuser is not there with the child. He or she feels totally alone. This reinforces the sense of unreality in what is happening (Furniss, 1991). The child may think that he or she cannot believe his or her own senses.

Perhaps the most dramatic phenomenon that happens in the World of Trauma is that the abuser is perceived by the victim to be a monster. Through the process of the entrance ritual, the loving individual in the shared reality is transformed into a monster (Furniss, 1991). So, the father who loves his little girl so much, more than anyone else in the world, the father who gives her presents, spends time with her, and makes her laugh—this father is not the abuser. The abuser is a monster, a not-father. Therefore, the little girl is in a bind. She wants the abuse to stop, and she wants to tell people about the monster, but, although young, she knows that if she tells about the monster, people would not understand. They would think she was talking about her father. They would take her father away together with the monster. That is not what she wants. She wants them to take away the monster and leave her father.

Dan, mentioned previously, could not bear the abuse anymore, and when he was eight years old he decided to tell his mother about it. He even took the chance that the monster would find him and break his arms, thinking that a better option than the continuing pain and the humiliating encopresis he suffered. However, when his stepfather was put in jail to await trial and was no longer at home to help with homework or play soccer with him, Dan regretted having told. He became depressed. He refused to cooperate with the investigation and told everyone he had lied because he was angry at his stepfather.

The victim in the World of Trauma is overwhelmed by pain, terror, rage, and helplessness. Physical pain does not always occur, but emotional pain certainly does—the pain of loneliness. During the abuse event, the adult loved outside the World of Trauma, having become a monster, is not someone the child can feel connected with. Since no one else is there to save him or her, the child feels totally alone. One is reminded of a scene from a science fiction movie in which an astronaut leaves the spaceship to repair something outside and the cable tying him safely to the ship rips apart and he can only grasp at the airless space as he drifts off into the emptiness and darkness.

The victim feels not just fear, but terror; not just anger, but rage. Not to mention the overwhelming helplessness of not being able to stop what is happening. All of these feelings are too intense for a child or young adolescent to bear, and the victim must dissociate and shut off his or her feelings to survive.

It is possible that the child merely stops feeling what is happening in his or her body. He or she knows that the body is being fondled or raped, but does not feel the physical sensations. The body is numb. For instance, Nurit's uncle intensified his abuse of her and raped her repeatedly between the ages of eight and twelve. She always remembered the abuse, but never understood why she couldn't remember how it felt. When she first told her therapist of the rapes she could only describe the sense of heaviness on her chest where her uncle laid his head when it was over. It was, to her, as if the rest of her body had just disappeared.

The child may also disconnect only from the emotions and is not aware of feeling sad, afraid, angry, or helpless, and is only apathetic to the experience.

"I got to the point where I didn't care what he did to me anymore," David said, when explaining in survivors' groups how he had experienced the sodomy he suffered at the hands of a neighbor. "I don't know how, but all of a sudden, it was as if I told myself that I didn't care what he did to me. All at once, I didn't feel anything. I just stopped caring about anything that happened to me—what the neighbor did, how I did in school, if my parents yelled at me, if friends wanted to be with me. Nothing mattered to me anymore."

Some young children disconnect from themselves to an even greater extent. It is as if they leave their bodies during the abuse and migrate to another part of the room, often the ceiling. They view the abuse from that angle. Some say that they look down on what is happening and feel sorry for that little girl or boy who is being so badly treated. Others feel disgust for that dirty little child and say they hate him or her.

When the abuse is over, regardless of the extent of the dissociation, the victim and perpetrator must return to the Shared World. They do this by use of an exit ritual (Furniss, 1991). A word, a sentence, a gesture by the abuser signals to the victim that the abuse event has come to an end. Then, the abuser withdraws from the scene, leaving the child alone to reenter the Shared World on his or her own. This further enhances the sense of splitting between the monster and the loved one, and between the unreality of the abuse and the World of Trauma.

After her father reached sexual satisfaction, he would say to Debra, "After I leave, you go to pee and then clean yourself up. You're such a mess!" Always the same words, as if a script, and knowing her part in the play, she would wait for him to leave the room then go to clean herself up. By the time she left the bathroom, she already felt that she had dreamed up the whole incident.

Joel was molested by an uncle who would bring himself to orgasm while fondling Joel. During the entire incident, his uncle never looked at him. Joel felt as if he did not really exist. When it was over, his uncle would wordlessly readjust his clothing and just leave the scene. Joel would force himself to fall asleep, if only for a few moments, and then he would wake up as if it had never happened.

The exit ritual means that another dissociative split has been successfully accomplished—the cutoff between the World of Trauma and the Shared World. Knowing that he or she cannot tell others about the abuse experience, it seems to be in the child's interest to split it off from apparent awareness. This is, perhaps, part of the mechanism behind the "forgetting" that many CSA survivors experience. It does seem to explain the ability of the child to get up, get dressed, eat breakfast, and go to school as if nothing had happened the night before. Understanding this dissociative split would explain how a child goes to a family celebration in the presence of the abusing family member without giving him or her away.

However, the dissociative split between the World of Trauma and the Shared World is not hermetic. A slow leakage of the abuse experience into daily life occurs in the form of symptoms that others can observe, even if they do not interpret them correctly. Much has been written about the symptoms of abuse. Boys have been characterized as "acting out" (becoming bullies, abusing animals, setting fires, engaging in criminal behavior), whereas girls are said to "act in" (hurt themselves, become depressed and/or fearful, feel suicidal, withdraw from social interactions). However, both boys and girls can exhibit any of these signs.

Today, with the growing awareness of CSA, children showing such signs of distress may be offered help by school personnel, neighbors, or other involved adults, and the abuse can be discovered in time to prevent further developmental damage. Nonetheless, some children do not disclose that they are being abused, even when asked, and other children do not show the common outward symptoms that can bring them to the attention of professionals. In these cases they continue to live a double life—with the dissociated World of Trauma lurking behind the mask they present to the Shared World. The next chapter addresses how this double life affects their continuing development.

Chapter 2

Trapped in the World of Trauma

Sheri Oz
Sarah-Jane Ogiers

It takes courage to grow up and turn out to be who you really are.

e.e. cummings

Most survivors of childhood sexual abuse (CSA) find that the trauma they suffered as children does not end when they leave the abusive environment. Rather, it accompanies their every move, seeping insidiously into different areas of their lives. It is as if survivors live in two dimensions simultaneously, with one foot in the World of Trauma and the other foot in the Shared World (see Chapter 1). They feel as if they are walking on a tightrope between the two, struggling to hold on to a semblance of sanity (Shared World), all the while feeling that any slight breeze will disturb their balance and knock them off the rope into insanity (World of Trauma). They are sure that should others truly get to know them, the charade will be over, and their "craziness" and "badness" will be exposed.

Even as adults the world is frequently seen through the eyes of the victimized children they once were, and this perception becomes the basis for decisions made and actions taken. Sarah-Jane wrote about this in her diary when she began to recognize the impact on her of her father's abuse and her mother's neglect.

This chapter, then, explores the effects of CSA on later development, looking at friendship, puberty and sexual development, partner selection, and parenting. The discussion is accompanied by clinical material drawn from individual therapy and group sessions in Sheri's

Overcoming Childhood Sexual Trauma
Published by The Haworth Press, Inc., 2006, All rights reserved.
doi:10.1300/5668_02

practice (all names used are pseudonyms and each client discussed here is actually a conglomerate of a number of individuals), and selections from Sarah-Jane's diary. During therapy, Sarah-Jane wrote about the consequences of the abuse she suffered as a child:

July 10, 1994

My abusive childhood has leaked into every part of my being—my relationships, my self-worth, my parenting, my personal development. It's like poison sprinkled from an eyedropper onto every part of me, soaking through the layers. I'm always terrified I'm going to be found out. In my mind it's only a question of time until everyone discovers how boring/stupid/bad/dirty I really am. I hate myself. I'm never pretty enough, sexy enough, clean enough. I'm not witty enough or intelligent enough. I don't know enough. I won't take college courses because I'm sure I'll fall short of requirements. At work, I'm terrified of failure and always make sure I cover my tracks after even the smallest, most innocent of mistakes. I don't allow myself to write seriously because then I'll be exposed for the fraud I really am. Then people will know that my so-called writing talent was just one big lie that I used to cover up my ineptitude in other areas, like math, physics, chemistry, etc.

I spend most of my life in a seething rage and frustration, but I come out in a cold sweat at the thought of confronting someone who has angered me. Anger is dangerous and destructive, and people punish those who show anger by rejecting them. When the anger does rise to the surface it is so intense that it pours out of me like acid.

I constantly berate myself for being a bad mother and wife. I displace my anger onto my children, scaring them, and then hate myself afterward for becoming a monster in their eyes.

My relationships over the years have been warped and my feelings toward people close to me have often been paranoid. I test people over and over again and scrutinize them closely so as not to miss even the slightest slip. They invariably do slip, of course, since no one is perfect, and when they do I laugh humorlessly, almost proud of myself for discovering yet again that there is no point in opening up or getting close to people, since they will always let me down. Even the most caring, patient of my friends will eventually slip up if I give them a hard enough test. I trust no one and nothing.

My reality isn't good enough. It always seems empty, and I use a myriad of techniques to fill that emptiness. Whether it be addiction to inappropriate, unhealthy relationships where I submerge myself in others to avoid thinking about my inner void, or overeating to compensate for the emptiness I feel inside, followed by more self-disgust at my lack of self-control.

Another way I avoid thinking about that void is by controlling everything around me. I must always have my way and get what I want. People often give in because my persistence wears them down. I don't tire because it's a matter of life or death for me. If I do come up against a person or situation that cannot or will not give in, I experience incredible panic and/or searing rage and frustration. It's like the ground is shaking under me and being pulled away. This control is the only way I stay sane. When it's taken away from me I feel my strength and power running through my fingers like water.

Hand in hand with the need to control is the need to keep tabs on every single tiny atom that makes up my environment. I've always been safe on the street at night because I'm totally aware of everything around me. When sitting in a room, I have to see the door—if my back is to the entrance I get a creeping sensation down my spine. I'm so hypersensitive that I tune into people in an exaggerated way and pick up on their moods the moment there is the slightest change. It's like those dog whistles that humans can't hear. Well, I'm the human who can hear them.

This incessant need for control Sarah-Jane writes about is a common theme among CSA survivors, and it is related to their experiences both in the World of Trauma and in the Shared World (described in Chapter 1). This experience is marked by dissociation or disconnections (Furniss, 1991)—the way perpetrators cut victims off from the Shared World in order to abuse them secretly, the way victims dissociate in various degrees from their own emotions and physical sensations during the abuse, the way perpetrators transform themselves in their victims' eyes from the caring individuals they are in the Shared World to the monsters they are in the World of Trauma, the way victims disconnect from the World of Trauma when they reenter the Shared World. The victim has no control over any of this. In an attempt to try to make the Shared World an orderly place, to hold surprises at bay, the survivor tries to exert some control over either the inner subjective world or the outer world populated by friends, family, peers, etc., or both.

CONTROL

Controlling the Inner World

Some survivors unconsciously attempt to control their feelings by engaging in addictive behaviors, by self-mutilation, or through obsessive-compulsive symptoms. These behaviors, which are destructive to the individual, can be seen as attempts to resolve certain psychological problems. For example, they may be attempts at "numbing," a means to block out the pain, anger, or helplessness associated with the unresolved traumatic memories (Briere and Gill, 1998; Haines and Williams, 1997; Sutton, 1999). In my clinical work I have found that the most difficult feeling to cope with, and the one that must be defended against to the greatest degree, is a pervasive sense of emptiness. CSA survivors speak about an inner emptiness that is both frightening and painful. It is similar to the emptiness of the World of Trauma, in which the only other person present is the abuser, someone the victim obviously cannot connect with.

Sometimes a trigger sets the destructive behavior in motion by arousing feelings similar to those experienced in childhood related to abuse or neglect. Dan, for example, grows extremely anxious when criticized, because criticism usually preceded a beating by his mother. After being criticized, even in adulthood, he goes off by himself and drinks. When night falls, Iris, whose father woke her at night to abuse her, feels an uncontrollable urge to cut her arms. In other cases, the triggers are not clearly related to anything particular other than feelings of anxiety that seem to arise from nowhere. Barb feels intolerable anxiety when a picture on the wall is crooked or she sees spots of dust on the floor or furniture. She gets a sensation of something crawling up her spine and the only way to get away from it is to clean incessantly. Generally, it is only through therapy that the triggers and/or anxiety or other feelings behind the addictions, self-mutilation, or compulsions are recognized and the relationship of the trigger to events or people from the abusive childhood environment understood.

On the other hand, these behaviors may be seen as diversionary. Cindy came to understand that her eating disorder kept her from thinking about the rape. As long as a problematic symptom drew a great amount of attention to itself the abuse issues could remain masked and out of awareness.

Other dynamics might also be involved. For example, self-harming behaviors may be seen as punishment (Sutton, 1999). Alternatively, a survivor may think, "If I hate myself for being addicted, then I hate myself for something that is within my control to stop. I should be strong enough to stop drinking/bingeing and purging/stealing from shops/sleeping around/etc., but I'm not—just as I should have been strong enough to have stopped my brother/father/teacher/etc., from abusing me, but I wasn't. I am bad because I did not stop him or her just like I'm bad for not stopping this addictive behavior now." It was important for the survivor to have believed this when still a child, as Nina's situation exemplifies:

At ten years of age, Nina was dependent on her older brother (then seventeen) since their mother was hospitalized frequently and their father was rarely home. It was impossible for her as a child to consider blaming her brother for sexually abusing her because she would have risked losing the one person who was taking care of her. Now, as an adult, any hint of the excruciating pain caused by his childhood betrayal of her trust arouses the same panic as she felt then and keeps her trapped in addictive, compulsive behaviors.

Controlling the Environment

Incessant cleaning or checking, coercing other people to do something they don't really want to do, hitting, or other forms of acting out can be seen as unconscious attempts to satisfy the need to control the environment and make it predictable. Given that the outer world during childhood was so unpredictable, the sexual abuse survivor cannot tolerate surprises or change. Even positive changes are likely to upset the abuse survivor. If the outer world has order to it, is predictable, it can be soothing to the CSA survivor whose inner world is now chaotic and overwhelming. Nurit, for example, had trouble with all her roommates in college because she was constantly cleaning up after them, straightening the pictures on the walls, lining up canned goods according to size with their labels facing "just so," etc. Any slight disturbance to her perfect order aroused in her a rage she found terrifying and inexplicable.

In contrast, some CSA survivors find it more calming when the outer environment is chaotic and therefore similar to the inner world, when subjective experience is mirrored in outer reality. For example, Jana, an unemployed single mother, did not have a regular schedule, and her children would fall asleep on the couch or on a rug on the floor whenever they got too tired to stay awake. Then, too tired to wake up in time for school, they were usually late. The apartment was messy, with soiled clothes on the bedroom floors, unmade beds, dishes piled up in the sink, and a collection of old newspapers gathering dust in a corner in the living room. She felt weighed down by the chaos around her, but if a friend came in to clean and organize the apartment, it did not feel as if it was her space until it was messy once more.

The Polarity Rule

Childhood for the CSA victim was terrifying and dangerous. Surviving required learning to adapt to a constant state of imminent or actual danger. Therefore, the victim, having to constantly assess levels of danger in the environment, probably did not learn to cope with ambiguity or distinguish subtleties in interpersonal communications. In addition, whereas children in relatively healthy environments find that their needs change as they grow and that the behavior of others toward them changes accordingly, the sexual trauma victim is less open to experimenting with new ways of interacting with others. This means that the individual remains frozen at child or adolescent forms of interpersonal interactions even into adulthood. Adult sexual abuse survivors often find themselves maintaining rigid and exaggerated modes of thought, feeling, and behavior.

Indeed, as an adult, the survivor is often not able to experiment with new ways of being, given that, as a result of the dissociation inherent in the abuse trauma, he or she may not have access to many memories, traumatic or otherwise, or even to some of his or her own emotions. People rely on their emotions and on memories of their past to provide them with enough information with which to make decisions in the present, for example, whether it is possible to trust a particular individual, how to respond when feelings have been hurt, and even determining their own likes and dislikes. If, instead of being able to consider what to do when insulted, the person is triggered by the pain of the insult into a flashback of some form (which may not involve remembering the abuse but perhaps only the accompanying emotional pain), then the adult survivor, absorbed in protecting himself or herself from the flashback, will not be able to think about how to react sensibly. In this way the dissociation that once helped the child survive by putting feelings and knowledge of traumatic events beyond awareness now handicaps the survivor by making these aspects of his or her identity inaccessible. Never knowing from which direction or at what time a flashback will be triggered means that life is full of uncertainty, something that is too frightening to bear.

The resulting need to control oneself and/or one's environment, as discussed in the previous sections, leads the CSA survivor to take up polarized positions (Pistorello and Follette, 1998) in a variety of interpersonal realms (such as constant rage versus never expressing any anger at all, being perfect versus being a failure, never trusting anyone versus trusting everyone). In contrast, those who were not traumatized throughout childhood find a balance between such extremes based upon their individual inclinations, developmental stages, and the particular situation in which they find themselves.

GROWING UP A SURVIVOR

The remainder of this chapter addresses comments made by survivors in individual therapy and in group sessions concerning what it is like to face the world outside of home while growing up. Essentially, what is explored is an answer to the question of how carrying a World of Trauma within himself or herself impacts the victim's continuing development and social interactions.

Because Sarah-Jane kept a diary from adolescence on, we have access to some aspects of her growing up as she documented it at the time. The following discussion is interspersed with selections from Sarah-Jane's diary, preceded by a date, together with reflections on her teenage years from her current perspective.

Friendships in Childhood and Adolescence

Many years ago, when I was leading a group for CSA survivors, I decided to give the participants a break from the heavy emotional material we usually discussed and raised the topic of social interactions and friendships during childhood and adolescence. That brought a gasp from the group and the exclamation that this was certainly not a "light" topic. Research does mention the difficulty CSA survivors of all ages have in making friends (e.g., Johnson, 2001; Trickett and McBride-Chang, 1995). Considering the importance of social support in coping with sexual as well as all kinds of trauma (e.g., Ahrens and Cambell, 2000; Muller et al., 2000), it is surprising that more studies have not been carried out in this area.

It seems that, as children, a large proportion of survivors felt they were different from others—freaks, or weird—and this often continues into adulthood. What makes them feel different? They see the reactions of their peers in a wide variety of situations, they read books, and they see movies. For example, Miriam knew that when you get a gift you are supposed to be happy. She never was. Even as a child she had to pretend to be excited. She always asked herself what was wrong with her—why couldn't she just be happy about gifts like a normal person?

Part of the pain involved in friendship during the school years is the jealousy that seems to have infected many survivors. Some speak of being jealous of others who had apparently normal families and parents who were loving and gentle; jealous of the homemade meals they found in other homes; jealous of other kids who had more freedom and spontaneity in their lives, not having to worry about a sudden explosion of anger on the part of a parent; jealous of those who just seemed to naturally belong to people and place.

Three possible ways to react to feeling different exist: (1) try to cover it up; (2) give up trying to belong a priori; or (3) act out even more, be even more different. All solutions are related to control, with the first and third solutions representing attempts to control the situation and the second solution being to resign oneself to absolute lack of control.

Joel talks about not having been able to participate in games during recess at school or be with classmates after school because he felt he was a misfit. "I was strange, weird. I didn't know how to act around people. So I just stayed away from other kids." Orli says: "Even when the whole class organized a party and it was obvious I was part of it, I still felt alone. They must have felt something because they would often forget about me and sometimes didn't relate to me at all."

Nina, on the other hand, tried to stand out: "Sports, music, art—I was good at all of them and I used them to put myself on center stage. I wanted everyone to admire me, to like me. But even when I was in the center of things I felt no true confidence in myself. I felt as if the real me was erased. Inside I was small and insecure, but always outwardly I projected confidence." Debra speaks of overcoming her sense of not belonging by having made herself useful to her peers: "I didn't have a boyfriend but I set everyone else up. I brought people together, made sure everything was okay. I was always mediating when there were conflicts, taking care of everyone."

"Friendship was something to hang onto," Carla recounts, "to pass the time. Our home was very open; we could bring friends home whenever we wanted. I used that—I invited all the gang and was afraid when they had to leave, afraid of being alone at home."

It is interesting to see that for those survivors who made friends, the relationships were not for the friendship alone, not for mutual support, having fun, and companionship, but rather were something that could be exploited to cover up a low self-image, feel significant or of use to others, or ward off danger. The polarity rule described earlier is also relevant with regard to social standing. For example, if a girl was the class princess or a boy the class prince, he or she would always know what was going on with everyone else, would have a handle on all the social interactions within the class, and would not be open to surprises. In other words, he or she would have a sense of control. On the other hand, if a pupil was the class reject, he or she would also not be open to surprises. The pupil would know that no invitations would be given to him or her. He or she would expect to be ignored or ridiculed.

For those who made friends, it seems that it was important to project an image very different from the way the survivors felt about themselves deep down. However, this created a tension between inside and outside, and the survivor was in constant fear of being found out as an imposter. For those who did not try to make friends, it appears that they projected an image consistent with their own view of themselves. Barb explains, "I never ever had friends. I was stupid, ugly, a liar. There was the gang at scouts, which was something large and not personal, and I went regularly to every activity, to feel as if I belonged somewhere. But I didn't dare open my mouth in any discussions. I was sure the others would laugh at the stupid things I would say. I was sure that everyone was smarter than me." Miriam always felt like the class reject. She was surprised, therefore, when near the end of school one year a group of classmates approached her and told her how they had thought she was a snob at the start of the school year and how glad they were to find out she was really quite nice. She was shocked by this revelation, realizing that for them to have thought she was a snob meant that they saw something in her about which she could be snobbish. This was the first time she realized that her inner feelings were not necessarily visible to others, and if that were true, then perhaps she had some control over what people thought of her.

Throughout her childhood and adolescence, Sarah-Jane always felt like an outsider, wherever she was and whoever she was with. It took her many years of inner work to begin to form friendships based on mutual trust and support.

January 25, 1975

I haven't any friends, except perhaps Lucy. Oh, I wish something good would happen to me. I'll probably still feel depressed tomorrow. I could honestly kill myself.

SARAH-JANE: My experience of friendship in adolescence was very much like my experience of relationships in general. I did not belong anywhere with anyone. My conviction that I wasn't good enough to be anyone's friend, and my consequent fear of exposure, meant that I was very lonely for a good number of my school years.

My sense of worthlessness was reinforced by my father, since I cannot remember a time when he wasn't telling me how bad and selfish I was. Once, at the age of twelve, when I was living with my mother in a town far from my father, I remember writing to him that I was lonely and miserable because I had no friends. He replied that it wasn't surprising, because no one wants to be friends with a self-centered girl who doesn't care about other people.

Outwardly, I was extroverted and sociable, sometimes playing the clown in class to make others laugh and notice me. But almost every friendship I made quickly fizzled out. I was so convinced that it was only a matter of time before my friends found out how boring, bad, and selfish I really was that every quarrel signaled that I had been "caught." I was hypersensitive and plagued with imagined slights. It just wasn't conceivable to me that friends could fight and make up. Once I fell from grace I could not get up and once they fell, neither could they.

February 27, 1975

Life is going okay, apart from lack of friends and a rotten personality.

SARAH-JANE: I found myself throughout most of my school years tagging on to already established friendships, and I was always either the third or fifth wheel. Looking back, I realize that this pattern, while painful, was also safe. As the odd man out, no chance of really close friendships existed, and therefore no danger of suffering betrayal and abandonment.

At thirteen . . .

April 23, 1975

Lucy has made up with Karen and she said she would still go around with me. I suggested a threesome. She thought it was a good idea, but I'll be pushed out as usual.

At fourteen . . .

March 2, 1976

Oh God! I'm so lonely. Help me, please. I haven't any real friends. Lynn just doesn't care about me, Vicky doesn't mean to leave me out but she does, Elaine is being horrible to me, without showing it to the others, and Mary blames me for everything. Today I found out that the four of them have made up a secret code between them, but they won't tell me what it is. And I'm supposed to be one of the gang!

And at fifteen . . .

March 25, 1977

Don't feel good today. There are bad vibes in the air. Julie and Gail announced that they will be taking acid at half-term. I'm sure Gail is persuading Julie to trip with her, so that it will all be very pally between them. Since she knows I'm not interested in drugs, this will completely exclude me, and that seems to be happening already. There are lots of whisperings going on between them. It just feels not good, not good at all. Christ! I'll be glad to get out of that school. I hate relying on those two for company.

May 2, 1977

It's quarter to eight in the evening and I am already in bed. I feel awful, and I'd love to stay off school tomorrow. But if I do, even though I got back to being really friendly with Julie today, Gail will use any possible chance to literally stop Julie being friends with me. I know it sounds childish but it's so necessary for me to stay friends with them both until I leave that school. I just don't want to be alone again.

SARAH-JANE: But, it wasn't all black. I did have one very good close friend—Maggy. We became friends when we were seven and we are still friends today, and although our teenage friendship, for me, was subject to the same fears of abandonment I felt with other friends, she was the only friend I ever felt was really mine, and I trusted her far more than anyone else. However, for three years of our adolescence we lived in different towns and saw each other only on school vacations. Even after I came back to my hometown, Maggy and I did not attend the same school, so I usually only saw her on weekends. During the week, at school, I had to survive being the odd man out. My friendship with her extended to her family, and I experienced the same longing that other abused children experience when they are shown a window into a "normal" family.

November 16, 1977

Last night I was so desperate with everything. My dad didn't understand about school and Gail and Julie. So I walked out, stayed at Maggy's, and didn't go to school today. We talked about it, and tried to think of somewhere else I could live, as I hate it so much at home—a hostel or something. It won't solve the loneliness problem, but I feel lonely at home anyway. I wish so much that I was living with Maggy's family. I can't think of anything I'd like better. I'd have someone to come home to who would understand when it went wrong at school. I'm so unhappy, yet if I killed myself, it would be such a waste of a life.

SARAH-JANE: Today, when talking to Maggy about her childhood, I hear a different story. Not a horror story, but by no means picture-perfect. But picture-perfect or not, her home was often the only light at the end of my week, and Maggy was my only true childhood friend. As an adult I find making friends easier and my close friendships are loving and mutually supportive, but I still tread carefully. As in all my relationships, I know that I need to trust more, and find a way to express my disappointment and disillusionment assertively and painlessly rather than muffling it or waiting for it to explode. It has taken me many years to accept that if a friend is in a bad mood and doesn't feel like company, it doesn't mean that I am being abandoned, and every conflict we have doesn't mean I am not loved.

Puberty and Sexual Development

One aspect of life that seems impossible to control is puberty. The body has a biological clock with its own internal timers. However, although the research is inconsistent in this matter, sexual abuse has been thought to cause early sexual development in some girls (Brown et al., 2004; Herman-Giddens et al., 1988; Romans et al., 2003; Schmidt et al., 1995). Perhaps this is a result of the psychological stress of CSA, which has been shown to impact the body's hormonal system (van der Kolk, 1994). Nobody knows yet for sure. Puberty and the concomitant surge of sexual hormones can be overwhelming for any teenager, but for the CSA survivor this period of time can be even more confusing.

Many female survivors seem to want to prolong childhood, whereas others want to leave it behind as soon as possible. On the one hand, the development of secondary sex traits causes embarrassment, leading one to buy a bra that was too small in order to flatten her chest, and caused others to hate summer and swimming pools. Some survivors had been tomboys, and puberty was seen as a betrayal, forcing them to face being female. On the other hand, other survivors found that menstruation gave them protection, the abuse having ended once the possibility of pregnancy existed.

Regardless of whether they want to remain little girls or grow up, survivors talk of difficulties with their femininity and disgust with their bodies that begin in midadolescence. They often do not feel connected to their "femininity," believing that for other girls being female is much easier. Amazingly, Iris thought her body produced only male hormones and she did not feel female at all.

Miriam actually did enjoy moving into womanhood once she came to terms with being a girl and was wise to stop playing touch football with the boys on the street. She felt awkward with her changing body and hated any attention she got from her father and brother (the active abuse had ceased before puberty), but she used her sexual attractiveness outside the home to feel wanted and liked.

Many female survivors have periods of being one of two extremes: either a "slut" or a "nun." Both are ways of gaining control over sex and men. In the "slut" stage, the survivor feels she uses her body for her own purposes and, rather than leaving open the possibility that men will use her, she uses them first. At the other pole, "nun," the survivor declares a moratorium on sexual activity and no man will touch her in any way. This is consistent with the professional literature that points out the possible impact of shame and guilt on a girl's developing sexual identity (Finkelhor, 1984; Howell, 2002; Noll et al., 2003). Others suggest that sexual acting out may be related to levels of dissociation (e.g., Trickett and McBride-Chang, 1995) or to a compulsion to repeat the traumatic experience (van der Kolk, 1989).

Biological sexual development and gender identity formation have not been well explored in the professional literature for either male or female survivors. Some research on the difference in the psychological impact of CSA on boys and on girls has been done (for example, Gold et al., 1999) and on the contrasting gender-specific neurophysiological impact of trauma (Perry et al., 1996). Some inferences can be made from these reports. For example, it is recognized that boys are more often abused by nonfamily members, whereas girls are more often abused by family members. In this way, boys do not have to deal with the same degree of betrayal issues as do girls. However, sexual abuse of boys is more often accompanied by greater overt violence than abuse of girls, in which violence is often threatened but not always acted upon. In contrast with girls, who grow up knowing that they can fall prey to sexual harassment and rape, boys grow up perceiving masculinity as having nothing to do with possible victimization. In addition, given that boys develop emotionally at a slower rate than girls, boys have fewer emotional resources to deal with the impact of the abuse than do girls of the same age (see Oz [2005] for a more detailed review of the differences between the sexual abuse of boys and girls).

What does this mean regarding puberty and sexual development for girls? Does a difference exist between how sexually abused girls and how girls who were not sexually traumatized experience breast development, menstruation, sexual desire, masturbation, etc.? Some evidence is starting to emerge that a difference does exist. Noll et al. (2003) found greater anxiety and ambivalence regarding sexuality for abused girls when compared with their nonabused peers, and Schmidt et al. (1995) found that abuse survivors were more positive about masturbation than nonabused girls, perhaps viewing masturbation as less threatening than sexual intercourse with a partner. This finding stands in contradiction to my clinical experience; most clients express disgust at the thought of masturbating. Unfortunately, these studies focus on sexuality from the perspective of sexual (dys)function, whereas sexuality encompasses far more than that. The emotional and psychological aspects of gender identity, body image, etc. remain to be explored.

What can we say about puberty and sexual development in boys? Does a difference exist in how sexually abused boys experience sexual urges, wet dreams, masturbation, growth of the penis, increased musculature of their bodies, etc. in contrast with boys who were not sexually traumatized? Do male CSA survivors react differently than other boys and men to our increasingly pornographic society ("family" movies with explicit sex scenes, television advertisements, violent movies, etc.)? Research beginning to explore this area shows that male CSA survivors find sexual arousal and masturbation to be confusing and anxiety provoking (Bramblett and Darling, 1997; Lew, 1988). Unfortunately, the general perspective of the literature on the male survivor focuses on a possible connection between CSA and later abusive behaviors. This needs to be expanded to include aspects of normative sexual development and behavior.

Dating

If friendships during the school years are fraught with difficulties and psychobiological sexual development is conflictual for the CSA survivor, then the idea of dating and mate selection is likely also to be a complex issue. How is dating experienced? What kind of partner would the survivor look for? Would the eventual partner match what the survivor thought he or she was getting? This area, as well, has not been examined much in the research literature. However, clinical experience points us in a direction that will be discussed here.

Dating for some survivors was something to avoid. "Men just didn't flirt with me," states Orli. "I was afraid of that someone would ask me out and I would only go out in groups, never when there was the possibility of couples forming." On the other hand, Jana always made sure there was someone on hand, a new love interest. She would go out with someone for a time, and as soon as he started getting more serious she would break off the relationship. She explained to herself that she was less mature than her peers, not ready for a serious relationship. Only lately did she wonder if this pattern was related to her traumatic past.

In the same way that Carla used girlfriends to protect her from being at home alone, she later used men to protect her from being alone in the world. "All my boyfriends were just there so that I could say I had someone. I didn't love any of them. I didn't even want a boyfriend. I fell in love with their parents and wanted them to adopt me so that I would have a decent family." Nina wanted a boyfriend to provide a protective shield against the world, saying, "As long as I had a boy beside me I was safe from everyone else." Barb wanted more than anything to belong, to be like everyone else. She did not really want a boyfriend for herself but in order to be like her peers so that no one would wonder if anything was wrong.

In contrast, some survivors enjoy the thrill of dating. For some it may be the excitement of being in love, a state that does cause hormonal excitation similar to that of risk taking (Marazziti and Canale, 2004) For Jana, it provided a sense of power, of being able to make someone fall in love with her.

Men report similar attitudes toward dating. Mike, for example, was afraid to ask anyone out. He felt so ugly and stupid that he was sure nobody would want to be with him. Rob was very popular in school and always had a date, but always with a different girl. He loved the feeling of falling in love, but once he began to feel comfortable with someone the excitement was gone and he needed to find someone new. Joel liked being an accepted member of a family that felt normal to him. He would find someone he trusted and just stay with her; it was safest that way. It is difficult to know how common these patterns are to all teenage boys and how much they relate to a traumatic childhood.

Sarah-Jane's experience of dating as a teenager was turbulent. Because she believed that she was inherently bad, she felt that she needed to literally annihilate herself and her needs to please her boyfriends. Because she related to the opposite sex from a place of low self-esteem, Sarah-Jane often found herself in dysfunctional, sometimes violent, relationships.

SARAH-JANE: As a teenager I was obsessed with the opposite sex. Sexually developed, vibrant, and pretty, I got a lot of attention. However, my sexuality was a constant source of anxiety for me. I could not get enough of the attention it afforded me and was intoxicated by the power I felt with the opposite sex, but I was indiscriminate about the boys I spent time with, and, drawn to any boy who was interested, I often found myself the recipient of sexual touching that I did not want. I could not get the attention I was so hungry for without it, but because I wasn't emotionally ready for sexual activity I was plagued with feelings of shame and worthlessness. At thirteen I volunteered at a youth club as part of a school community project and got mixed up with a group of gypsy boys who spent time there.

December 12, 1974

I don't feel I can go back to the youth club. I met some more boys and walked home with four of them. Tony asked me out so he could have a bit. Honestly! Boys either think I'm a tight virgin or a fucking slut. Now he'll tell everyone what happened. They'll just laugh but they won't like me anymore.

December 25, 1974

Tonight I kept thinking about all the boys I'd been out with. A lot of them only wanted a bit of the other. That makes me a slut. I can't be anything else because I haven't got a personality. Inside I'm nothing, just a body.

January 6, 1975

Gym club cancelled, so I swallowed my pride and went to the youth club. George showed he liked me, but it might just be my body.

SARAH-JANE: In spite of all the attention, I was frequently treated badly. But, in my mind, just as attention and sexual touching were one and the same, there was no difference between affection and abuse. They were as closely entwined as the roots of a tree.

March 11, 1975

Terrible day, great evening. Enid said she asked George if he would go out with me and he said "Fuck off." I went to the youth club anyway and it was alright. George was still hitting me, but he's done that before. Affection is sometimes shown through violence. He was nice to me as well.

SARAH-JANE: My definition of a great evening at age thirteen was being hit by a boy I liked. And this was just the beginning. As time went on, I was always being humiliated in relationships. Boyfriends repeatedly stood me up, and I, helpless in the face of their indifference, would continue to make dates that they would not turn up to. It never occurred to me that perhaps I was choosing inconsiderate, even cruel, boys. Every time it happened I was thrown into self-doubt, convinced that I wasn't good enough, attractive enough, or intelligent enough. At fifteen, I was depressed and lonely, living with a father who abused me both sexually and emotionally. When life got too much I would dissociate from reality:

February 6, 1977

Everything's bad today. Bad, bad, bad! Nothing in my life is good. I enjoy sex but I can't do it right. I'm a failure at school, at home. My father hates me. I know my mother loves me, but because I don't often see her, I've lost touch, I don't communicate at all anymore. Tonight was horrifying. It was about eleven o'clock. I was coming home from Maggy's. At the bus stop there were two guys. One just stood there, the other kept staring into the sky. Then a drunken man went past muttering. He looked so weird. He kept swaying and I thought he'd knock into me. On the bus—a normal bus!—I kept hearing whispering, singing. First it came from the guy next to me, then the driver. Everything was distorted. I hate the world. I hate me.

SARAH-JANE: At the time, I was involved with a twenty-year-old man who drank too much and took drugs. Desperate to fill the void inside me, I believed, like so many codependents, that straightening him out would bring me peace and make me feel whole.

April 9, 1977

Shit! Jim hasn't phoned. God! I feel so depressed. So does he. I mustn't show how I feel. He's the most screwed up person I've met. I must try to make him happy. If I can do that, I'll feel I've achieved something. It's such a big thing to have to do. Everything is getting on top of me. I don't know what to do. I wish somebody would help me.

May 13, 1977

Jim said he'll stop smoking dope and speeding. And also stop relying on tranquilizers. I must straighten him out. Have you ever tried to straighten someone out when you're mixed up yourself? God, it's hard!

May 22, 1977

Nice evening. Spaghetti bolognese for dinner. When we were with the others, Jim got very angry and hit me, but he hardly touched me really, and we made up. Then we spent about an hour in the bathroom with the door locked. Lovely!

July 6, 1977

Last week I thought my depression had reached its peak and was going to decline. But now it's so bad, that if it gets worse I'll go silently mad. Jim told Maggy on Saturday that he wasn't strong enough to cope with me. I'll die. I really think I'll die. I'm now going to throw so much strength into my relationship with Jim that some must reflect back on me. If it doesn't then I'll decide how to commit suicide in one easy lesson.

August 14, 1977

Jim said he is not capable of loving and he doesn't want to be tied down. I realize what a mistake I made now. I look back on everything we said. I should have agreed to an easygoing, lighthearted relationship. I mustn't force him into anything or make demands on him, or else he will reluctantly stay in this relationship and that will cause bitterness.

August 30, 1977

Today has been a horrific, hellish numb nightmare. Just one big low. Jim finished with me last night, giving me all sorts of confused reasons. He's not interested and there's sweet fuck all I can do about it. I feel sorry, because he knows I've straightened him out a lot so far, but he doesn't realize that he *needs* me for the one thing he wants: "to sort himself out." Oh, sure, with will-power and strength he'll manage it, but it would be so much easier if I could help him.

SARAH-JANE: Where was I in all this? It's not surprising that I never once considered my own needs, for at fifteen I felt as empty, as devoid of personality, and as worthless as I did at thirteen. And so began a long string of unsuitable, unavailable sexual partners and lovers. Sometimes I would even end up in bed with guys who did not attract me sexually, then either have sex with them out of politeness or feel guilty about not having sex with them! I was a magnet for men who put me down, could not commit, and were careless with my heart.

June 5, 1980

Steve: I'd love to tell you how I feel, but I know deep down that, at best, you would pity me and, at worst, you would run from me with contempt. I'll never have you I know. All I can hope is that I'm important enough to be spared a thought now and again. Could I be falling in love again? I'd forgotten how miserable it is when it is unrequited. But hasn't it always been miserable and unrequited with you?

October 18, 1980

Feel happy. Just because I slept with Steve last night. Still don't know what he feels as he won't talk, but he wasn't well last night. The worst thing was that we were in a place I didn't know at somebody's house. It brought back how sordid it was at the beginning, screwing in places we didn't know. I cried most of the night and nearly went home because he ignored me. It was very selfish of me because he was tired. Still he didn't hear me, which is just as well. I think he *must* know how I feel now. Is that good or bad?

SARAH-JANE: The only stable element in this chaotic string of relationships was that I practically erased myself to meet the needs of every boy or man I dated or slept with. As time went on, I became increasingly anxious about showing my feelings. Cynical about love and distrustful of the opposite sex, I began to shy away from any hint of emotional involvement. Eventually I insulated myself so successfully from my feelings that I eradicated any affection and warmth from my interactions with men, whom I had sex with but never made love to. As an adult, after years of therapy, I have gradually learned to celebrate my sexuality, a sexuality worlds away from the sexual persecution of my childhood. As for combining sex and love, progress is slow. The damage done to my ability to trust a sexual partner is enormous, but looking back over the past ten years it is clear that I am learning. It might take me the rest of my life to get there, but I know that the journey itself will be as rewarding as all the other journeys I've made.

INTO ADULTHOOD

Partner Selection

What kind of committed partnership does the CSA survivor actually enter? Little research has been done on this topic. However, if we look at the most important factors in mate selection we can extrapolate what an intimate relationship may look like for the adult who was sexually abused during childhood (see Chapter 3 for an in-depth discussion on couples' relationships). From my clinical work with couples, I have found that the most important elements in mate selection are self-esteem and ability to form trusting relationships. Both elements are seriously affected by having grown up sexually traumatized. When the child is not properly cared for, he or she doubts his or her lovability. The child, feeling unworthy of love, anticipates that all close relationships will lead to disaster—either he or she will be hurt very badly or he or she will be abandoned. This is obviously not a solid basis upon which to form meaningful relationships.

SARAH-JANE: My choice of a partner was definitely influenced by my abusive childhood. After years of fruitless dating, I met Avi, my future husband. Although I was attracted to him, for the first time in my life I did not jump into bed on the first or second date. We became friends over a period of several months before I committed myself to the relationship. Perhaps I waited because somewhere deep inside I knew he was the man I would marry, or maybe he became the man I was going to marry because I got to know him first. One thing I'm certain about is that he wasn't like the other men I had known. He was neither "commitment phobic" nor strung out on drugs and alcohol.

We were together for more than twenty years, and the relationship was not perfect, but looking back I know exactly why I chose him. He was dependable, responsible, and solid as a rock—the antithesis to my parents. I knew he would always provide for his family, that he would stick by me through thick and thin, and most important, he would not sexually abuse our future children. Is that enough to base a marriage on? Probably not, but as a survivor of childhood sexual abuse, and before even beginning to work on resolving the abuse, I made a surprisingly good choice. We had our ups and downs, our fun and our tears just like any other couple. Intimacy with a man is still a fraught issue for me, and to be honest, although I chose my husband carefully, I probably would have chosen differently had I not been abused. But no one can guarantee that it would have been a better choice.

Parenting

In this section we will look at parenting from the point of view of CSA survivor parents and their concerns about their ability to raise healthy children. Chapter 8 will explore the impact on children of having a CSA survivor mother or father.

When they set out to build their own families, where do CSA survivors find role models on which to base their own parenting skills? How can they protect their children when they themselves were not protected? If inappropriate sexual behavior was the norm in their family of origin, how can they relate in a healthy way to their own children? If they were abused how can they stop themselves abusing in turn? It emerges that here, as in other aspects of life, the polarity rule affects the adult CSA survivor's parenting. In other words, either an inordinate emphasis is placed on protection or the parent is resigned to feeling as if they cannot ever protect their children. A parent can remain in one position or the other throughout his or her life span, or flip back and forth between these extremes when the children are at different stages of development. And, of course, it is obvious that some CSA survivor parents do neglect their children or abuse them emotionally, physically, or sexually—mothers as well as fathers.

What about other aspects of parenting? How are pregnancy and nursing experienced? How does the CSA survivor parent handle hygienic care of their children? Sex education? Does being a parent affect the CSA survivor's interactions with the spouse or other relations differently than for the parent who was not abused? What is it like for the CSA survivor to raise teenagers?

The information we have on survivors as parents comes mainly from survivors in therapy who agree to participate in research and from anecdotal reports of therapists working with survivor parents. Probably similar to that of other therapists in the field, my clinical experience concerns mostly mothers. Most of the male survivors with whom I have worked clinically are children, adolescents, or young and still unmarried adults. Older male survivors are still very reluctant to disclose their stories of abuse and, therefore, are seen less in therapy.

The need for control shouts out at us from survivors' descriptions of their experiences of motherhood. Notice how here, as in other areas, control can express itself either through an inordinate need for order and compliance on the part of others or in the absolute relinquishment of control to others.

Nurit says the whole issue of motherhood scares her. It seems too much responsibility exists over the life of another human being. She would not know how to keep her child from harm. She may be an example of what Professor C.M. Willems (2005, personal communication) calls "conscientious objectors," survivors who decide not to have children as a means of preventing the next generation from being abused.

Barb (now a mother of two) expected motherhood to make her life perfect. She imagined family walks in a pastoral setting, similar to the movies, planning the picture down to the finest detail. She got pregnant as soon as she wed, feeling a deep need to see if "something" she could produce could come out normal. She did not really believe that a baby of hers could be okay, yet she was determined that everything had to be perfect. She stopped smoking the moment she knew she was pregnant—she stopped smoking two and a half packs of cigarettes a day in a moment! It was as if her control over something such as smoking gave her control over everything else as well.

Jana enjoyed being pregnant. It made her feel as if something was filling up the "black hole" in her gut. In contrast, Orli did not think about motherhood at all. Even when she was pregnant she had no feelings one way or the other toward the coming baby. She felt disconnected from her body, disconnected from her life. It was as if she was fulfilling expectations others had of her, nothing more.

For some mothers, the baby was seen as a strange, incomprehensible creature with incomprehensible needs, sometimes even an enemy. Motherhood was foreign; the mother felt helpless and did not know how she was supposed to behave. Some recent research (eg., Buist, 1998) shows that postpartum depression may be more common for women who were abused than women who were not. The impact of depression can be debilitating, and the mother's self-esteem will suffer as a result. Nursing in this case can be incredibly difficult (Kendall-Tackett, 1998). Nina felt she was being torn up inside when her baby nursed. Nursing for Iris was something that just had to be done, something that was instinctual, automatic. It is interesting to note the dissociation in Iris's relationship with her baby: on the one hand she responded to him as if from a place of deep connection, an instinctual bond with the child, while at the same time she felt emotionally remote, as if on automatic pilot. For others, motherhood was a natural state, something they slipped into easily. At times an overly symbiotic relationship existed in which the mother overidentified with the child. For example, it took Miriam and Jana about a month before they were able to call their children by name and not see their daughters as an extension of themselves.

Unfortunately for Barb the reality after her child's birth was so different from the dream that she was left with feelings of rage. In spite of her fear that nothing she produced could be normal, her children could be nothing less than perfect, and when they weren't she was angry. Sitting with other mothers she would listen to them telling stories about how wonderful their children were, and she had nothing to tell. Everyone else's children were great; only her children were not. She felt she was such a failure—every woman knew how to be a mother, only she did not. This is consistent with the results of a study by Fitzgerald et al. (2005), who found that CSA survivor mothers tended to be overly critical of their parenting behaviors.

After her son was born, Orli understood she had to protect him, but she still operated robotically. Living with her in-laws, she let others do everything instead of taking responsibility herself. When she and her husband were able to move into their own apartment, she understood that she would be on her own and thought she was prepared. However, once alone she found that she could not function at all. Suddenly, she was overwhelmed by flashbacks of the abuse without understanding at the time what they were. She could not bear the sound of the baby's crying. It frightened her and she felt out of control, and being unable to tolerate the feeling of fear, it turned into anger. She felt like a lion in a cage. She would sometimes shake the baby. Once, when she felt she was losing control and could really hurt him, she put the baby down and went into another room. She knew she must never hurt her child. In order not to hurt the baby, when she needed to release her rage, she would scream at the dog and kick the sofa. When her son was a year old, she recognized that she needed help. She went to social services and asked for help to learn how to raise her son safely. Luckily she was treated with respect rather than suspicion. Today, Orli's posttraumatic reactions to childbirth are recognized by professionals (Kendall-Tackett, 1998) even though a clear need for more research in this area exists.

In contrast, when her daughter was born she did not let anyone else take care of her. This was very different from her first time. She no longer had problems with the crying. However, this time she jumped to the opposite extreme of motherhood and she was always around, did not let both her children out of her sight. Nina is also overprotective, warning her children constantly to be aware of others. If it appears that one of her children is upset, she immediately interrogates him or her, making sure no inappropriate touching had happened.

Whereas some mothers keep their children close to them, want to know at all moments what is happening and will not leave them with babysitters, other mothers may leave their children with others too easily. Barb is sorry now that she used to leave her children with her parents even though her father had abused her. When her children were young, she was aware of his severe physical abuse of her but had not remembered the sexual abuse. After his death the memories came back. Now she is left with remorse for having entrusted her parents with her children, and even though they deny that her father ever touched them inappropriately, she is not without guilt. Nina is afraid that one can never truly protect one's children. The world is a dangerous place and no real protection can every truly be offered.

Being a mother of girls is different from being a mother of boys. Iris was happy to have given birth to sons and not daughters. However, when her sons began to reach puberty she began to fear them just as she fears men in general. It has taken a great amount of work for her to neutralize the fear of her own sons. Barb found that she was fearful for her son and daughter in different ways. She was worried that her son would become homosexual. She wanted him to be a "man," but perhaps because she feared nothing of hers could turn out "normal" she was afraid he would not be straight. Apprehensive of her daughter's growing maturity and the sexual attention she could draw, she would buy clothes that were too large for her. Furthermore, she never let her husband walk around the house in any state of undress and always observed his relationship with the children.

Sarah-Jane put a great deal of work into her relationship with her children. In fact, this was the initial reason for her decision to go into therapy. In the following account she describes her experience of motherhood and her struggle to be what she calls "good enough."

SARAH-JANE: I became pregnant during my first year of marriage, and if being in a serious relationship was difficult, becoming and being a parent was no less so. Being emotionally unstable and immature, my mother had been unable to provide a safe environment for me to grow up in. She submerged herself in me and my siblings when we were born, reveling in the symbiotic state of mother and newly born baby, but she retreated from us once we showed signs of independence. Although she tended to our basic needs and there was always food and clothing, on a deeper, emotional level she was not present, and this was one factor that made it possible for the abuse to take place. I found myself, as a small child, thrown to the wolves, unprotected by the one person I trusted and loved.

So, having had little or no experience of competent parenting, as an adult I did not have a healthy role model to refer to in my own experience as a parent. I found myself lost, bewildered, and terrified when I gave birth to my first child. I kept my daughter fed, warm, and clean, but most of what I remember from the first few years of mothering was a never-ending power struggle, revolving around how much of my attention my daughter was going to get. The baby was restless and demanding, and I, miserable and frustrated by my inability to give my daughter enough love and attention, felt inadequate and hopeless.

In addition to feeling trapped and overwhelmed by my daughter's incessant demands, I found myself plagued with severe anxiety and fear that something terrible would happen to her. From the moment I knew I was pregnant I was frequently bombarded by frightening scenes in my mind that materialized suddenly and apparently out of nowhere. In these scenes, either my baby was in danger and I could do nothing to protect her, or I myself was hurting my child. Although I loved my baby deeply, this fear and anxiety only served to push me farther away from her.

The years passed and I gave birth to another daughter. My first-born continued to be demanding, and the resentment I felt at having to constantly engage in the attention power struggle began to turn into anger, and eventually into an all-consuming, barely controllable rage. Eventually, when my eldest daughter was four, I realized that I was in danger of causing harm to my children. I hooked up with Sheri through a friend and began the long journey toward mental and emotional health.

A major consequence of the abuse that I found to be prevalent in my life as an adult and a mother was a powerful life or death need to control my environment:

December 2, 1990

I'm driven by this gut instinct to control everyone in my life—my husband, children, and most of all, myself. My life has to be methodically organized. Everything and everyone in my surroundings is rigidly controlled, and others are forced to fit into my routine. My violent feelings toward my child don't fit into all this, since they are almost impossible to control. I hang on to my self-control by a thread. So here, into my perfectly controlled life comes a burning hot, raging emotion that needs all my energy to control. Am I trying to tell myself something?

Perhaps my obsession with control is the reason I can't get in touch with my feelings. I put so much effort into organizing my life to a tee, filling my day with chores and activities down to the last minute, that I make absolutely sure that I won't have time to feel.

SARAH-JANE: Once in therapy, I gradually began to connect with the void that my childhood had left me with. It became clear that one of the main obstacles in my struggle to be a good mother to my children was that I simply could not give what I hadn't received.

June 9, 1991

Several times today I wanted to escape, to run away from the responsibility of mothering. I wanted to be a child, spoiled and mothered. Which would explain my blowing up at my daughter all day. She needs my mothering and she doesn't care if I happen to be rebelling against motherhood on a particular day.

SARAH-JANE: One of the first issues addressed in therapy was my expectation of the mother/child relationship. Since I had no role model of motherhood I could turn to I had very unrealistic expectations. I lived in a world of absolutes and was unable to accept anything less than perfection, both in myself as a mother and in my children.

Also, although I was aware that something had been terribly wrong in my childhood and that I had received inappropriate caretaking I did not yet remember all aspects of having been sexually abused. Although I had always had memories of my father's inappropriate sexual behavior, I did not see this behavior as abusive. So I believed that my rage and violent feelings toward my daughter could only be the result of a fundamental flaw in my character. I began to work on my rage in therapy, but in the beginning my feelings of self-hate were worse because I still held on to the ideal of a picture perfect mother, and therapy was supposed to help me achieve that. So when things did not change immediately and completely for the better I felt myself to be even more of a failure— impossible to help, beyond saving.

September 17, 1991

Now I sit here despairing, quelling the urge to cry because I've lost my newfound affection with my child, not to mention her trust that I'd started to build over the past three weeks. I look back and remember how good I felt about her and myself as a mother and feel the pain people feel when they remember a lost love.

SARAH-JANE: Today, several years after therapy, I know that no perfect people and no such thing as perfection in human relationships exist. If I'm not a perfect mother that doesn't make me a pathetic failure or an evil person with a deeply flawed character. Now I know that life and relationships are full of bad days and good days, and the relationship between parent and child is no exception. However, I believe that as long as the child's needs are answered within a healthy, functioning framework and bad days take place in the context of a basically loving, warm, and supportive relationship, then the damage is not permanent. In the past I believed that if I was the epitome of the perfect mother (and nothing less!) for three weeks and then had one day during which I lost my temper, then the three weeks were erased as though they had never been. Eventually I began to question my unrealistic model of motherhood. Bad days continued to happen but a perceptible change occurred in my response to them. Instead of just wallowing in desperation at another bad moment, I would try to rectify it:

November 18, 1992

I got into a spiteful rage because my daughter forgot her homework, which ended with me calling her a stupid brat who shouldn't be allowed in school and throwing her schoolbag the length of the room! Later, after I'd put her to bed, she called me in and I stroked her face and said I was sorry and she wasn't stupid, but the cleverest child in the world. I'm glad I can admit I'm wrong to her, but I wonder if it repairs damage done.

SARAH-JANE: I spent years in therapy, taking a break of less than a year, before finally going back to resolve the trauma of my childhood abuse. On the one hand I had to work through memories of the horrific and sadistic abuse suffered at the hands of my father while on the other hand I had to face the terrifying void left inside me as a result of my mother's neglect and failure to keep me from harm.

As the therapy sessions took me deeper into the world of past abuse, and closer to the insanity prevalent in that world, I found myself retreating from my husband and children. My marriage suffered enormously and times occurred when I believed that the damage to my relationship with my husband was irreparable. I managed to maintain a tenuous connection with my children, but most of the time I put nearly all of my energy into pushing through the enormous pain caused by reclaiming ownership of long-buried childhood memories. Functioning in other areas of my life was down to a bare minimum, and my life was a mere skeleton of what it had once been. I began to feel as though I was imprisoned in a transparent cage, looking at family, friends, and loved ones through a glass wall.

October 31, 1993

I have this feeling that I'm always writing about panic and depression. I'm surrounded by people who love and care for me, deeply. Why can't I touch their love? Why can't I take it? My husband and children offer me their love every hour of every day. Their hands are open toward me, palms face up and the love is piled upon them, just waiting for me to reach out and touch it. They never retract it, never draw back. I stand and watch them offering me their love, through a glass wall, and only sometimes I allow myself to feel the warm rays that it projects on to me.

SARAH-JANE: This family I loved so much, the family denied me as a child, the family I had yearned for, now became, paradoxically, part of me yet alien to me. And when I looked at them it was as if I were looking through a window into another world. It was as though I had cut myself off from their world in order to rebuild myself. I needed to recognize and fill the emptiness inside me before I could come back and be a fully functioning member of my family.

December 14, 1993

Today was a miserable day, but in spite of this I came home and managed to bathe the girls and read them both stories of their choice. I put them to bed after looking over homework and helping to organize schoolbags. These motherly duties are now so rare and foreign to me (and probably to them!) that I realized how much I missed them and my role as a mother. All the same, even though I enjoyed it, I'm still not ready to go back entirely, and I mustn't get overenthusiastic or push myself too much, otherwise I'll only frighten myself and lose the satisfaction I get from these small insights into mothering.

SARAH-JANE: Now, looking back, it is clear to me that I could not go on being the mother I was—physically present, emotionally distant, and overwhelmed with rage at my daughters' vulnerability, with each new anxiety attack pushing me farther away from them. I had to learn how to be a mother from scratch. I needed to build a new image of parenthood, my own model, not based on the dysfunctional parents of my childhood and the poison of my abusive past. I had to throw away the old model, completely dismantle it, and start anew. However difficult it was for my children and for me it was the only way I could break the chain of abuse and neglect.

Eventually I found healthier ways to deal with the legacy of rage and fear from my childhood instead of projecting them on to my children. The anxiety attacks did not disappear, but they became less frequent and, more important, I knew where they were coming from. In time, I stopped perceiving them as terrifying, incomprehensible scenes thrust unbidden into my consciousness and saw them for what they were: flashbacks from my nightmare childhood. I made mistakes as a parent, but my world did not crumble around me each time I made them. Being able to pick myself up and forgive myself made it easier for me to go back to being the loving mother I wanted to be, and understanding the reasons for the mistakes often made it possible for me to avoid similar behavior in the future.

May 14, 1995

I took the children to Sheri about a week ago. She said they'd be alright, that they are strong and that my encouraging openness and honesty was a great help. Since this meeting I have become closer to them. Although there have been some crazy moments when their vulnerability terrified and enraged me, I have allowed myself to feel love for them.

SARAH-JANE: Having come from a place where my own vulnerability was exploited and abused, the innocence and fragility of my daughters had always driven me to distraction, but I had reached a point where I could still stay connected to them in spite of my fear, and this was an incredible achievement for me.

July 9, 2004

In the diary entry at the beginning of this chapter, written in July 1994, I spoke of poison soaking through the layers of my being. Now, ten years later, I see that with each journey I made, at least one layer was reclaimed. There is still work to be done, but the healing process is just that: a process.

SARAH-JANE: My daughters are teenagers now. Strong and independent, they are a source of great happiness to me, and although the anxiety I felt in the past at their vulnerability still peeps out of my subconscious from time to time, I recognize it instantly, and soothe it with calming thoughts. I'm a good enough mother, but not perfect, and one of the most valuable insights from my journey of healing is that I do not have to be.

Parenting is known to raise issues for parents that have still not been resolved from their own childhoods. In responding to the needs of their children, adults have the opportunity to look at their own parents' behaviors from a new perspective, hopefully finding a way to accept their parents' shortcomings. However, when parenting was so noxious that overt abuse occurred or an environment was created in which abuse by another was possible, then resolution and forgiveness are not simple and perhaps not even possible (see Chapter 6). The full impact of this on the CSA survivor parent's parenting values, approaches, and behaviors are still not clear. The consequent impact on the next generation will be explored in Chapter 8.

Still more questions than answers exist regarding the impact of CSA on social and sexual development. Understanding this impact could help survivors feel less "weird" and less judgmental toward themselves. With the self-hate mitigated in this way, their ability to actively engage in therapy and work through the trauma would probably be enhanced because they would understand more easily how it is possible for the therapist, and others in their lives, to value them as human beings. Being valued by self and others (or at least believing that this is possible) provides the motivation for the hard work of therapy, described in Chapters 4 to 7.

Chapter 3

Intimate Relationships
and the World of Trauma

Sheri Oz

One of the most valuable things we can do to heal one another is
listen to each other's stories

Rebecca Falls

Some child sexual abuse (CSA) survivors tell their partners about
the abuse as part of their growing intimacy before they have made a
formal commitment. Others do not share this fact, leaving the partner
puzzling over seemingly incomprehensible behaviors and responses.
In Chapter 2 we looked at subjective experiences of survivors in a
number of areas that are pertinent to mate selection and committed
relationships. In this chapter we will look at some of the factors at
play in couples relationships based upon theoretical views. Little research has been done on this population and most of that has been for
the heterosexual couple. Hopefully this discussion will be useful for
the same-sex couple as well. All examples described are conglomerates of couples in which one partner was in therapy with me.

THE CSA SURVIVOR
IN AN INTIMATE RELATIONSHIP

The betrayal inherent in CSA means that intimate couples relationships will probably be even more challenging in some ways than for
partners who both grew up in fairly healthy families. For one thing,

Overcoming Childhood Sexual Trauma
Published by The Haworth Press, Inc., 2006, All rights reserved.
doi:10.1300/5668_03

trust, as discussed throughout this book, is not easily handled by the
CSA survivor (DiLillo and Long, 1999; Johnson and Williams-Keeler,
1998; Kirschner and Kirschner, 1996; Serafin, 1996). Given the polarity rule noted for this population (discussed in Chapter 2), we would
expect the CSA survivor to find it difficult to develop healthy levels of
trust. Instead of taking the time to get to know the potential partner, the
CSA survivor may jump in with both feet or, alternatively, withhold
trust to an exaggerated degree for years. Lacking the skills to assess
trustworthiness, the CSA survivor could find himself or herself in a relationship that is emotionally, physically, or sexually abusive. This
would reinforce the survivor's belief that nobody can be trusted.

Survivors have problems communicating feelings (Bacon and Lein,
1996; Johnson and Williams-Keeler, 1998; McCollum, 1993; Nelson
and Wampler, 2000; Pistorello and Follette, 1998; Serafin, 1996). They
may explode in a rage that is out of proportion to the situation (Bacon
and Lein, 1996), or be unable to express anger in any way. They may
cry at the slightest provocation, or be unable to cry at all when crying
would be an appropriate response. Several reasons for this exist.
First, dissociation during the abuse event in childhood cut survivors
off from their feelings, and many remain dissociated into adulthood.
This leaves them confused about what they feel and unable to label
emotions or talk about them. Second, it may be frightening either to
acknowledge to themselves what they feel or to express this to others.
Some survivors are afraid that if they start to lift the lid off their pot of
feelings, a dam will burst open and emotions held in check until that
moment will surge forth out of control. Other people, therefore, may
find them to be cold and unfeeling. Third, for some survivors, any
emotion may be expressed as anger. Jana, for example, was not aware
until later in her therapy that when she thought she was expressing
sadness or hurt feelings, others backed off in apprehension of what
they experienced as her anger. Fourth, the low self-esteem of the CSA
survivor may lead him or her to feel undeserving of any supportive attention or consideration and certain that no one would be willing to
listen to his or her feelings.

Sexuality, another aspect of an intimate relationship, is a veritable
quicksand for CSA survivors. Not allowed to grow into their sexuality at their own pace, they find this a painful part of couplehood (Button and Dietz, 1995; Maltz, 2001; Westerlund, 1992). Some survivors
may suffer from an aversion to sex (Buttenheim and Levendosky,

1994; Maltz, 2001), or conversely, they may use sex compulsively much as others use alcohol or other addictive behaviors (Scharff and Scharff, 1994). Since trust, communication and sexuality are the basic foundations upon which a good relationship is built, quite a challenge is in store for the CSA survivor and his or her partner.

COUPLES RELATIONSHIPS

Couples enter into a contractual relationship whether they get married or not. Every relationship, in fact, has a "contract" of some form in that each person has expectations of the other. Some of these expectations are overt and discussed openly; other expectations are more subtle, and the individuals may not even be aware of them. Overt expectations may include such issues as where the couple will live, how they will spend their money, division of labor regarding household tasks, how many children they will have, if any, who they will count among their conjoint friends and which friends will not be part of their joint social circle, etc.

It is unlikely that partners will agree on all of these issues. They need to negotiate to come to a compromise that will be satisfactory to both of them. This requires them to know what they want and to have communication skills, assertiveness, and flexibility. CSA survivors may have difficulties with any of these qualities. As children, they were unaccustomed to having their personal needs or desires taken into account; therefore, as adults they may not even know what they want. Sometimes they do not have the ability to stand up for themselves or, alternatively, they do not have the flexibility that enables them to compromise. Here again is evidence of the polarity rule. For instance, as soon as she married, Miriam was suddenly unable to make even the simplest of decisions, such as choosing a movie or restaurant. A successful professional who had regarded herself as a strong, capable woman before marriage, she saw herself defer to her husband and lose personal power almost immediately. In contrast, Barb needed to make all the family decisions. She would get furious if her husband insisted on anything against her wishes. As discussed in Chapter 2, we can understand these extremes as being the way each of these women found to deal with the need for control: Miriam gave up the chance of ever having any control and Barb demanded absolute control. No room existed for maneuvering and both women were under a great deal of stress, as were their husbands.

Sometimes apparently overt expectations are comprised of other, more subtle issues. For example, in deciding where they would live for the next ten years, Nurit and Suzanne thought they were making a rational decision based solely upon technical matters, such as distance from work, housing costs in relation to expected income, and type of neighborhood. However, they continued to fight and were unable to agree on which apartment to take. After discussing the issue in therapy, Nurit became aware that the area Suzanne was enthusiastic about reminded Nurit of the neighborhood in which she grew up, and as they looked at one apartment after another Nurit was being triggered without understanding the cause. As a result she would lash out at Suzanne in anger, unable to talk about it but upset with Suzanne for "causing her to feel that way." Once she understood this, Nurit told Suzanne and they found it easier to discuss whether they would seek housing in a different neighborhood or whether Nurit, now knowing what was triggering her anxiety, would be less affected.

The second section of the couples agreement deals with the "love contract." Each partner has his or her own expectations about how love will be expressed. In couples' workshops I have participants write on an index card an answer to the question "How do I know I still love my spouse?" (To date, I have only conducted workshops for heterosexual couples.) Typical responses given by husbands are: "I still have a ring on my finger," "When she's sick I like to pamper her," "When I have to go on a business trip, I miss her almost as soon as the plane takes off," "Even when I see women younger and prettier than her, she's the one I want to make love to," and "When something good or bad happens to me, she's the first one I want to tell." Typical responses by wives are: "I look forward to him coming home in the evening," "When he's late, I worry about him," "I know I love him when, after all these years, he still turns me on," and "He's my best friend."

These responses can be divided into three categories: emotional intimacy or friendship, sexual attraction, and commitment. Individuals differ in the emphasis they place on each of these categories, and these may change over time. Sexual attraction, for example, may be more important for one partner at the beginning of the relationship when newness is exciting, whereas the other partner may find that when aging causes physical changes that affect self-esteem, sexual relations take on a significance that did not exist earlier. For the CSA survivor the "love contract" may be complicated because sex and love have been confused for him or her by the perpetrator. Debra, for example, decided that if her partner loved her enough he would be willing to forgo having sex with her altogether because of the anxiety it caused her.

The psychological contract is the most difficult contract to discuss because it involves largely unconscious wishes and needs. A committed relationship can be considered a form of therapy, since partners are frequently selected on the basis of unresolved psychological issues from childhood. In my clinical experience I find that people often choose partners who present them with the same challenges they faced with the parent they found most difficult. Apparently an unconscious hope exists that it will be possible to gain mastery over problems originating with this parent when in a relationship with someone who is supposed to be one's equal, one's partner in life. In fact, mate selection may be an accurate unconscious identification of complementarity (Dicks, 1967). This complementarity does not mean that the partners are opposites in the sense of being characterologically different, but rather that they are "polarized variants of the same conflict" (Miller et al., 1988, p. 107).

For the CSA survivor, these conflicts probaby revolve around the pattern of victim-abuser that results from growing up with abuse and/or neglect. Individuals who grew up in abusive environments internalized the roles of abuser, victim, "blind" bystander, and rescuer. They will play out these roles in a variety of relationships throughout their life until they resolve their own abuse and learn how to get out of this vicious rectangle. If the survivor has more issues with an unprotective parent than with an abusive parent, then he or she may get involved with a partner who is largely unresponsive to his or her emotional states. This person may be stable and trustworthy so that at first the relationship feels safe and the partner is perceived as a rescuer. However, unable to sustain deep emotional communications, the partner can later be experienced as abandoning or neglectful. The survivor attempts to engage the partner emotionally, yet he or she remains aloof. After some time this feels abusive to the survivor who feels victimized by the partner's coolness. The survivor lashes out at the partner, who then feels victimized himself or herself, a situation that can cause the survivor to feel guilty and apologize. The partner, happy to have life return to the status quo, is once more steady and calm and the situation settles down—for a while, until the survivor once more needs the partner's emotional support.

On the other hand, if the CSA survivor was drawn to someone who represents an abusive parent then the partner may appear strong, harsh, and easily angered. The survivor feels that his or her love will be enough to make the partner change and lose his or her aggressive manner. In other words, the survivor will rescue the partner from his or her "bad habits." This, of course, does not happen, and the survivor can end up feeling victimized by the partner. The survivor may punish the partner either by withdrawing or by being more aggressive. Thus the survivor is perceived as abusive and the partner feels victimized. The vicious cycle continues.

Partners who themselves were traumatized to some degree are likely to be especially vulnerable to the abuser-victim-bystander-rescuer pattern. It is not surprising, then, to find that women who are CSA survivors marry men with PTSD, such as war veterans (Nelson and Wright, 1996), other childhood trauma survivors, etc. In these cases, complementarity exists in that both partners probably have problems with self-esteem, trust, emotional expression, intimacy, sexuality, etc., and by either rescuing or being rescued by the partner an attempt is made to resolve childhood problems (Oz, 2001).

Being in an intimate relationship with someone who suffers from the aftereffects of chronic childhood trauma can result in a "sharing" of trauma symptoms, even if the partner has no personal trauma history. In response to symptomatic behavior on the part of the CSA survivor, the partner may experience inordinate stress and anxiety, and some partners may themselves develop symptoms associated with posttrauma (Chauncey, 1994; Maltas and Shay, 1995). This is referred to as *vicarious traumatization* (Pearlman and Saakvitne, 1995).

After some time, equilibrium is reached. When the couple is flexible they develop a relationship whereby each can support the other according to need. When one partner is in distress, the other can put aside his or her own needs and provide support with the secure knowledge that, when required, the partner will do the same for him or her. However, many CSA survivors and/or their partners lack this flexibility and find themselves stuck in a pattern whereby the survivor either constantly rescues or is rescued by the partner. In these relationships, in which the spouses take on polarized positions, a lack of intimacy exists. With no freedom of movement spouses cannot support and be supported; no real closeness, no authenticity exists in their relationship, they are playing roles rather than being whole human beings with both strengths and weaknesses. A truly intimate relationship includes confidence that if one person needs the other, the partner will be supportive and not belittle him or her or use knowledge of the weaknesses as a weapon. It is likely that the model of the codependent couple first recognized with regard to alcoholism and drug abuse is relevant here.

Codependency means that neither partner stands firm on his or her own two feet. To feel good about himself or herself the seemingly healthier spouse needs the partner to remain weaker or more problematic. Dan finally understood how his wife used his dissociative problems to maintain her own sense of self-esteem. He would often forget things he or others said or did. This made him fear his sanity and he was always sure he was on the verge of a breakdown. His wife recognized this and used it to her benefit. She could tell him anything she wanted or do anything she pleased and convince him that if he remembered things differently or not at all it was because he was crazy. Knowing that he did have a problem with memory, he believed her. Only when faced with undeniable proof that she had lied to him was he able to confront her. Faced with a stronger husband, she suddenly fell apart and was unable to function both at work and at home. Dan realized that her apparent mental health had been bolstered by his apparent madness. Still, the "pull" back into this crazy pattern was very strong, and he felt guilty for her breakdown. It required much support from people who cared for him for Dan to maintain his gains and wait for his wife to decide whether to work on herself, and for him to decide what he would do if she did not.

Cindy, another example of a "weaker" partner, was confused most of the time. She had no family and had adopted her husband's family as her own. She felt unable to make decisions on her own and relied on her husband for everything. She would not even buy a piece of clothing without his prior approval. Feeling herself unworthy, she was grateful to him for having married her. He felt like a knight in shining armor.

Not all couples become embroiled in this pattern of interaction. For these interactions to take place, both partners must be drawn into the current, because if one partner does not play the complementary role these scenarios will not develop. For instance, although Fay was similar to Cindy, her husband did not want to be a "knight," and when she felt insecure he refused to do her tasks for her. They fought often, but he was as willing to hold her when she cried as he was to stand firm before her when she railed at him. Their arguments were loud but respectful, they did not swear at each other or use weaknesses as weapons to hurt each other. Their relationship developed over the years into one that was mutually supportive and satisfying.

On the other hand, it may be the CSA survivor who is the seemingly healthier spouse. Remember that the polarity of the CSA survivor can push him or her into either overfunctioning or underfunctioning as a response to the need for control. Carla, for instance, married a man who earned a good living but who could not cook or change a light-bulb. He relied on her to take care of everything around the house. Whenever problems with the neighbors, handymen, and even his parents occurred, Carla took care of it. She felt strong and important to him. He felt taken care of. These same patterns will be found for same-sex couples and when the husband in a heterosexual couple is the CSA survivor.

CHANGES IN THE RELATIONSHIP DURING THE CSA SURVIVOR'S THERAPY

Some partners feel betrayed when confronted with the abuse (Button and Dietz, 1995; Follette and Pistorello, 1995), either when they are told about it some time after having made a commitment to the relationship, or when faced with the inevitable yet unexpected changes in their relationship patterns during the turmoil of the therapy process. Other partners, however, feel honored by the trust such sharing entails (Davis, 1991; Follette and Pistorello, 1995).

The therapeutic process is draining on the survivor. Initially, it may be calming as the client-therapist relationship is beginning to form and hope for a better future exists. However, within a relatively short time tension begins to grow (as described in Chapter 5). As the client moves closer to the Wall of Fear, mood changes can become more extreme, and the survivor may feel as if he or she is in constant crisis (see also Buttenheim and Levendosky, 1994; Button and Dietz, 1995). Seemingly innocuous events or objects can become triggers, setting off anxiety or panic reactions. Flashbacks may be overwhelming, symptoms grow in intensity and the survivor suffers from increased suicidal ideation.

Couples are confronted with a situation in which they may need to change their original couples contract to correspond to the changing nature of their interactions (Chauncey, 1994; Kirschner and Kirschner, 1996; McCollum, 1993; Serafin, 1996). When a partner used to taking care of the survivor is unable to rescue him or her from crises that arise during therapy, he or she may feel guilty and inadequate. Being unable to meet his or her own unrealistic expectations can be disillusioning and lead the partner to withdraw from the relationship. Alternatively, the partner may match the survivor's increasing neediness by becoming increasingly helpful, thereby intensifying and further solidifying the original marital contract (Oz, 2001).

Often the abuse becomes the only topic of conversation of interest to the survivor. When the partner inevitably tires of this, the survivor may turn to friends and perhaps members of a survivors' group, leaving the spouse to feel rejected and lonely (Button and Dietz, 1995). At the same time, unrelenting demands may be placed upon him or her for absolute understanding and complete support.

Sexual relations, regardless of how little or how much the survivor enjoyed them before therapy, often become impossible at some point in the process (Chauncey, 1994; Maltz, 2001). The partner may be treated as if he or she were the abuser for even wanting to hug or hold hands. Partners may grow angry with the survivor for not "doing therapy" quickly enough, thus prolonging the nightmare that their lives have become (Oz, 2001). In some cases they may wish to escape the relationship and consider separation (Chauncey, 1994). The slow pace of healing can frustrate even the most supportive partner. Moreover, the duration of therapy can be a serious drain on the family's financial resources, either via the direct costs of therapy itself or indirectly through lost income if the survivor finds himself or herself temporarily unable to function at work (Bacon and Lein, 1996).

As a result of the growing inability to maintain a balance between the survivor's needs and his or her obligations as a partner and/or parent, the home may cease to be seen as a safe place. Perhaps the only safe place the survivor finds is in bed, alone, with the covers drawn up over his or her head (Oz, 2001).

It is painful for the partner (as well as the children) to observe the increasing difficulties the survivor has in parenting the children. In extreme but not necessarily rare cases the survivor may neglect the children, unable to relate to them at all, or may react to them only with rage. In some families the partner must take over full responsibility for the house and children for at least part of the healing process (Barcus, 1997). For Jack, Cindy's husband, this did not entail a significant change from their pretherapy relationship; however, for a partner such as Tom, Carla's husband, who previously relied on the survivor's strength and organizing abilities, the change in the relationship pattern and demands upon the partner are extremely distressing.

For both Tom and Sam, Fay's husband, this was a difficult time, and both wanted to speak with a therapist to understand what was happening and what they could expect. Sam continued to meet with a therapist on an as-needed basis. Tom was angry and tried to get Carla to stop therapy, hoping that that would bring her back to her previous level of coping. He saw therapy as having changed his wife for the worse. When she would not leave therapy, as some survivors do under such pressure, he had the choice of withdrawing from her or working with her to develop a new contract for their relationship.

Although it is important to try to keep couple communication lines open, this point in therapy is not the appropriate time for working on the relationship. Johnson and Williams-Keeler (1998) provide moving examples of couples work that show how it is possible to find emotional safety within the intimacy of marriage; however, the articulation of needs and desires or having to respond to such disclosures from their partners can be threatening to survivors (Buttenheim and Levendosky, 1994; Chauncey, 1994; Serafin, 1996) when it occurs too early in the therapeutic process. Moreover, not all survivors feel safe enough to discuss matters with their partners (Reid et al., 1996). After all, the betrayal of intimacy was a significant part of the original trauma (Follette and Pistorello, 1995; Freyd, 1996), and even when survivors are open to couples therapy, their partners are not always willing to consider that option, just as in other potential couples therapy cases in which CSA is not an issue (Oz, 2001).

Whereas before crossing the Wall of Fear the survivor expresses a great amount of tension and depression, on the other side of the Wall is more anger, followed by sadness and crying as the survivor moves into the mourning stage of the healing process. At some point the survivor begins to feel stronger and makes plans for the future. Sam was still putting his own needs on hold, waiting until he could be sure that Fay was strong enough to carry her share of the load. Tom was somewhat mollified at this point, seeing that his wife was beginning to return to "normal." She was not pleased, however, that he just expected everything to go back to the way it had been before therapy. She wanted a more equal partnership.

At this point Jack was becoming upset. Until then he had taken care of everything and Cindy did not make a decision without him. Toward the end of her therapy, however, she began to come out of her cocoon. She started to be more aware of her own desires and needs and was beginning to practice asking for what she wanted. Jack was threatened by her growing strength. He resisted giving up the role of rescuer, not out of malice, but from insecurity, since this position was important to his self-esteem. In attempting to maintain the pretherapy status quo, he claimed, patronizingly, that her anger was part of still-unresolved abuse issues. By this time, however, she was aware of other influences on her development, apart from the abuse, as well as aspects of the marriage that she found unsatisfactory. Jack's refusal to move beyond the abuse and take her disagreements with him seriously infuriated her.

Follette and Pistorello (1995) present a sensitive and comprehensive approach to working with couples in which one of the partners is a CSA survivor. Called *acceptance and commitment therapy*, it promotes a growing ability to come to peace with one's history and its impact upon oneself and the relationship. Using this approach, couples learn to appreciate the roles they played at various points during the relationship and become open to more flexibility.

Usually the CSA survivor is able to begin working on the sexual relationship with his or her partner only after crossing the Wall of Fear. The following discussion explores the complexity of sexuality and sexual relations for the survivor.

SEXUALITY

Sexual relations are a minefield for the CSA survivor. Here, as in other areas of their lives, survivors may find themselves governed by the polarity rule, either constantly turned on or perpetually turned off, or they may flip back and forth between these two extremes, unable to find a balance where they feel desire but are not overwhelmed by sexual urges. Some can only enjoy sex within the framework of "forbidden relations," such as affairs outside the committed relationship, sadomasochistic interactions, or compulsive, robotic masturbation that may include self-inflicted pain, or they may be unable to enjoy sex in any shape or form.

Some survivors find themselves feeling sexually aroused at all hours of the day and in situations that are not normally considered sexual. This may make them feel crazy, dirty, and ashamed, and it may evoke the guilt they felt if they were aroused during the sexual abuse itself. Having little or no understanding of healthy sexuality, they could misinterpret the sexual arousal as something that is "attacking" them rather than as something that happens to all people at different moments. They may think that spontaneous sexual urges and sexual thoughts occur only to them, constituting evidence of their depravity. In some cases the sexual urges may subside naturally as the trauma is worked through; in other cases it will have to be directly addressed in clinical sessions. Sadly, because of the shame involved, they may not feel able to raise this issue in therapy on their own initiative.

If sexual urges are regarded by some survivors as unnatural and evidence of wickedness, then masturbation is seen as a necessary evil for dispersing the sexual tension, so masturbation is not experienced as self-love but rather as hate, or alternatively as something mechanical that must be endured. Some survivors reading this will balk at the suggestion that masturbation can be an expression of self-love, but through the process of reclaiming, from the clutches of their abusers, ownership over their hijacked body and sexuality, masturbation will take its rightful place as one more healthy behavior in their sexual repertoire.

Perhaps one of the most disturbing phenomena is that of sexual fantasies. Sexual fantasies are recognized as a normal part of healthy sexuality for men and for women (Abraham, 2002; Nutter and Condron, 1983; Stoller, 1976; Trudel, 2002), and some people cannot reach orgasm without fantasy (Sholty et al., 1984). However, given that in CSA the perpetrator invaded the child's boundaries with overstimulating sexual touch and introduced the child to sexual responses that were beyond the child's capacity to assimilate and cope with, the child's trajectory of sexual development was irrevocably altered and his or her sexual fantasies sometimes reflect that. CSA survivors' fantasies have been reported to be violent and sadomasochistic (Maltz, 2001; Westerlund, 1992). Maltz (2001) suggests ways to stop these humiliating, frightening fantasies and perhaps replace them with more "acceptable" fantasies. Although some survivors learn to modify their sexual fantasies on their own and others can be taught to do so in therapy, this approach will not help everyone.

It is recognized that fantasies do not necessarily reflect an individual's sexual orientation or personal preferences whether he or she is a CSA survivor or not (Bramblett and Darling, 1997; Keating and Over, 1990). For example, heterosexuals may have same-sex fantasies and homosexuals may have opposite-sex fantasies. People may imagine themselves in romantic, sensual interactions with a famous actor or actress without it detracting from sexual enjoyment with his or her partner. A woman may fantasize about rape without it being an indication that she wants to be raped, and, a man may fantasize about raping without the slightest inclination to commit an actual rape outside of his imagination. One difficulty with accepting violent fantasies is that sex offenders often have them, and changing these fantasies to nondeviant ones is part of their therapy. However, because deviant sexual fantasies do not inevitably lead to sex offenses (Curnoe and Langevin, 2002; Howitt, 2004; Stoller, 1976), it is inappropriate to indict the fantasy; it is the behavior of the offender that is indictable. Furthermore, we do not know what proportion of the population, male or female, has rape fantasies or sexual fantasies involving children, who do not, however, act upon them (Bramblett and Darling, 1997). Therefore, in my opinion, it is not the objective content of the fantasy that is problematic but rather the subjective experience of the person who has the fantasies.

Fantasies can be disturbing to an individual when he or she feels controlled by them or when they reduce sexual arousal rather than enhance it. It is important to help the survivor recognize the source of disturbing fantasy material and, although it is regrettable that he or she may never know sexual pleasure without the "stamp" of the past trauma, it is possible to learn to accept it. The CSA survivor can come to terms with the images of the abuser or the abuse being part of his or her adult sexual repertoire. This can lead to a very different subjective experience for the survivor, in contrast to one of Westerlund's (1992) research participants who wrote:

> It makes me angry that my mind isn't free of degrading and humiliating fantasies. They're an intrusion and I feel helpless against them. I feel attacked by my own fantasies and yet the only way to orgasm is to give in. (p. 76)

Part of resolving CSA trauma is recognizing those symptoms that can be alleviated and those that cannot. Just as therapy cannot provide the survivor with the childhood and parents he or she should have had, so therapy cannot entirely undo the imprinting of the traumatic sexual experiences. Sexual arousal and/or orgasm may forever be linked with trauma, but that does not mean that the survivor has to be doubly victimized—once with the abuse itself and then in feeling guilty for a phenomenon that possibly cannot be changed. Working on changing fantasy scripts, if unsuccessful, leaves the survivor with the burden of an odious fantasy coupled with the belief that something is wrong with him or her because he or she is not able to change it, and, feeling ashamed, he or she may not share the failure with the therapist. I believe that scripts that can change will change on their own as the trauma is worked through, perhaps even long after therapy has ended.

It is important to distinguish between sexual fantasies that contribute to excitement and orgasm, and flashbacks. Whereas the former is a natural part of a survivor's sexuality, as discussed previously, the latter hinders its expression. The survivor does not have to remain tortured by flashbacks, but overcoming them even within the context of a loving relationship takes communication, time, and effort on the part of both partners. Although Maltz's (2001) book is a useful guide for the lay person as well as the professional, many people feel safer working with a therapist (also see Dolan [1991], for other suggestions for therapeutic work).

The timing of the work on sexual relations will vary from individual to individual. Usually at some point close to the Wall of Fear CSA survivors declare a moratorium on sex and cannot bear any kind of touch. They are strongly reconnecting with the child they once were, and sex and childhood do not go together. Therefore, they need space clear of sexual demands or expectations. I have much respect for the countless partners of CSA survivors in therapy who put their sex lives on hold until the survivor is able to initiate lovemaking.* When I led psychoeducational groups for husbands of clients I felt bad for those whose wives were beginning therapy (and they were still having sex) when they heard how long some of the other men had gone "without"—one year, two years, five years! I could see their mouths drop in horror. I would not expect a different response from wives whose husbands are survivors, or same-sex partners of either sex. After all, a great deal of self-esteem is connected with feeling sexually attractive and desirable to our partners. Some couples during this period of abstinence find their emotional intimacy deepens because of their need to find other means to communicate their love, whereas other couples grow more distant and do not manage to bridge the gulf, even with the help of couples therapy.

Some time after passing the Wall of Fear, having mourned their losses, survivors begin to reemerge into life, and a rekindling of sexual feelings usually occurs. This is often expressed as a willingness to start to explore touch in a nonthreatening manner. Now is the time to start reading the books and practicing the exercises, or to enter couples therapy.

MODIFYING THE COUPLES CONTRACT

Not all couples will survive. This is true for couples in which a partner is a CSA survivor just as it is true for couples in general. In some cases divorce will happen; in other cases the partners will live separate but parallel lives for convenience sake, without a formal change in status.

Where flexibility exists in the couples' relationship, some change may have already been taking place over the course of the CSA survivor's therapy. Where respective roles are rigid, a great reluctance to change may exist. However, this can be looked at in two ways: on the one hand, the "weaker" partner may resist giving up being taken care of and; on the other hand, the "weaker" partner may actually be helping the "stronger" partner maintain his or her self-esteem by remain-

---

*Although this chapter deals with couples relationships, obviously some survivors are not in a relationship. This does not preclude them from resolving sexual issues resulting from the abuse and working toward a healthy sexuality on their own. For, after all, when learning to love themselves they open the door to loving another.

ing needy, thereby allowing the "stronger" partner to feel needed. Or perhaps the weaker nonsurvivor partner remains weak in an unconscious attempt to help by diverting the survivor's attention away from his or her increasing anxiety and fear as he or she approaches the Wall of Fear.

This reminds me of the couple in which the husband complained that his wife's sexual appetite was too low. He criticized her almost constantly. She happily embraced celibacy later during therapy and resisted any attempt to work on their sexual relationship. Her subsequent sexual awakening came as a surprise to her, and when she finally felt desire for her husband she discovered that he had had a problem with premature ejaculation long before he met her, and exposure of his problem left him temporarily impotent! With her previously low sexual desire and consequent lack of enthusiasm for long sexual encounters his problem had not come to light.

In other words, not all change, even change that one or both partners want, will necessarily be easy to adjust to. Relationships should be continually evolving as each person continues to grow and develop, and that entails continued conflict and negotiation as they learn to accommodate each other over the years. Conflict is not bad in and of itself—conflict is sometimes the mechanism that alerts the couple to the need to reexamine their relationship and check for signs of growth and change.

As the survivor moves from the mourning stage of therapy back into the "world of the living," with the World of Trauma shrinking back into the past as a sad, sad memory, he or she becomes more assertive and communicative and hopefully so does his or her partner. The polarities that once characterized their relationship, at least in part, become more balanced and the relationship more egalitarian. In this way, their couples contract, in all its sections and paragraphs and subparagraphs, remains a document that is under constant revision.

PART II:
THE JOURNEY

Chapter 4

Choosing a Therapist:
A Client's Perspective

Sarah-Jane Ogiers

There are two ways of spreading light: to be the candle or the mirror that reflects it.

Edith Wharton

THE BASICS

Choosing a therapist is, of course, very individual. Obviously you need to take care of the basic criteria and make sure that the therapist you find is properly qualified and experienced, and is getting training in working with trauma survivors. And, of course, he or she must be ethical—although this is something you can only have partial knowledge of before you reach those points in the therapy process where you find yourself in crisis with your therapist. If absolute privacy is not an issue, a recommendation from someone whose opinion you value is very helpful.

No less important than this criteria is the personal chemistry between client and therapist. I feel that this can only be evaluated in a face-to-face meeting, not on the phone, and usually the first meeting will give you plenty of information. Before you meet a therapist for the first time, think of what is most important to you, and keep this in mind during the meeting. For instance, do you feel at ease in the room with the therapist? Is his or her manner empathic or cool? Is he or she

Overcoming Childhood Sexual Trauma
Published by The Haworth Press, Inc., 2006, All rights reserved.
doi:10.1300/5668_04

too "bubbly" for you, or alternatively, too reserved? Can you see yourself sharing intimate information with this person?

Although rapport between client and therapist is essential, I do not put much weight on my therapist having the same life view and value system as me. Frankly, although it's nice to have, it's not crucial. If your therapist is ethical, which we have already established is part of the basic criteria, you will not find yourself embroiled in squabbles about politics. Neither will you be expected to justify or defend your behavior. This brings us to another "must" that you can only partially assess until you have been in therapy for a while: no judgmental therapists. Judgmental behavior in a therapist is a deal breaker. And no, constructive criticism is not judgment, not when given in the context of a caring relationship from a therapist who accepts the client, along with all of his or her strengths and weaknesses.

KNOWING A POOR FIT

How do you know when the therapist is wrong for you? Fortunately, I have not had any experience with abusive or exploitative therapists. However, the first therapist I went to see in Israel, more than twenty years ago, was unfriendly to say the least. I walked two miles uphill to his clinic on a hot summer afternoon, and needless to say by the time I arrived I was parched. Immediately after introducing myself and sitting down I asked for a glass of water. He refused. I was taken aback but didn't insist or ask why. I then noticed that although plenty of daylight was still outside, none of it penetrated the room. Blinds were shut, curtains drawn tightly, and the only source of light was a tiny, dim lamp in the far corner of the room. I dislike dark rooms, and I quickly felt suffocated, but having had my request for water refused I dared not ask for more light. The unfriendly atmosphere did not improve as the meeting progressed. He asked me the usual therapist questions, but was as cold and aloof throughout as he was when I first came in. At the end of the meeting he referred me to a woman colleague of his for a psychological evaluation (the evaluation probably had a fancy name, but I cannot for the life of me remember what it was). I departed feeling that I must be the worst person in the world for a complete stranger to be so unpleasant to me. Not a very promising start.

Wanting to give it a chance I made an appointment with the woman he had referred me to, and a few days later arrived at her home. She was pleasant enough, but when I said "hello" to her family, whom I passed on the way to her office, she became agitated and hurried me through the house, holding up a protective arm between them and me. I have the utmost respect for people's need to separate work and personal life, but this psychologist's clinic was in the middle of her home! If her clients have no choice but to walk through the living room to get to her office, it seems unreasonable to treat them like lepers if they smile and greet family members they meet on the way. Anyway, I completed the exam and left, careful not to make eye contact with anyone on my way out.

The results were sent to the therapist who referred me, but by the time I met him for a second session I had already decided that I did not want to start therapy with him. Nothing about him was abusive or exploitative, he was just wrong for me. If I had been more experienced in "therapist hunting," had prepared questions in advance, or had just had an inkling about what I wanted from therapy I could have saved myself a second session with him, not to mention the uncomfortable and expensive visit to his colleague.

Trust your gut feeling when you are looking for a therapist. I know that when it comes to judging people CSA survivors have had their natural instincts damaged, but if you feel uncomfortable, beyond the usual awkwardness of a first meeting, you are probably in the wrong place. Beyond a polite "no thank you" you owe no explanations.

THE IDEAL THERAPIST

Now that we have covered the fundamentals of "therapist hunting" I can tell you about my own personal deal makers. Again, I stress, it is individual. I will be using the feminine gender as I talk about my ideal therapist, but not because I don't believe that men can help CSA survivors to heal. I know women survivors who have had supportive, compassionate male therapists who fulfilled all the requirements on the "must" list. It's just that therapy with women works better for me.

My therapist has to be very perceptive, and the farther I travel up the spiral of healing, the more perceptive she has to be. As I reach more advanced stages of my journey I want to spend less time fumbling around for answers. I have higher expectations of myself and usually live up to them. Answers come faster, my dream life cooperates, and my subconscious snaps to attention, alert and ready to provide information. When I go down, I come up faster, spluttering and gasping, ready to fight another day, so I have similarly high expectations of my therapist. I expect her to keep pace. I rarely had to wait for Sheri to catch up, and she was often one step ahead. I hardly ever have to wait for my present therapist, Sary, either. She is always on her toes, providing metaphors and interpretations that keep me thinking until our next session and then bowl me over when I "get" them. I believe that this kind of perception can only come from a therapist who has a great deal of confidence in her intuitive ability to give the right information at the right time.

Although I will not get hung up over my therapist and I having different values, I will be far less tolerant of a lack of a sense of humor. At difficult points in therapy my humor is sometimes so black that it's difficult to find people who can bear it, let alone appreciate it. But for me it is indispensable, and I do not think I could have gotten through therapy without it. I am careful not to laugh at the pain of others, but sometimes the soulful look other people give me when hearing about my childhood, even though well-intentioned, is so tiresome that I have to crack a joke. Of course the well-intentioned listener will invariably recoil, their soulful look becoming one of bewilderment if not horror. But not *my therapists*. They do not flinch. Not even momentarily. They even join in when appropriate. What is an appropriate moment? Well that is the beauty of having a similar sense of humor. You just *know*.

A sense of humor is important as a defense mechanism during the heavy moments of therapy, but what happens if sometimes it cannot keep the monsters at arm's length? That brings me to the next quality on my "must" list, which is just as if not more important. My therapist has to have two strong arms—figuratively and literally. Strong enough to pull me out of my black hole of depression, or just hold me in her arms when I'm not ready to come out; strong enough to contain the moments of madness that ricochet, like stray bullets, from my past; and strong enough to stay connected to me and reassure me that although my childhood was insane, I am not. I sometimes think about how hard it must be for my therapist to share those moments of horror and communicate empathy without showing fear. But, to be honest, a therapist who freaks out on a regular basis is of no use to me in my journey.

As therapists, Sheri and Sary are more than capable, and they are also extremely strong women. Perhaps this explains my choice of female rather than male therapists. My mother was weak, putty in the hands of abusive men, and unable to protect her children. In my eyes, she was not a woman I could identify with *and* use to build a healthy image of womanhood for myself, so by choosing powerful women to heal with I get the added bonus of having positive role models while I work to build a stronger self-image.

A perceptive, powerful woman with strong arms and a sense of humor. That is my therapist "must" list in a nutshell. Now that I have painted the portrait of my ideal therapist for you, what happens if she falls off her pedestal? What happens when she makes a mistake?

I need a guide, not a guru (and in my experience therapists do not appreciate being called gurus, even in jest). Gurus do not make mistakes. As a survivor of childhood abuse, being in any kind of relationship—which therapy is—with an infallible figure of authority is a repeat performance of my childhood. My mother was a compliant and angelic victim. It would have been a sin to find fault with her. My father was a tyrant beyond judgment. When they did bad things to me, it was because *I* was bad; *they* never made mistakes.

Therapists do make mistakes. They are living, breathing people, not gods. What is important is that they admit to, and rectify, their mistakes. For me, the honesty of my therapist during a crisis in our relationship makes me feel more comfortable about seeing and pointing out mistakes that she makes, without fear of abandonment. For this to happen, we must already have established a relationship based on trust. In my experience, the occasional mistake made, then discussed and resolved in a safe environment, can strengthen the therapist-client relationship and help define boundaries. I find it to be a liberating experience. Being able to criticize a person of authority and have that person stay is soothing balm to my heart. Once, during our long journey together, Sheri and I found ourselves in such a crisis.

I was at another very low point in therapy. I cannot put a date to it, but I remember the experience clearly and I remember the feelings of anxiety and panic I had then, so it was obviously before one of the several Walls of Fear I had to climb over, tunnel under, walk around or, when all else failed, break down with my bare hands. I called Sheri, feeling that I was losing my mind, and this time she told me that she didn't know what to do and suggested hospitalization. I was stunned. The familiar, heart-lurching feeling from my childhood that signaled abandonment engulfed me. Yet again I was too much to handle. Yet again I had to be shunted off to someone or somewhere else. Was I insane? Is that why Sheri suggested hospitalization? If she could not help me, could anyone? Was the hospital the only place left for me? Sheri was the rope that moored me to the shore of my life, the rope that pulled me back to reality when the memories and dreams became too painful to bear, and suddenly I was set adrift in the middle of the storm. In short, I felt betrayed.

I arrived to the next therapy session feeling anxious and lost. However, Sheri and I already had a solid relationship built on mutual respect and trust, so it was not hard to discuss what had happened. Without going too deeply into her own feelings, Sheri admitted that she had felt overwhelmed by the prolonged intensity of my emotions and had sought supervision to deal with the crisis. Sheri's honesty about her mistake shifted the "blame" away from me and reassured me that the pain that prompted me to call her was not insanity. Furthermore, by seeking help she proved that she was not an infallible guru, and she displayed a sincere wish to acquire the tools she needed to help me. Perhaps most important, that she *did* acquire those tools reinforced my previous belief that she was strong and capable enough to contain the horror of my apocalyptic childhood.

Today, in therapy with Sary, my practice with confrontation with Sheri bears fruit. Alien as it felt then to confront a figure of authority—or anyone in fact—today it comes easily. I challenge Sary on a regular basis, apologizing only if I raise my voice, reminding myself that it will not help me get my point across.

In the past I dealt with conflicts by either spitting poison at people or throwing my self-respect at their feet, begging forgiveness for having displeased them. Now I have begun trying out the new skill I learned in therapy with the people closest to me, who I trust the most. As a woman of extremes it is always challenging for me to find the middle road, but finding a balance between raging and whining when in disagreement with people actually seems to be going quite well.

So, the right therapist for you can be more than just a guide on your healing journey. He or she can be someone who teaches you new communication skills and provides you with tools for dealing with the ups and downs (especially the downs) of life. I suppose this is why the client-therapist relationship is often equated with the child-parent relationship. Similar to good-enough parents, good-enough therapists do more than just comfort us when we are down: they encourage growth and development and teach us how to stand, walk, and then run. Then they let us go. And we, like children, take our newfound abilities and knowledge and rush off to try them out on the rest of the world.

CODA

Sheri Oz

As a therapist, I like clients to be informed consumers, and the first question facing a prospective client is how to select the therapist with whom to team up in doing battle with the ghosts of the past. It would be helpful, I think, to know how other people handle this situation. Do they find their therapists by referral from acquaintances, their family doctor or another professional, or from an agency such as a rape crisis hotline? Do they check the yellow pages or the Internet? How many survivors referred by professionals or hotlines consequently make an inquiring phone call or first appointment? Do clients actually think about their expectations in advance as Sarah-Jane suggests, or interview the prospective clinician as recommended by various Web sites (e.g., Frawley-O'Dea, 2004)? How much do they know about therapy before they begin? How many survivors feel they have the right to question the therapist about his or her approach, experience, and whether or not he or she is in supervision? How many times do they start therapy before they find someone with whom they are satisfied? What is the difference for clients between a clinician in private practice versus a public agency? Unfortunately, research on the topic of therapist selection from the point of view of the therapy *client* cannot yet be found in the published literature.

Clinical experience of many therapists, as well as data from a preliminary study (Gavish, 2005), point to many survivors having been in therapy repeatedly since childhood or adolescence without the abuse history having come to light. Gavish (2005) found that therapist selection seems to be more random than carefully considered, with the survivor acting on recommendations that do not necessarily reflect their own particular needs or likelihood of a personality "fit" with the therapist. She does note, however, that in contrast with older clients who sought therapy before CSA was widely recognized, younger clients are being referred to professionals with expertise in the area such that the sexual trauma issues are now being addressed to a greater extent.

In contrast with the dearth of client-oriented research, numerous studies have explored factors affecting the success or failure of therapy. I will briefly discuss the professional literature and then talk about what that means for the prospective client. The research includes looking at the effectiveness of different forms of psychotherapy (e.g., Carbonell and Figley, 1999; Chambless et al., 1998; Seligman, 1995), therapist and client variables that enhance the therapeutic relationship (e.g., Hersoug et al., 2001; Joyce and Piper, 1998), the impact of client and therapist values on engagement in therapy (e.g., Geert et al., 1997), therapist and client genders (e.g., Simpson and Fothergill, 2004), therapist decisions regarding the type of therapy offered (e.g., Scheidt et al., 2003), and therapist interpersonal relationship skills (Caspar et al., 2005; Hardy et al., 1999).

The overall impression is that the most important elements in therapy are the clinician's interpersonal skills (Lambert and Barley, 2001; Lampropoulos, 2000) and relational style (Bennet-Levy, 2006; Casper et al., 2005). Hersoug and colleagues (2001) suggest that clients respond more positively to a therapist who is active and warmly supportive, who explains symptoms and develops therapy goals together with the client as opposed to a therapist who may be experienced and competent but is reserved and distant. It is interesting to consider what *therapists* look for when they seek therapy. Not surprisingly, they themselves select clinicians who are warm and open, individuals who will help them with their problems within caring, respectful relationships (Norcross et al., 1988).

Much of contemporary research focuses on the effectiveness of various therapeutic methods. Although studies suggest that in the treatment of trauma cognitive-behavioral techniques are more effective than psychodynamic therapy (see Glossary for definitions) (Carbonnell and Figley, 1999; Chambless et al., 1998), CSA cannot be compared with the trauma of car accidents, natural disasters, or war;

CSA happens within a relationship and healing from it takes place in a relationship. Therefore, in the search for therapy approaches that can be statistically proven effective, if the therapist-client alliance is not one of the variables studied, then not only is the research ignoring the findings of more than thirty years of study (Henry, 1998; Lambert and Barley, 2001; Norcross, 2000; Saakvitne and Gamble, 2002) but also it is probably irrelevant to CSA therapy.

Because cognitive-behavioral therapy is generally more short-term than psychodynamic psychotherapy, the trend in today's world of managed care in the United States and government-subsidized psychological treatment in other countries is to favor the former. Predictably, Seligman (1995) found that clients did worse when their choice of therapist or length of therapy was controlled by insurance considerations.

For the CSA survivor this is of utmost importance, because therapy can take time. If you do not have the financial resources to pay for therapy beyond the time allotted by medical insurance or mandated by the public clinic, then you need to decide whether to embark on therapy at all, or perhaps you need to define goals that are more appropriate to time-limited clinical work. Some clinics offer fees on a sliding scale according to household budget, so try to make a fair assessment of your ability to pay for the course of therapy and openly discuss this issue with prospective therapists.

It is important to remember that you are entering into a business arrangement (Morrison, 1991). This can be confusing as you may get the impression that you are paying for friendship or attention. This is not so. You are paying for expertise and professional services that should be delivered with warmth and caring (Simone, 2005, personal communication). You are paying for a guide into the inner reaches of your being. So, although the therapist is your teacher, so to speak, and thus in an authoritative position, the therapist is also your "hired help." It is a delicate balance to maintain, perhaps even more so if you are paying a reduced fee.

In their training, therapists learn all about beginning therapy, developing the therapeutic relationship, different techniques for promoting healing, and about ending therapy. They learn that different stages of therapy require different approaches, both to the therapist-client alliance as well as to technique (Prochaska and Norcross, 2001). Clients do not have such training. This means that you may find it difficult to assess whether problems that arise between you and your therapist are part and parcel of therapy and, therefore, something to be worked on (Frawley-O'Dea, 2004; Safran et al., 2001), or if they are a sign that therapy is not working and it is time to leave (Saulny, 2005). Of course, this is best handled by discussing your feelings with the therapist, but it is not easy to do so. You may not be used to having someone else care about how you feel or about what you want.

For you to take the risk of being open with your therapist he or she must be respectful toward you. The well-known trauma expert, John Briere (2002) says it so well when he writes that instead of regarding the posttrauma symptoms as signs of "pathology" they should be regarded as natural attempts at finding a solution for the pathological childhood. Therapy brings the survivor repeatedly in contact with pain and fear in order to heal from pain and fear. "As therapists," he continues, "we should not forget what we are asking of our clients in this regard, lest we lose track of the courage and strengths that they inevitably must bring to the treatment process" (p. 24). I wish all survivors the good fortune of finding a therapist who never forgets this, for this is a clinician who will regard you as an equal partner in the therapy venture and will not patronize you.

The therapist who respects your strengths and expects you to express your wishes and needs as well as your feelings about therapy and about the therapist is someone who will help you ease yourself into therapy and with whom you can develop a way of working that is a synthesis of both your ways of working. This is also a therapist who will help you think about how to make various decisions, including whether or not to leave therapy, even if he or she feels it is premature. Remember, when you enter therapy you do not sign a contract promising to agree with everything the therapist says or offers, nor do you agree to stay in therapy until the therapist says you're done (you even have the right to run away from therapy in fear or take a break to catch your breath). You sign a contract promising to work on finding your own voice and the confidence to use it. Keep looking for the right teammate until you find him or her.

Chapter 5

Stages of Therapy:
Breaking Through the Wall of Fear

Sheri Oz
Sarah-Jane Ogiers

The woods are lovely, dark and deep,
But I have promises to keep,
And miles to go before I sleep.
And miles to go before I sleep.

Robert Frost, "Stopping by Woods on a Snowy Evening"

Survivors of childhood sexual abuse (CSA) seek therapy under a variety of guises. Some start therapy with memories of abuse and a clear and determined desire to get help in overcoming the ravages of the phenomenon. Others may not remember having been abused, or they may be too scared or humiliated to discuss it in a straightforward manner. They may ask for help with relationship problems, psychosomatic ailments, or parenting. Alternatively, they might be unable to point to anything more than a general sense of dissatisfaction with life. Some survivors request therapy for serious problems, such as addictions, compulsive behaviors, depression, suicidality, or phobias.

Regardless of what brings them into the clinic, the basic path to recovery from CSA is the same. This chapter will discuss that path. Sarah-Jane's diary entries and reflections on her process of healing, together with the drawings of one other survivor, will illustrate how clients may experience therapy for childhood sexual abuse. Throughout this chapter Sarah-Jane's diary entries are preceded by a date and accompanied by commentary from both authors.

Overcoming Childhood Sexual Trauma
Published by The Haworth Press, Inc., 2006, All rights reserved.
doi:10.1300/5668_05

SARAH-JANE: I first went into therapy with Sheri in 1990, seriously worried about my inability to control my anger around my children. For a year and a half we worked on my parenting skills. The therapy was mainly behavior oriented, with little delving into the source of my never-ending, exhausting rage.

When I left therapy, equipped with the tools to help me be a better mother, Sheri, I later learned, had already made the connection between my dysfunctional behavior and the abuse of my childhood. At that point, memories existed that I had always had but did not yet recognize as evidence of abuse, and the memories of my father's more sadistic exploitation of me were not yet accessible to me. Although the symptoms existed, I was not yet ready to confront the truth.

In the spring of 1993, I went back to therapy to work on my marriage. Very soon the subject of sex came up, which opened up the Pandora's box of sexual abuse. I was able to face the abuse at this point, even though I sensed that it would take inordinate strength and courage to deal with the monsters waiting to crawl out.

For me, therapy proved to be similar to giving birth. Once on the delivery table I could not turn back—once my monsters started emerging from their dark confinement of twenty years, I could not push them back into the box. For three years I gave birth—to my monsters, to my pain, to the terror of my buried childhood, but also, eventually, to hope, to light, and to the ability to live a full, satisfying life.

THE MAP OF THE THERAPEUTIC PROCESS

Figure 5.1 presents schematically the stages of the process of healing from childhood sexual abuse. In fact, this is essentially the same process of healing from all kinds of traumatic events. We will refer to this map throughout the discussion of the therapeutic process.

Using the map metaphor, the healing process can be compared to a car trip through unfamiliar terrain. We know where we are starting from and we know our destination point, but we do not know exactly what we will find when we get to the end, nor are we sure of the path we need to follow to get there. To help us find our way we have a map and we know that we cannot just skip from the starting point to the

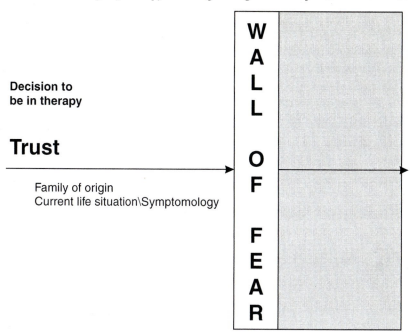

FIGURE 5.1. States of therapy.

end; we need to go through all the landmarks along the way. We also do not know what awaits us at these landmarks. This is a voyage of discovery, and what the survivor is discovering is himself or herself.

This journey is not fun. It is not easy. Many people do not do it in "one go." Some people start the process, take a break, and continue later. In some cases clients return to the original therapist, others may start with one clinician and continue with another, or, perhaps, participate in different types of therapy. The map does not have to be followed in one set way.

SARAH-JANE: Very soon after I returned to therapy my subconscious gave me a clear signal that my "journey" was about to begin. I dreamed I was in the house I lived in as a child. I knew I had done something wrong and it was only a matter of minutes until it was discovered and somebody would be after me. I ran away from the house, and over to the big green park nearby. When I reached the other side of the park I found myself in an unfamiliar place: a small, tourist village with a few shops and a railway station clustered around a square. I approached a man in the middle of the square and asked him where I was. He said it was a place between two other places. But I didn't understand the names of any of the places he mentioned and I asked him how I could get to my home town. He vaguely pointed the way and when I walked in the direction he pointed I found a tollgate, where I had to pay. I met a lorry driver there, and he said I could ride with him. I took out all the money I had and gave it to him. The dream ended.

STARTING THE JOURNEY

Trust

When we book a cruise, we trust the travel agent who assures us that a ship exists that is going to all the places indicated on the itinerary, that the ticket sold to us will be recognized at the embarkation point, and that the guide on board really is familiar with the sites we will be visiting. When we buy a product in a store, we trust the salesperson's word and the writing on the box that the product will do what it claims to do. When we sign up for a course in a foreign language we trust that the teacher really is an expert in that language with the skills necessary to help us learn it.

However, therapy offers no detailed itinerary, no writing on a box explaining the product, and no language tapes to compare our instructor with. In therapy, the client buys the services of an individual who claims to be an expert, and the product the therapist sells is a therapeutic *relationship* built on trust.

How are sexual abuse survivors to judge trustworthiness? After all, they were betrayed by the very adults who were supposed to protect them, regardless of whether the abuse occurred in the home or not. When home is not a safe place—either because the child is being abused there or because he or she cannot talk about abuse suffered elsewhere with any hope of being heard and protected (in other words, the child suffers from a degree of emotional neglect)—then that child needs to find a way to resolve the problem of not having a dependable adult upon whom to lean. The resolution of this dilemma is either to decide that it is not safe to trust anyone and to become prematurely self-sufficient, or to continue to hope that the abusive or neglectful adults will come to their senses, and cling to them until that time. Whichever of these two extreme solutions a particular individual finds, this will then be repeated throughout life with other adults in the family, with teachers, with therapists, with marital partners, etc.

Therefore, the first task of therapy is to establish the groundwork for building a relationship of trust between the client and the therapist. This is done during the initial stages of the therapy process in which clients share their life story, including family background and current life situation, such as employment, couple relationships, children (if any), friendships, symptoms, and clients' understanding of their problem. Clients note how the therapist relates to them and to the information that is unfolding before them. Does the therapist listen respectfully? Is the therapist judgmental? Is the therapist cold or empathic? How does the client feel when in the room with the therapist?

However, abuse survivors have difficulty assessing how they feel with a therapist. After all, as children they were led to believe that they could not trust their own senses. The abuser may have told them that what was happening was love and therefore not wrong, or the neglectful, nonabusing parent may have said something such as "Your uncle would not do such a thing! You must have misunderstood." Clients who gave up and decided that nobody is worthy of their trust expect to be disappointed again and again, yet they crave the experience of being able to relax and rely on another human being to take care of them. Clients who trust blindly need to learn to withhold absolute trust, and test trustworthiness instead. Thus, the polarity rule with respect to trust governs the starting point of the therapeutic relationship.

SARAH-JANE: When I came to therapy with Sheri for the first time, I was open about my fear of doing harm to my daughters because of the incredible rage I felt. During our first meeting Sheri listened empathically to my fears but made it very clear that she would immediately take steps if she felt that my children were in danger. It was very distressing to even consider the thought of losing my children, but Sheri's honest approach made me feel that I could trust her. No unpleasant surprises were waiting for me along the way since she was up-front about her intentions. Furthermore, Sheri explained that if she felt that my violent feelings were escalating we could take steps that could relieve the pressure, such as increasing the frequency of our sessions. This was reassuring, and surprising, since up until then my rage and intense emotions had been, at best, a puzzle to others. People had shunned and deserted me over the years, feeling intimidated by my mysterious anger. This was the first time that anyone offered to help me contain my rage.

For a year and a half we worked on my parenting skills, and another element in learning to trust Sheri was her nonjudgmental attitude, which was crucial in enabling me to reveal my deepest fears. I was often ashamed of the difficulty I had controlling my rage, and if I sensed anything judgmental in the attitude of my therapist I would never have been able to work through my violent feelings so successfully.

As mentioned earlier in this chapter, during my first stint in therapy, Sheri had come to understand that my rage and fear of being violent with my daughters were related to an abusive childhood. However, she did no more than hint at the possibility, and at the time I was not ready to consider it. This respect for my boundaries was one of the most important elements of building trust in our therapeutic relationship. Sheri did not push me to continue therapy—she let me go and waited for me to come back on my own.

Trust is not a commodity that, once acquired, remains constant. At each new stage of therapy clients will test the therapist again in order to verify whether or not he or she is able to guide them safely through the impending challenges.

SARAH-JANE: The second time I was in therapy with Sheri it was clear that this time we would be dealing with my abusive childhood. We had already done the groundwork the first time around. I was already familiar with different therapeutic tools, and I had worked on my parenting skills, so the contrast between my parents and my own parenting was striking. I no longer considered my childhood "normal." I was all set, so to speak. Consequently, I found myself dealing with painful memories very quickly. Each time we worked on a new memory my anxiety would escalate until I needed to speak to Sheri several times a week on the phone. These were very intense, intermittent episodes in the therapeutic process, and stretches of time occurred in between where my weekly session with Sheri was enough. However, Sheri's willingness to be available during these very dark times was essential to me in my struggle to relive and assimilate each new memory that demanded attention. Her soothing, reassuring voice calmed me, and her objectivity and guidance gave a sense of proportion to my trips into the past. Knowing that I could trust her to be there for me helped me face the truth about my childhood.

It is important to note that not all therapists are trustworthy. Unethical therapists exist just as unethical people exist in all walks of life. Some therapists sexually abuse their clients, and this abuse can take many forms: On the one hand, the client may be duped into believing that sexual activity somehow advances the therapeutic goals, if, for example, resolution of sexual problems is one of the stated goals of the clinical work. On the other hand, the therapist may claim to have fallen in love with the client or to be otherwise unable to resist his or her charms. The therapist does not have the luxury of not being able to resist the client's charms since the therapist is responsible for the well-being of the client, which a sexual relationship with a client would endanger. In fact, cases of a therapist actually raping a client in the middle of a flashback have occurred (Salter, 1995). Not all exploitive behaviors on the part of a therapist are sexual, and a therapist may use the therapy session to tell the survivor too much about his or her own problems. Alternatively he or she may ask the survivor for advice in the survivor's field of expertise, thus altering the relationship from strictly therapeutic to one in which the therapist's needs are present to an untherapeutic degree (Yahav and Oz, 2005; see also the discussion of boundaries in Chapter 9).

Getting Acquainted

All therapists have their own unique way of beginning therapy, a stage that involves a process of familiarization for the client and therapist. The therapist learns about the client's life story, the client's symptoms, and the client's strengths. The client learns about the therapist's style of working and relating.

At an early stage of therapy I ask my clients if someone they knew during their childhood valued them. Most of them can confirm that at least one such individual existed. In this case, I assume that this client knows how it feels to be positively regarded, knows how it feels to trust, and I can build upon that.

SARAH-JANE: Throughout my life I looked for and found people outside my family I could trust. At any moment of my life I could point to a person who gave me love, warmth, respect, and encouragement and who made me feel good about myself without demanding I pay a heavy price.

From a very young age and for many years I had a best friend, Maggy, whose family, and mother in particular, were a very positive element in my life. Throughout my life Maggy loved me and stood by me, and never let the thread between us break. Even now, when we live in different parts of the world, it is as though our friendship is engraved in stone. Her mother was probably the most trustworthy adult in my life during my miserable childhood and adolescence. She was a vibrant, caring woman, full of love, with plenty left over for me. I was accepted as part of her family, and their house was a frequent sanctuary to me over the years.

At sixteen, my first serious boyfriend was another positive part of my life. He was my first love and one of my closest friends. I drove him crazy with my roller-coaster moods, not to mention my scathing verbal attacks directed at him just because he was male. But he knew I was suffering, although in those days neither of us understood why, and accepted me, with all my failings, giving me that elusive, much-sought-after unconditional love.

Later, in Israel, I found myself a string of good, kind, open-hearted people to lean on in times of trouble. When I first arrived, a penniless tourist with holes in my shoes, I "adopted" a family. They were so good to me that I sometimes wondered if a limit to their love and generosity even existed. They took me in, embracing me as a member of their family while they found me a job and an apartment. After I was settled, they continued to welcome me into their home on weekends and holidays, until I married and built my own home and family.

As for my ex-husband, we had our ups and downs, and I know that my depression during therapy scared him to death, but he held on, even though the ride was bumpy and I steered us around some pretty scary corners, sometimes at breakneck speed.

Of course, I had Sheri, who patiently and tirelessly walked me through the world of my destroyed childhood, with all its horror and insanity. When I needed to be prodded, she prodded. When I needed space, she provided it. When all she could do was stand and watch and wait for me to find my way, she did that too. She was accepting and nonjudgmental, but she gave me tough love too, when I needed it.

Another lifesaver during therapy was my good friend and neighbor, Mazi. Even though she did not always understand what was going on, she was always accessible and always listened. She held me for hours as I cried, made my children dinner when I could no longer function, and let me obsess, rant, rave, or just stare, glassily, at the television while she made me coffee and fed me perfect sandwiches.

If I had to characterize what all these people have in common, it is this: they never let go of my hand, even when I was hateful and obnoxious, weak and foolish, bad-tempered and inconsiderate. Even when I was depressed and so absorbed in the pain of the past that it was impossible to communicate with me, I sensed their presence. Squinting through my haze of misery I could barely make out their forms, but they were there.

Was it luck? Was it fate? Did some higher power notice me? Maybe. Or perhaps, somewhere deep inside me, a healthier me, with a relentless instinct for survival, made sure that no matter what misery I was drowning in at the time, someone would always be there who would never let go of my hand.

Although most of my clients have had the good fortune to find at least one trustworthy individual with whom they were able to feel trusted and cared for, for some the world contains only hurtful, exploitive, or uncaring people, both in the past and in the present. For these clients, the therapist knows that he or she will have to single-handedly fulfill a role that would be better shared among several individuals within the client's own social environment until the client can develop an independent support network.

I have clients do several exercises as part of the process of getting acquainted (two of which are described in Appendix A). For example, after the first or second session I assign the kinetic-HTP (house-tree-person) drawing (Burns, 1987) as homework: the client draws a house, a tree, and a person, with movement in the drawing. The main reason for this task is to set up a baseline against which the client can compare his or her psychological state at later stages of the therapy. Most clients feel stuck at various points along the path and do not believe that they are making any progress at all. When I have them repeat the original drawing assignment and then show them the series of drawings, they can see for themselves that progress has been made, and that the process is dynamic.

Hodaya's first drawing is shown in Figure 5.2. When she entered therapy Hodaya complained about her father's abusiveness and described being overwhelmed by her uncontrollable rage. In Hodaya's first kinetic HTP, we see the figure running toward the house with arms outstretched. It is not clear if the arms are showing anticipation about arriving home or a need for self-defense. It is clear, however, that the figure, lightly drawn and hollow, is the least emphasized element in the drawing. The house, on the other hand, is heavily shaded and outlined. In the windows are curved lines implying unrest within the home. The door is emphasized in such a way that it appears to be inviting, but at the same time is barred, indicating that it is not necessarily true that one can enter the house or that what happens in the

FIGURE 5.2. Hodaya's kinetic HTP drawn at beginning of therapy.

house can be shared with others. The tree overhanging the house appears to have legs but it is not clear in which direction it is running—toward or away from the house. The overall impression of the drawing is one of anxiety, insecurity, and invisibility.

Moving Along

While the client and therapist are getting to know each other and growing used to working together the client usually feels an initial sense of relief. Starting therapy raises hopes that life can be better, that problems can be solved. Now that he or she has a place to talk about what is distressing and difficult, the loneliness that the CSA survivor feels is relieved somewhat. He or she now has someone who cares, someone who understands. After a short while, the week begins to revolve around the day of the appointment. No longer is the week from Sunday to Sunday. If the therapy session is on Tuesdays, for example, then the week is from Tuesday to Tuesday. The client says "I'll wait and tell that to Sheri on Tuesday." Dreams are frequently dreamed the night before therapy. These are signs that a relationship is forming, a relationship in which the client depends upon the therapist.

That dependence means that the relationship with the therapist has become important to the client, yet clients can experience this as dangerous. They can feel they are losing control and giving it up to the therapist, and since the abuser had control and maliciously exploited it, this can be particularly frightening for the client. Some clients do not manage to deal with this fear and pull away from therapy again and again, therapist after therapist, despairing of their ability to ever heal.

Most clients, however, do manage to cope with this growing dependence and accept it as part of the therapeutic process. At this time, therapists help clients find ways to handle overwhelming emotions. They teach self-soothing procedures that clients can apply when beginning to feel loss of control out of session.

Ways for accomplishing this are varied. Some therapists use guided imagery with or without relaxation audiotapes. With this method, the client closes his or her eyes (or looks down) while the therapist helps the client focus on areas of tension in the body and find ways to relax that tension. The client goes into a somewhat meditative state of which he or she has total control. It is important to emphasize that this is not something the therapist does *to* the client but rather something the client learns to do for himself or herself.

Other therapists work with a technique called EMDR, eye movement desensitization and reprocessing (Shapiro, 1995). EMDR has been studied extensively and found to be valuable in working with individuals who suffer from trauma and phobias, among other disturbances (see Glossary). Recent research shows its effectiveness with adult CSA survivors (Edmond and Rubin, 2004). Part of working with this clinical tool involves helping the client to modulate the intensity of overwhelming emotions (e.g., Omaha, 2004).

As therapy progresses beyond the initial period in which clients feel hopeful about healing and relief at having a place to talk about distressing issues they notice that pressures build up once more. Symptomatic behaviors that may have decreased at the start of therapy once again grow in intensity and may impact day-to-day functioning more seriously. Clients start to feel gradually more and more fearful and sensitive. They may cry more, get angry more, or alternatively, become more disconnected and unresponsive to others and to stimuli in the environment. They are moving along the path toward the Wall of Fear. Some clients do significant work on themselves before coming to therapy. In such a case, they may already be standing close to the Wall of Fear at the start of this new therapeutic process.

THE WALL OF FEAR

Generally, the most intense and distressing part of therapy is the issue of crossing the Wall of Fear, and the greatest amount of time and energy in therapy is spent standing in front of the Wall. Clients know that they have to cross over to the other side of the Wall, even though the thought is terrifying. Some clients describe it not as a wall but as a cliff from which they know they have to jump. The frightening aspect is that no one knows what lies on the other side of the wall or at the bottom of the cliff, and, although staying in place is more and more unbearable, at least the pain and other emotions are familiar to the client. When I ask clients what they anticipate lies on the other side of the Wall, all invariably reply with one or more of the following: death, insanity, or emptiness. It is not surprising, then, that in order to continue through the Wall they must fight hard against all of their most basic survival instincts.

The experience of approaching the Wall of Fear involves increasing intensity of the symptoms that originally plagued the client when beginning therapy. Depression becomes deeper; suicidal thoughts may be dangerously frequent, dominating thoughts and fantasies; anxiety attacks grow more serious; obsessions become more pervasive; and self-injurious and other compulsive behaviors are even more difficult to control. Those with eating, substance abuse, and obsessive-compulsive disorders find that, although they may have gained some control of their impulses in the initial stages of therapy, the battle is much more difficult as they approach the Wall of Fear. The risk of suicide is greatest at this stage of therapy. It is not surprising, therefore, that the therapist who is inexperienced in this area of work fears client breakdown or wonders if therapy is hurting rather than helping the client. Although increasing symptom intensity near the Wall of Fear has not yet been recorded in the research literature, supervisees and other colleagues have also observed this phenomenon. It is hoped that appropriately designed studies will confirm its existence. The client feels himself or herself approaching the Wall of Fear and bouncing back from it in panic. This happens over and over again. Clients often feel that they will never be able to get beyond this point, and many despair of ever getting control of their lives.

At this point I generally ask clients to redraw the kinetic HTP and the tree drawings that they did at the outset of therapy. Hodaya's drawing is shown in Figure 5.3. We can see many interesting elements in this drawing compared with the first one: the heaviness of the lines and shading show a great deal of anxiety, much more than was present at the start of therapy. The figure remains in the same pose as before, but it has more "presence": it is no longer hollow, has been clothed, and has hair and some sign of facial features. An additional figure now stands in the doorway. Is this the client's mother? Perhaps it represents the therapist. The house has changed and seems to be the client's current home, one built alongside the original house on the farming community where she grew up. The windows still show evidence of a storm inside the house, and great attention has been given to detail. The client is becoming more aware of her inner life and more in touch with her feelings, which necessarily corresponds with an increase in anxiety.

FIGURE 5.3. Hodaya's kinetic HTP drawn when approaching the Wall of Fear.

Here I teach clients to be ducks. A duck can dive into the water, be totally surrounded by water, and yet emerge dry. The same can be said of emersion in the fear, which may be experienced as a huge wave threatening to engulf the client with overwhelming and unbearable terror. The client runs away from that fear in different ways: increase in symptoms that take attention away from the fear, sleeping much more than usual, dissociating more, being busy at work. However, when clients learn to be ducks they can face the approaching wave of fear, trusting that they will emerge unharmed, as a duck emerges dry from the water.

The fear is a message from the inner world of the client letting him or her know that the time has come to learn something new about himself or herself or about the abuse. For some clients, crossing the Wall of Fear results in recalling a forgotten aspect of the abuse; whereas some clients reconnect with the feelings they felt at the time of the abuse. For others, crossing the Wall of Fear brings into their awareness the complicity of an adult who witnessed the abuse but did nothing to stop it. Other clients are certain that if they continue they will be confronted with proof of their own guilt and will learn that they are as evil as they feel. In my experience, what they actually confront is that they were all alone and totally unprotected. Until clients are prepared to accept the particular message contained in the wave of fear that threatens to annihilate them, they will continue to be pursued by the fear.

What Hodaya's drawing shows us graphically, and Sarah-Jane's diary expresses in writing, is the torturous world the client lives in at this point of therapy. Due to Sarah-Jane's previous round of therapy with me, she was already approaching the Wall of Fear when she came back a second time, so she reached the Wall very quickly.

September 6, 1993

Sheri said to write when I panic, because my putting myself into a panic mode is a way to stop thinking. Now I'm afraid to stop writing. I'll do anything to keep myself occupied and stave off the fear. It tears into me like some wild animal pulling me to pieces inside. Clawing at me, eating me empty. I'm using all my energy and strength to prevent myself from screaming. The panic rises and rises and sticks in my throat. My chest tightens and my body tenses. How can I keep this inside? The last time I saw Sheri I told her that I couldn't live in my body. No place gives me peace. I want to leave my body and fly away. I want the pain and the panic to stop! I can feel the panic rising up. It starts in my stomach, spreads over it like a cancer, but fast, rises up through my chest, making my heart beat faster, then goes straight for my throat, choking me. My breathing becomes rapid and uneven. I shift and move in my chair but can find no position that I can tolerate. My inner being is bursting against the walls of my body, trying to push through the pores of my skin. I hold my shrieks and screams inside me. They pile up against my throat and under the roof of my mouth. My teeth are clamped shut, making my jaws ache, just in case the screams should try to explode from my mouth. Why won't the panic go away? I'm writing aren't I? I'm tired, so tired, I want to cry. Where will I find the strength to overcome this pain? Now I'm at the bottom of the pit, groveling aimlessly in the dust and dirt. There's nowhere to go but up. I wait to rise up to the light and enthusiasm of living.

SARAH-JANE: When I look back it surprises me how quickly after the onset of therapy I moved into panic mode. The anxiety attacks materialized so fast and they were so intense that it took my breath away. No gradual increase in intensity occurred, no time to get used to the idea was allowed. What is even more surprising is how long I stayed in panic mode, how long it took me to face the memories of abuse and stop fighting my fear of the feelings associated with them.

October 1, 1993

One day someone will find this diary and think that it's an account of a mad person, of someone losing her mind. I'm at the bottom of the pit. I look up at the tiny pinpoint of light. Is it growing smaller? Could there be worse? God, no, please! The only thing that keeps me holding on with my teeth is the knowledge that I can't go any lower. I walk along the street, I sit in the cab, I walk through the corridors at work and my face is totally distorted with the effort of holding in the shrieks and tears that I know will erupt from me if I let up for a minute. I have to pull myself, drag myself, through this somehow.

This is also the most difficult stage of therapy for therapists. In addition to the fear that clients may commit suicide, it is excruciating to watch the pain and despair they experience. This is also a precarious point in that clients are tempted to leave therapy, feeling no help for them exists. The client's trust in the therapist is crucial at this point to enable therapist and client to work together in dealing with the Wall of Fear.

November 15, 1993

I feel as though I'm drowning in a whirlpool of emotions. I'm totally overwhelmed. I just don't know what to do. This myriad of feelings is drowning me, spiritually, physically, and emotionally. I want my life back! I want to be out the other side and back in my life, inside Sarah-Jane, with my children and husband. More than I've ever wanted anything in my life, I want this pain, this agony, this torture to END! Meditation, sport, writing, therapy—none of these techniques work. None! None! None! I can't see the world without panic anymore. I want to break something, rant, rave, cry, but I can do nothing, except boil away inside until there's nothing left. Again I find myself wondering if this is the end of my life, my world.

SARAH-JANE: During this stage of therapy I found numerous ways to deal with the pain, panic, grieving, emptiness, and terror I felt (discussed in detail in Chapter 7). I would write, draw, meditate, and take long walks in nature. I would work out fanatically and spend days under the headphones of my Walkman. I cried for hours on the phone to friends and stared glassily at sitcoms for entire evenings. I went to healing sessions and bought mystical crystals to hang around my neck and place under my pillow. I did everything and anything to get through the day, the night, the next minute. But times occurred when none of my remedies worked, and no matter how hard I tried to avoid it I could do nothing except sit with the pain until it passed.

November 21, 1993

I spent the entire day in my now usual state of anxiety and panic. I finally called Sheri and she said she was glad I'd called her because it meant I was reaching out for help and allowing myself to be needy. She said that these are old feelings that I felt as a child and locked away for years. What I'm feeling is the old panic that overwhelmed the child then. It has nothing to do with anything in my present reality.

SARAH-JANE: As my journey progressed I became more dependent on my therapy sessions and on Sheri. I would call when the panic and fear became too much and ask Sheri time and time again when it would end. She would tell me that it had to get worse before it can get better. As to "how much worse can it get?" she would say that when I reach the point where the pain is so unbearable that I feel I cannot stand it another minute, then it would start to let up. What amazes me now is how many times I felt that way and thought it was over, only to find that more existed, that the pain could get worse, that I could suffer extreme emotional and mental pain without going insane.

December 3, 1993

Today was better than yesterday. But then, what is "better"? I guess it means that I'm not actually groveling around at the bottom of the pit, trying desperately to go down farther, but just sitting there wondering what to do. The pain is still there and cuts deeply into me like a knife. I wait for numbness. I keep telling myself to be patient and concentrate on the little windows that afford me a glimpse of the life that awaits me should I choose to enter it again.

December 17, 1993

My misery weighs me down with incredible persistence. There are days (most of them!) when I feel as though some invincible force is piling rocks onto my already heavy load, making me crouch farther and farther down under their weight. The panic totally overwhelms me. I feel like a bird in a cage. I just want to fly out of my body. But I can't. I have to stay inside it in order to solve the turmoil and misery heaving around inside.

December 22, 1993

It's like there's nothing in my life anymore except the panic and depression overwhelming me and my constant struggle to get through each minute of each day and function, just function. I don't know how I do it; I don't know where I drag out the strength from some place deep inside me to get me through the days. What power is it that forces me out of bed every morning and into my daily routine? Maybe it's just habit, or maybe somewhere at the core of my being I have reserves of energy I didn't know were there. And always, always there's the fear that I will use up those reserves or the habit will dissolve into nothing. Then I will just lie in bed like a zombie in a coma.

January 1, 1994

Well, another year has passed. God! I hope this one will be better than the last. It couldn't be worse, could it? Last night I came home sad and defeated after a nice movie and glass of wine with a friend, sad and defeated because I carry my dull ache with me everywhere. After I fell asleep I had the strangest dream. I was in my old room, in the house I lived in as a young girl, getting ready to go to bed. I was apprehensive and afraid. I knew my father was downstairs, and for some reason I was afraid to get into bed and sleep because I thought he would come upstairs. I couldn't think of any reason why he should but the feeling was there in my gut and I was getting more terrified by the minute (there was some confusion as to my age, because I knew I was grown up, but I felt like a child, with a child's feelings). I walked down the stairs and when I got to the bottom I looked around and the house seemed bigger. It looked as if it was being renovated. All the time I was aware of my father in his room. As usual, in my dreams about him I can sense his feelings without him saying a word, even if, as in this case, I can't even see him. I could tell he was angry about some noise outside keeping him awake. Then the dream changed. I was back in my room, asleep. Something must have happened because I woke suddenly in my dream, which caused me to wake up for real.

January 11, 1994

A beautiful day—sunny and happy. Outside, at least. As for me, I woke up today with a heavy feeling of depression. Somehow I made it to the shower and got the girls ready. At work things got slightly better, but only enough to allow me to function. I'm so terrified this won't end, that I won't love Avi again or get my life back. The only thing that interests me on the home front is Eden and Ofek. I wonder if I can hold on to that. Actually, looking at it objectively, there has been a distinct improvement in my relationship with my daughters over the last six months. I manage to connect with them. I take time out from my ongoing private hell to play a game or draw with them. I even try to teach them what I am finally learning: that their body belongs to them alone and nobody has the right to touch them without permission. But no improvements give me any joy. Nothing looks good or positive. Everything seems black, or at best gray.

February 9, 1994

Whenever there is a family occasion coming up my heart sinks because I know what an ordeal it's going to be for me. Today, I tried to convince myself that it would be okay, that I would be able to enjoy the company of Avi's family who've been a part of my life for so long, but as the time neared I became more restless and unable to function. A few minutes before leaving the house I got a bad anxiety attack. I felt panicky, almost desperate. My mind started to race, thinking "how can I get out of this?" I felt trapped, paralyzed, so I tried to put off our departure. I looked at Avi pleadingly and he was understandably impatient with me, for we go through this every time. I sat in the car on the way over, almost in a state of coma. When I arrived I said my hellos and sat on the edge of the sofa, holding my bag. It wasn't that bad (it's never as bad as I imagine) and soon I let the strap of my bag slip off my shoulder. But, as usual I came prepared with a book, notebook, and pen to counter the anxiety should it raise its ugly head.

SARAH-JANE: Unsocial behavior and intense discomfort around others was a frequent problem during this stage. Once sociable and pleasant, I became withdrawn and unresponsive to others. I didn't smile and my face was so sad that my eyes sometimes betrayed my inner anxiety, and people were startled at the pain in my expression.

March 23, 1994

Same old stuff again. At least I know where it comes from now. I read a good book over the weekend: *Survivors and Partners—Healing Relationships After Sexual Abuse* [Hansen, 1991]. It gave me great insight into a lot of my behavior over the past few months. Running away from the house at every opportunity, needing more space, fanatically withdrawing from Avi. The panic, when it comes, is no less frightening but I know it's there for a purpose, even though I'm exhausted after I've been through it.

As clients deal with the Wall I draw them an illustration of the stages of recovery (Figure 5.1), explaining to them the stages up to the Wall of Fear. Then I redraw the figure illustrating the nature of the trauma (Figure 1.1, Chapter 1) to demonstrate that the Wall of Fear is actually the boundary around the World of Trauma. Remember that at some point the child dissociated out of the World of Trauma in order to survive; the child felt that if the abuse lasted one more second he or she would either die or go insane, and dissociation was the spontaneous defense mechanism that saved him or her. Now, as the client progresses in therapy, he or she comes closer to the World of Trauma. In other words, the client must reconnect with the experience of the abuse, to survive the experience without dissociating from it. This means that moving along the route of therapy brings the client backward in time through the dissociative state to a moment that represents the first dissociation. The client must reconnect with the split second before dissociating out of the horrors of the abuse. This empowers the client, who learns that he or she can live through the intense emotional experience without either dying or going insane. He or she can feel all the terror, rage, pain, and helplessness and not fall apart.

The best tools for working on moving through to the other side of the Wall of Fear are EMDR, traumatic incidence reduction (TIR, French and Harris, 1999), or some forms of body-oriented approaches (see Glossary). I learned EMDR in 1994 and TIR in 1999. Had I had these tools from the beginning of my work with Sarah-Jane, I would have started applying EMDR at the start of therapy to help her contain the overwhelming emotions and then used EMDR and TIR for crossing the Wall of Fear. Although these clinical tools do not help everyone, when they do, they can significantly shorten the length of time it takes to deal with the Wall of Fear phenomena.

May 5, 1994

I cannot imagine myself without this gaping hole inside left over from my childhood. Nobody filled it for me then, and certainly nobody is going to fill it for me now. I'm the only one who can do that. My life is a grave at the moment, filled with pain and anger that will not die, despite the fact that it has been buried. It claws up and out of the earth and chokes me mercilessly, trying to pull me down with it, as if it is saying "You want me to die and leave you in peace, but I will only die when you do. You were not destined for a happy life." Well, I can't just lie down and accept that anymore. It is my birthright to find peace and happiness. I did nothing wrong. The responsibility lies squarely on the shoulders of my inadequate parents.

June 22, 1994

Yesterday I felt the shadow of my childhood hovering around me, and when I tried to peep at it, it looked like a black hole, a monstrous black hole that I couldn't even bear to look at. When will I have the courage to step into it? As soon as I get to the edge, a force stronger than me throws me back. The little girl inside me is still protecting me the way she protected herself all those years ago. People around me are too much to bear, interaction is excruciating, and the touch of my sweet children fills me with rage, as though my boundaries are being invaded.

SARAH-JANE: The "monstrous black hole" that I refer to is an apt metaphor for the Wall of Fear. The other side of the Wall of Fear holds black, never-ending emptiness and loss, and this legacy of nothingness from the abuser to the victim is what makes crossing the Wall of Fear so unbearable. By this time I was not only aware of the Wall of Fear I was also well aware of what lay on the other side. To finally face the deathlike emptiness I had avoided for so long was unthinkably painful. I didn't believe that I could survive that much agony.

We can see in Sarah-Jane's writings that she moves back and forth between panic/fear and pain/emptiness/sadness/aloneness. In other words, she manages to cross the Wall of Fear in part. Some clients experience crossing the Wall of Fear as a one-time event that puts the fear, suicidal thoughts, and depression behind them, whereas other clients experience the Wall of Fear as a series of walls, some higher, thicker, or harder than others. In this case, they flip back and forth between "before-the-wall" feelings and "after-the-wall" feelings. Getting through the Wall of Fear initially brings a form of relief, and survivors are glad to see that neither death nor insanity waits for them on the other side. But when they experience a series of walls as Sarah-Jane did, what they often feel instead of the relief are a few unexpected moments of rest now and then from the terror and horror.

July 5, 1994

As I move forward, the memories grow more and more intense and harder to deal with. At first, the picture of me at age five comes up. I'm crouched down, watching my father masturbating, then finally ejaculating and dirtying my dress and skin. His black eyes bore into my bewildered, frightened ones. This scene came up time and time again and each time I had to deal with the fear, loneliness, and anger that I felt then and denied for so long. Now the scene of me as a teenager comes up over and over again. I am pinned down, but struggling. I feel each thrust like an electric shock. And his mouth is wet and repulsive as he insists on kissing me.

Had a pretty awful weekend. I start to cry now in inappropriate places and at inappropriate times. Everywhere I go, everything I do, my misery haunts me. I feel pain, disappointment, anger, and panic, a myriad of feelings, all within a short space of time. I can't let the kids come near me or touch me and it breaks my heart. I wake each day with a now familiar feeling. It starts before I even open my eyes. I feel a panic cruising through every muscle making my heart beat fast and my body hot. I feel disconnected, as though floating, and after I open my eyes I'm either exhausted or very irritable. Lovely way to start the day!

Everything is a struggle. Going to work, taking care of the house, talking to the girls or Avi or anyone in fact. Every interaction is a struggle. Just getting through the day is a monumental effort.

July 19, 1994

Today I called Sheri, in tears, and told her, among other things, about the scene of me lying spread-eagled on my back at five or six years old with my father touching my genitals. I told her I had pushed it away, rationalizing that it was my imagination. She said that if I stay with the scene I will know if it's imaginary or real. My intuition will tell me. She convinced me, yet again, that I wasn't crazy, that although I feel that my life is worthless and empty I do, in fact, have incredible resources inside me. She told me again that I would get through this pain and come out the other side. I went home and spent fifteen minutes lying on my bed, crying and hugging my pillow and letting the picture come up. It was hard, and even harder to let myself feel the little girl's feelings, but I managed to do it for a few moments and felt some of her fear and loneliness.

I see my children more clearly now. Ofek turns her face up to look at me and I am touched by the innocence and pure happiness that radiates from her, from her eyes, from her smile. I should have been like that. Was I? Did I look like that until my father used me and took advantage of my purity? Maybe he thought that no child is allowed that innocence. Maybe because he didn't have it. He had no right. He is an evil man.

July 28, 1994

Every morning I wake up and don't know how to get through each minute, but I do. Somehow I get to the end of the day and somehow I manage to fall asleep. My sleep is light and fearful. I wake too early and sometimes manage to doze back to sleep, but usually I can't. It's like a shadow that stands be-hind me. Like a heavy boulder on my shoulders, weighing me down. Like a ghost that haunts me. Twenty-four hours a day, seven days a week, I live with this pain. I'm so tired. I feel the pain filling me up, until it chokes me and threatens to spill out of my mouth. It is black and dense and heavy. It is like mercury. The drops run in all directions and spread out, until they cover the floor.

August 4, 1994

Yesterday, after work, I had to go to a birthday party for children of a friend. I sat and watched the guests. Again, I felt the panic and loneliness that I feel in crowds of people. It was as though I was looking at them through a glass wall, from another world. It suddenly hit me how lonely it is to be where I am now in my life. I realized the extent of my isolation from everybody else. I was overwhelmed for a moment with sadness. I can't believe that I'm so in-credibly alone. But when I look back at my life before therapy I realize that it has always been so. Deep down inside I have always felt completely alone, not good enough to truly be a part of society. All the parties and friends and flatmates, most of it was just a mask—a mask I needed in order to hide the emptiness inside me. It's not surprising that I'm sad. My entire life before I decided to deal with the abuse was make-believe.

August 11, 1994

I don't feel so good today. I can feel the panic rolling around inside of me. It's the beginning of something. . .

Later: as I lay in bed I had this strange feeling, like my father was close by and his presence was threatening. Suddenly, I remembered my recurring dream. The one where I'm pacing up and down in my room in the house I lived in as a child, afraid to go to sleep because he would come to me. When I finally fell asleep I dreamed I was having sex with a lot of different men, one after the other. I was sickened by my behavior and ashamed of what I had done.

August 14, 1994

Another terrible dream: I came up the stairs of my childhood home and found Ofek standing against the wall, and I knew that Eden was around somewhere. My father was angry about something I'd done and was ranting and raving. He said that he'd teach me a lesson by not giving the girls their presents. Ofek was looking very frightened and I was desperately trying to think of a way to stop him shouting and frightening the girls, but I felt so help-bless, unable to protect them. I took the girls upstairs to my old room and started packing our stuff, but everything was mixed up and I couldn't seem to get organized. I was getting more and more anxious about my father coming up to see what I was doing. It was like I couldn't just walk out the door. I had to "escape."

SARAH-JANE: Wanting to continue my journey toward health, I had no choice but to go on crossing each new Wall of Fear as it presented itself: memories, dreams, and physical sensations connected to the abuse became more frequent and more intense.

However, little by little, I started to feel happiness again. It started with the most basic and simple things. I would look out at the ocean and it would take my breath away. I would listen to a piece of classical music and my heart would fill with joy. Experiences that had never moved me before suddenly became sources of intense pleasure. And the one feeling that characterized all these moments, however few and far between, was the sense that I was experiencing them all for the first time. It was like being born again.

September 9, 1994

The last couple of weeks have been strange. In spite of my pain, which is still very much present, and my anger at my father for using me, I have actually had a few moments of happiness. I sit at the window, listening to Bruckner and watching the birds diving and soaring in the sky against the backdrop of the sea in the distance, and I smile. The smile is a new smile. Not forced, not the result of ecstatic happiness or passion, just a smile of appreciation of the good in life. Or I sit listening to Joe Jackson and watching the sun set, with this singing feeling in my heart. The intense and simple beauty of these moments is so great that I almost cry. The bottom line is that although there is a lot of pain, anger, and depression in my life, and days when I barely get out of bed, there are also beautiful moments. Sometimes even on the same day! This morning, while having my coffee and cigarette at the kitchen window, I saw a white butterfly and smiled.

SARAH-JANE: These glimpses of the good and beautiful around me were crucial in that they gave me well-earned breaks in the battle with my past. Nevertheless, these moments were still infrequent, and for every smile there were scores of sad, angry, and terrifying moments.

September 17, 1994

Last night, after I told a friend from the therapy group that I felt that something was going to come up, something did. I lay on the sofa, unable to speak to anyone, brief pictures of my father forcing my legs open, like clips from a movie, flickering in my mind. I spent the evening angry at him. And I suddenly realized what survivors mean when they talk about grieving for the loss of their lives. In addition to messing up every relationship I ever had because of the abuse, I never made anything of myself, because I was always being put down. Every idea I had for a career my father just laughed and said I couldn't do it. I left home at fifteen for reasons I didn't fully understand then. So I had to work for a living and couldn't complete college. There was no family backbone to support me in seeking a higher education. I thought about this and got so angry that in the end I wrote my father's name in red and black on a sheet of paper and burned it. Very satisfying!

October 2, 1994

I had an interesting session with Sheri on Friday. She learned this new technique, EMDR, in a workshop in England and we tried it. It's supposed to enable people to digest traumas they've been through and see them in a different way. I brought up a memory of being a little girl, in which I usually feel guilty that my body had enjoyed my father's abuse to a certain extent. I started to shout at him in my mind and for the first time I saw it all from the little girl's viewpoint. I could hear myself speaking like a little girl. "You're bad and evil, you're a bad man. You're my daddy. You're supposed to look after me. I hate you, I hate you. I'm not a bad little girl. I'm a good little girl. I do nice drawings and I make Mummy laugh." It was an interesting session, but I've been a basket case ever since.

SARAH-JANE: I found EMDR to be an intense experience, extremely tiring but very effective. In the previous case it helped me to finally internalize that my father had selfishly used me to serve his own needs.

October 6, 1994

Yesterday was the beginning of the peak in my latest nightmare. Ever since the session with Sheri where we used the EMDR technique, every day is worse than the one before. I left work at three in the afternoon because I could barely move. When I got home I lay on my bed, cried a little, but mostly just sat in this sea of panic and pain. I feel like I'm walking in the valley of death, like I'll never touch life again—but I will. I must believe that. When I finally fell asleep I dreamed of my father: We were sitting in a plane and I was talking to him about a man we knew. I was telling him what a hypocrite he was for being nice to him when he'd always said he despised him. I was really provoking him, prodding and pushing him for a reaction, but he just looked ahead. I felt him threaten me. But, as in previous dreams, he didn't actually speak, he just transmitted his feelings. I was afraid. I knew he would hurt me, but I couldn't stop goading him. Suddenly we were sitting in someone's house and it was morning. I realized that we'd been sitting there all night and that I hadn't gone to sleep for fear of what he would do to me if he caught me unawares.

October 12, 1994

The girls and I slept at my in-laws last night, on the recommendation of people who care about me. Avi is in reserve duty and people are afraid for me to be on my own. To tell the truth, so am I.

October 17, 1994

I don't write anymore, I don't work out, I don't draw, I don't read stories to my kids. The important things have dropped out of my life. I have an appointment with a psychiatrist today, which, hopefully, will result in mild medication to keep my feelings under control.

Last night I had a terrible dream: I was sitting in Sheri's office. I looked down at my thighs and they had turned into a kind of mosaic, like tiny cells. I panicked and screamed, but Sheri couldn't understand why it bothered me so much. Anyway, the rest of the dream was me losing my mind, running around dark streets, calling for help. I'll have to bring that up in my next session with Sheri.

Meanwhile I have the meeting with the psychiatrist to worry about and I haven't the faintest idea how to go about explaining my frightening experience with suicide thoughts.

October 18, 1994

Yesterday I arrived at the psychiatrist in a completely suicidal frame of mind, so no need to worry about not being able to explain myself. Words were unnecessary. He only had to look at me to see what was going on. He listened, nodded, and asked the occasional question, as shrinks do! He decided that my case was reactive depression, not clinical depression, and he is giving me a minimum dosage of antidepressants.

October 27, 1994

At my session with Sheri we used EMDR to explore my cell phobia. I started to feel incredibly tense, especially in my shoulders, as though they were caving in. I saw myself as a child. I curled up so my father couldn't touch me. But he uncurled me. My whole body was tensed up the way people's bodies resist when someone moves a part of them they don't want moved. The tension was incredible and eventually my whole body became frozen.

This happened twice. The first time Sheri helped me to move. The second time she asked me to do it myself. It was an incredible effort. The second time I could hardly breathe when I was "frozen." I could only take really short, shallow breaths. I wanted so much to take a deep breath, but when I tried I got terrible shooting pains in my chest. It was like there was an incredible weight on my chest, making breathing painful.

November 8, 1994

In therapy this week we discussed two dreams I'd had. In one dream I was a little girl looking for my mother in a prison. I dressed up as a prison warden otherwise they wouldn't have let me in. I walked around looking for my mother and discovered that the place was actually a psychiatric ward. There were lots of women with children but I can't remember the rest of the dream, whether I found my mother or not.

The following night I dreamed that I was at the Dead Sea. A Muslim family had married me to their son. He took me to his village where I lived with him as a submissive, Muslim wife. Suddenly I remembered that I had left my daughter, Eden, behind. I asked him if I could bring her to live with us and he said no. But he must have become sick of my nagging, because after a while he divorced me and said I was free to go.

SARAH-JANE: These dreams came soon after the EMDR session during which I finally realized that my father had exploited me solely to satisfy his own needs. The dreams are clearly connected to my discovery that, as a child, my welfare and interests had been disregarded.

November 9, 1994

I can feel something coming on. I have that old familiar feeling of panic. It's almost as though my subconscious gives me a break when things get totally unbearable. When I say unbearable I mean almost suicidal. So I get a break, but my subconscious only gives me just enough time to muster up the strength to cope with another black period and then sends me sliding back down into hell. Yesterday I tried several meditation techniques, but by evening the panic and restlessness inside me was so great that these methods were really only keeping my head above water. Now, sitting in a cafe with Ofek, by the window, in the sunshine, drinking hot chocolate and eating croissants, it is almost impossible to believe that my life lies in fragments at my feet.

November 14, 1994

The days pass and I feel that is all I'm doing: passing the days and trying to survive. I've come to the conclusion that outside my glass wall everything is sunny and bright and happy and everyone else is allowed to be there except me.

November 20, 1994

The panic attack is in full swing. I started going down into my familiar black hole on the morning of the day of my session with Sheri, and it's been depression on and off ever since. I'm filled with anger and anxiety most of the time and at one point today, when I tried to rest, I started to feel like I was dissociating, that same feeling I've had since I was a child but very strong. It was like my surroundings and I were totally out of proportion in relation to each other. And since my eyes were closed and I couldn't see my surroundings the feeling was much stronger. Some of the time I couldn't feel my body and some of the time parts of my body felt too small or too big. The picture of my father came up. I was a little girl crouched on the floor and he came into the room. I started to scream in my mind and I could feel my screams filling my head.

November 30, 1994

I'm feeling a little stronger and am getting through the days. I can see the sunlight here and there, but am still waiting for it to come out long enough to warm my skin.

SARAH-JANE: When the panic attacks first appeared it was difficult to gauge how long they lasted because they were so close with so few breaks that my whole life seemed like one gigantic panic attack. But as therapy progressed, the interludes between the attacks grew longer and I started to feel significantly better during these breaks. The previous panic attack seemed to last just over two weeks.

The Other Side of the Wall

Shortly after crossing the Wall of Fear, whether this is one wall or a series of walls, clients are overwhelmed by deep sadness. This is no longer depression, but sadness. The crying now is not merely tearing up but deep sobs that come up from the abused inner child who is finally able to release the pain. The crying brings a sense of relief, yet, at the same time, the emptiness that the client anticipated feeling does, in fact, overtake him or her. This is the emptiness of not having had anyone to take care of him or her as a child, for even if the abuse occurred outside the family, the child who felt he or she could not talk about what was happening was a very lonely child who lived in a world that did not take care of him or her.

Depression, which can lead to self-injury and suicidal thoughts, is actually a form of self-anger, perhaps resulting from the guilt the child feels thinking he or she was responsible for his or her own abuse. After crossing over to the other side of the Wall of Fear, the self-directed anger changes into anger toward those directly responsible for the abuse and toward the adults who were supposed to have protected the child and did not. Thoughts of revenge may come up and murder fantasies replace suicidal ideation (see Chapter 6). Managing the anger and desires for revenge is easier than dealing with the depression and suicidality—for the therapist if not for the client.

December 21, 1994

Everything's just too much. I don't function at home and I barely function at work. I feel like I'm in another world. The world of pain and despair, rage, and terrible, terrible sadness and loneliness. I guess that's why I stay in another world so that I don't infect the people who love me. The weekend was a living hell. The kids screaming all day. Me crying at the kitchen table, me crying on the sofa and finally, me crying under the bedcovers. Wailing and wailing, lamenting and grieving. The tears come and come and I feel the screams inside my head, begging for someone to take the pain away. I want a new life. I want to run away, away from this agony, this crying, desolate misery.

January 7, 1995

Here I am at Mum's house on my second day in England. Coming here was a spur-of-the-moment decision, a result of the black hole that I found myself in yet again!

SARAH-JANE: Although I was as miserable during and after my trip to England as I had been in previous months, it was an important milestone in the healing process. It was a necessary break from my everyday life of painful therapy and struggling to function at home and at work. In addition to the significant step of seeing my father for the first time since I had started to deal with the abuse, it provided me with some breathing space to take stock and try to make some decisions about the direction I wanted my life to take. Although I did not implement my decisions immediately, because I still had the pain of past memories to deal with, they were in the back of my mind, and gradually I began to take tentative steps toward rebuilding my life.

January 10, 1995

I've been out of the real world for almost two years now, walking with the dead in a desolate, gray graveyard of broken dreams. I visited the real world from time to time but it was inconceivable to think about staying there. God forbid the poison of my past should leak out of my fingertips onto my children. But when I went for a session with Sheri last week I felt like a veil was slowly being pulled away from my eyes. As we talked of my abuse, abuse in general, the therapy group, and me going back to school, suddenly I saw the rest of the world, the world where I could succeed and build my life however I chose. This feeling carried on through the weekend, before and after I decided to go to England. I looked at my home, my family and friends, and realized that I had discovered a small opening in the thick glass wall that had separated me from them, and now all I needed to do was step through this opening and join the world that has been waiting patiently for me to come back to it for two years. The thought of taking that first step is terrifying. It would mean taking the pain of destroyed childhood with me and hope that it won't poison anybody over there in the real world. Whatever happens, whatever I decide to do, I cannot leave that heavy burden behind. It has to go where I go, as an integral part of me, my past, and my life.

January 16, 1995

Came to Brighton to visit Maggy for a few days. It's been so good seeing all my old friends here and it makes me reluctant to leave. Of course, part of my reluctance is having to go back to Israel and face reality: therapy, my job, and my wavering relationship with Avi. I also know that when I go back something has to change. If I want to bring my girls up in an emotionally safe home, somehow I have to find a way to shift slightly off the track of my present self-destruct mode. I can't go on any longer feeling crippled by my past.

January 23, 1995

Well, I'm back in Israel. My last few days in England were depressing and subdued. Most of the time I didn't speak. I was wrapped up in my disappointment that my two-week break in England hadn't changed everything. I guess I had the illusion that by the time I came back a great weight would be lifted from me, but as the end of my holiday drew near I started to feel depressed and hopeless. It started to dawn on me that I had only jumped out of my life and into a vacuum of total rest for a short time, and that it was all still waiting for me. I could picture coming home and having one weight after the other heaped onto my shoulders: therapy, Avi, kids, work—it was all there just waiting for me to pick it up and carry it while I continue my journey through that familiar wall of pain that seems to be thicker than forever. On the plane I was so unhappy with myself and apprehensive about my return that I just curled up in the corner and cried.

In spite of my sadness I was happy to see Avi when he met me at the airport. He had promised the girls that I would wake them when I got home. When they saw me they were overwhelmed with happiness. Ofek couldn't stop hugging and kissing me. She was lost for words and just kept saying "Mummy, Mummy, Mummy!" over and over. Eden threw her arms around my neck and told me she loved me. As I lay in bed next to Avi, I had this incredibly safe, warm, and happy feeling. Thoughts of the abuse kept trying to butt in but I silenced them. Nothing was going to spoil that warm coming-home feeling!

It can take months for the sadness, pain and anger to begin to subside. During this time clients also deal with the sense of not knowing who they are. They recognize that until now they had an identity tied up with being a victim that is no longer appropriate, but they do not yet have an alternative identity. They feel that they were not allowed to develop into the individual they were born to be. So a great deal of energy is invested in discovering a new identity based on survival and strength.

February 11, 1995

My days go up and down, up and down, like a merry-go-round. Although functioning at work and at home has become possible, even to the point where I am actually working toward some kind of personal fulfillment, it is still all an incredible struggle. Every day is an effort, a battle against the black cloud that drifts around me. I wondered today how long I'll be able to keep this up, this daily battle to keep moving forward. I've been existing like this for over a year and a half now. Some days are blacker, some are brighter, some are unbearably painful, a few are filled with enthusiasm. But how much longer? When will it let up and life become easier to cope with? When will I be able to truly enjoy my children again and not just simply gaze longingly at them from my glass prison? What will become of Avi and I? Will I ever again be able to live through one single day without feeling that my heart is being cut out of my body?

February 26, 1995

Next week I start studying a course in mathematics to get myself ready for the psychometric exam. I needed so much courage to make this step. I feel as though I am constantly forcing myself to ignore that little voice inside me that says: "Don't bother, you're bound to fail," like I'm shaking my head to drive out the negative thoughts.

SARAH-JANE: At this point I was struggling to reclaim my life, but this was far from easy. I did not just step out of a negative self-image and into a new identity. No sudden metamorphosis occurred. At first, each small step I took toward a healthier life threw me back into the black hole. It was as though my past was hounding me relentlessly, trying to sabotage any chance of growth and happiness.

March 16, 1995

Ever since the session with Sheri last week, when I saw my father's angry, contorted face as he shoved his fingers up inside me, I've been unable to get the picture out of my mind. Even when I don't actually see it clearly, it's there in the background. It got worse and worse as the week went on, and I moved farther and farther away from reality until the night before last when I felt like I'd finally entered the realm of insanity. Everything was distorted and I felt like I was in another world. I cried on the phone for half an hour to a friend from the group, and when the girls came home I lost control and screamed at them. By the time I reached Sheri on the phone I was in an insane rage. I screamed on the phone that I wanted my father out of my head. I wanted to die. I just can't stand this amount of pain anymore. She said that although I feel like I'm regressing because each time I go into the black tunnel I go deeper and get closer to the torture and insanity of my childhood, it is in fact progress and that the only way to get to the light is to push through this wall of excruciating pain.

March 17, 1995

Today, by the time I arrived at Sheri's, I was back in my distorted world, looking at reality through an impenetrable wall of glass. We looked at one of the abuse memories that recently became clearer to me and managed to make a "movie" out of it, a sequence of events. It was horrific, and when it was over and time for me to go and meet a friend for lunch I felt like I couldn't take one more step in my everyday life, but yet again I proved to myself that I can do it. I had a nice lunch with my friend, and although we discussed the abuse, which isn't exactly time out from my pain, I enjoyed our time together. When I got home I even cleaned the house and finished my math homework.

March 25, 1995

This morning I awoke miserable and depressed about my pathetic excuse for a childhood, but now I'm sitting on the grass watching Avi and girls playing ball and enjoying the spring sunshine.

April 27, 1995

It's been a while since I've written. I wish I could say that everything's better now and that I feel healed, but I can't. I have been studying almost nonstop since I started the math course. I think I can honestly say that it has kept me alive during the past weeks. The concentration required to solve math problems has given me a welcome rest from the terrible flashbacks to my childhood.

May 15, 1995

What can I say about the memories? Except that each one is worse than the one before, more sadistic, more perverted. Sheri went overseas last week and before she left she spoke to my friend Mazi and wrote me a letter. When I received it I cried. I was so moved by this woman who never gives up on me and respects me so much. She wrote that I show my strength by choosing people like Mazi, who is gentle, patient, and trustworthy. So, here I am, still in the middle of it all. Everybody's rooting for me as I sit in the dark and wait for the sunshine.

May 21, 1995

Still struggling with the memories. I've become so expert at this that I have started to notice the signs. I was already irritable with the girls last night and this morning even more so. This evening at my math lesson, little snatches of memories, seemingly innocent, popped into my mind, and then I suddenly recalled how my father had caressed my school friend and I when we were fourteen. Before therapy it had never occurred to me that there was anything wrong with a middle-aged man fondling two adolescent girls dressed in bikinis. But now I look at this scene from my warped childhood and I am overwhelmed with rage.

May 25, 1995

I was just thinking yesterday that I have reached a place in my life where I only have a skeleton network of people close to me. Everybody else has either been cut out of my life or put on hold. It's like I've done a massive spring cleaning and mercilessly cut out everything that isn't absolutely essential. I stay close to Mazi when I'm home and I have my daughters with their never-ending love and affection. Of course there is always Sheri, who cushions many of the knocks and bumps I get while I move through this passage of hell.

May 30, 1995

Because I've been able to have the memory of the abuse present in my life sometimes, without collapsing into a suicidal heap, I feel like I've been on vacation. This vacation has made it possible, for the first time in months, for me to review the past two years and see my progress. My relationship with my children has improved greatly. When I'm not rolling around in my black hole we have a warm, loving relationship. I've been able to filter people out of my life who I feel exploit me, however painful that was. And I also feel that I have worked through a lot of the pain from my childhood. Today, I know when I'm going down. I know the process, the signs (I feel like I'm on the way down now actually—either a new memory is surfacing or an old memory is coming back in a new way). I have had a couple of moments of looking out at the world and seeing incredible beauty. It takes a long time to get to these moments, but when I do it is a fresh unknown feeling that makes me realize that life is worth living, even mine! Yesterday, on the way home in the taxi, listening to my Walkman, I looked at the people around me and watched them smiling and laughing together and realized that for the first time in two years I was feeling pleasure at seeing others smile. For so long now I have watched people smiling from inside a cocoon of pain and felt resentful and bitter that they have happiness that I don't. When I go down this time I will try to remember how I felt during these two weeks and maybe now that I have written proof it will be easier.

June 4, 1995

Well, I've gone back down into the pit. I can actually feel myself spiraling down into the depths and, if previous experience is anything to go by, I won't stop until I'm sitting right smack in the middle of the shit. What's interesting is that, unlike previous times, when I suddenly just find myself at the bottom of the pit without the faintest idea of how I got there, this time I can feel the process. I can feel myself going down but I still can't do anything to stop it. I feel my grip on reality slipping. I feel the chasm opening up between me and my girls. I see my math homework through a haze. I can't see the sunshine anymore. The light seems to have been just blotted out. I can't touch any of the good things that I've been feeling recently. It's like they've been taken away and placed on the other side of the glass wall.

June 13, 1995

Well, here I am, in one piece after my marathon weekend session with Sheri. We decided to do this after my recent descent into the black hole. It was intense but comfortable, and I got a lot of information about my child-hood. On Friday evening a memory of myself, at five years old with my hands tied, came up and the scene was so sadistic that I couldn't fully connect with the little girl's terror. In the morning we explored my experiences as a teen-ager. I discovered that as a teenager I had felt immense guilt at feeling sexual pleasure. I felt that my body had betrayed me. I realized that my in-ability to enjoy warm and loving sex is because my first experiences with sex were abusive and violent. When it was time to go Sheri told me that she feels I am closer to the end of the healing process than I think, and that I may be holding back because I'm afraid of the separation from her. Food for thought!

June 22, 1995

The days go by and in spite of the fact that I am stronger I still feel that I'm living my life with my head barely above water and that one slip would result in disaster. As for the abuse memories that I worked on recently, I think that I haven't fully absorbed them yet since there are no serious aftereffects. I guess it would be wishful thinking to believe that maybe these memories don't effect me so badly anymore. That *would* be tempting fate.

The World of Trauma begins to slide back into the past to the pro-portions that those events actually had. In other words, if the abuse occurred over a span of five years, they are now seen as five years that happened long ago and are no longer experienced as something that exists parallel to current day-to-day life. Past events—those that the client never forgot, those recalled more recently, as well as those still coming into awareness—begin to be truly experienced as memories of the past.

This change in time perspective has a dramatic effect on the survi-vor's sense of self. Hodaya's redrawing of the kinetic HTP (Figure 5.4) demonstrates this. Here we can see that her anxiety has lifted. The person is much fuller than ever before with clear facial features and a smile. However, the tree is gone and the house appears to have lost the fury from the windows. As a matter of fact, the windows in this version no longer exist! Attention has shifted from the house to the self. Surprisingly, the door of the house resembles either a bed or a grave. Perhaps one can say that the abuse has been "put to rest" or

FIGURE 5.4. Hodaya's kinetic HTP drawn when she left therapy.

buried. However, it is clear that a new identity has not yet been solidi-fied. A therapist looking at only this drawing may come to the conclu-sion that Hodaya needs therapy. So how did we decide that therapy was, in fact, over? Mainly because Hodaya herself felt that she had completed therapy. She had no more interest in coming to sessions, feeling she had the tools she needed for tackling life's problems.

For many clients, as they begin to emerge from the sense of empti-ness, this is the time to reexamine decisions made in the past and to evaluate whether or not those decisions are still relevant for the future. Some clients decide to change careers, others wonder if their mar-riages are still tenable. Some enroll in assertiveness training seminars or other forms of interpersonal communications workshops. They de-cide whether or not to confront their families and/or the abuser and decide what kind of relationship they want to maintain with their fam-ilies (see Chapter 6).

July 29, 1995

I don't know whether this is just another break or whether my private hell is finally coming to an end. It feels different from the other breaks. The changes in my behavior feel more deep-seated. The contact with my girls is holding up, and even though it's terrifying I manage to stay connected while being fully aware of the "price" I pay by allowing myself to feel love and warmth toward them. There is always the danger of something terrible happening to them. The same can be said of being in touch with the outside world. It's dangerous, filled with pitfalls, and the daily news is heartrending, but I make small tentative steps into reality, like five minutes of news on the TV or one page of the newspaper. I hear of children dying in a car accident and teenagers being trampled to death at a pop concert, and I cry and feel that familiar inner panic, but it doesn't send me scuttling back into my safe inner world. As Sheri says, there will always be pain in life; the only thing you can change is how you cope with it. I take more risks at work. Sometimes I succeed, sometimes I fail, but I feel alive. I look around now at the debris after the storm and thank God for the people who stayed by me. As much as I can believe in anyone they have won my trust.

August 16, 1995

I received my math grade yesterday: 100!! After all those years of never trying because I was afraid of failing, I showed myself and everybody else that with hard work and willpower almost anything is possible. I can't express how empowering this is. The feeling of achievement. The feeling that I'm not a piece of shit, worth nothing. This is one of the biggest steps I've taken to getting my life back.

SARAH-JANE: Several months after my visit to England—which I consider to be a major turning point in my journey—I had concrete proof that I was indeed taking my life back. I had completed the first step toward acquiring the university degree I wanted so much. However, since this isn't a fairy tale, my life did not miraculously change when I started to reclaim it. Plenty of pitfalls, setbacks, and black days occurred, but gradually my dependency on Sheri lessened and I became able to spread my wings and survive outside the nest of therapy.

CONTINUING THE JOURNEY

One year after leaving therapy, Hodaya phoned me to wish me a happy holiday. I took the opportunity to ask her to send me a new kinetic HTP drawing. In this drawing (Figure 5.5) we see lines that are clear and not overly shaded or emphasized. The figure walks nonchalantly in a stance that is relaxed and assured. The house is decorated with flowers and the windows no longer show signs of any storminess within. The tree is clearly alive and youthful in appearance. A letter accompanying the drawing describes how, at the end of therapy, she was still tense and would explode in anger at members of her family. However, gradually she felt herself strengthening from within, growing calmer. Her compulsive housekeeping eased up by degrees and she developed a stronger relationship with her husband and children. Finally, the raging disappeared. This emphasizes that a kind of inertia to the therapeutic process exists by which change continues even after formal clinical work has ended.

For Sarah-Jane, the therapeutic process also continued, and some of the coping techniques she used during clinical work with me were instrumental in her posttherapy endeavor to rebuild her life.

FIGURE 5.5. Hodaya's kinetic HTP drawn one year after having left therapy.

SARAH-JANE: Moving into the last stage of therapy with Sheri was gradual. Eventually, the sessions petered out and the day finally arrived when hardly anything was left to talk about.

Leaving the sadness and grief of that place on the other side of the wall was much like emerging from a storm. The winds had died down and the rain had stopped, but my life lay in tiny pieces at my feet. The thought of dealing with the debris was daunting, but I tackled it with a new energy. I knew that every relationship, behavior mode, opinion, or value I had held on to up to that point were based on the self-image of a victim and fostered by an unhealthy way of relating to the world. So, almost all of these tiny fragments from my life had to be picked up, examined, and be either discarded or put in my pocket for use in the future.

About a year after leaving therapy it was clear that the growing pains compelling me to change my life were powerful and insistent.

November 10, 1996

As I walked today I felt this incredibly strong desire to be free, to burst out of my mold. It's as though I have a bird in my chest, a big colorful bird that lies crouching inside me, growing bigger and trying to open its wings, and still I sit in my little box only big enough to let me wriggle. I wriggle and squirm, looking up and down and to the sides, looking for a crack. My muscles ache from sitting in the same position for so long. I long to be free of the walls of this box. I feel like Alice in Wonderland when she grows big and her arms and legs are sticking out of the windows of the house, with her face scrunched up against the ceiling. I am too big for the box now and it has no more use for me.

SARAH-JANE: Eventually, the walls of the box collapsed and my bird unfolded its wings, stepped out, and tilted its head to feel the warmth of the sun. It was time to get back to work. But this time, instead of assimilating the past, I was rewriting my present and looking to my future.

However, life after my journey with Sheri was not the rose garden I had envisioned. In fact, this expectation, and the consequent realization that life is far more complex than that, was a recurring pattern during this phase of my healing process. Problems did not just evaporate or cease to appear, and the aftermath of the abuse was still a part of my life.

March 7, 1997

It seems that my life posttherapy is neither smooth nor painless. I always thought that, once healed, a new world would suddenly open up before me, problem-free, without pain, and that I would no longer have to battle with my past, but apparently life is not so black and white; there are crises, obstacles, and problems. Now I must learn how to live in this world. I have to teach myself to deal with my problems and solve my conflicts without using the old unhealthy tools that belong to the past. When I feel threatened in the present, I sense the trigger that sends me back to the old ways of dealing with the situation. I feel the mechanism quickly rolling into place, and then I am either paralyzed or I attack. I can't escape the old feelings. The trigger and the danger of slipping back into old ways will always be there. Sometimes I just have to be on my guard, learn to identify the potential swamps before I'm in them, or deal with them differently if I do fall into them.

SARAH-JANE: The bad periods decreased in frequency, and the breaks between them became longer. I had more time and energy for rebuilding, and surprisingly I found myself using some of the tools I had employed during the dark days in therapy.

One of the methods I used in "reinventing myself" was the introspection I employed while coming to terms with my childhood. The hours and days of silent self-examination I had used while working through painful memories were just as useful when I had to decide who I wanted to be, how much of my past self I wanted to hang on to in my present self, and how much of my present self I wanted to keep for the future.

Coupled with my need for introspection was an almost spiritual communion with nature. During therapy I had frequently taken time out from the pain and anger I was feeling to meditate on the beauty and simplicity of even the tiniest aspect of nature. Butterflies, birds, clouds, sea, trees (and even houseplants!) were like balm on the cuts and bruises I accumulated on a daily basis, and after recharging my batteries I would resignedly return to work. Before therapy I had barely noticed the world of nature, and I often wonder whether the incongruous combination of vitality and serenity inherent in that world but so lacking in my own life was just too alien for me to connect to. But once I had made the connection, this newfound communion was of great help during post therapy rebuilding.

November 17, 1997

I have quite intense moments where I glance out of the window and see clouds of all shades of grey tumbling and rolling across the sky, and I stop and stare in joy, taken in completely by the magnificence of it. Or at the end of the day I leave the doors of the sterile hi-tech world and there in front of me, over the sea, is a perfect painting of a sunset with beautiful feathers of crimson and orange across a half-white, half-gray sky. Gazing out of my window at home I watch the white birds from the coop next to the house down in the valley fly round and round their owner's house, one minute swooping up, silhouetted against the blue sea in the distance, the next coming to rest on the house, and then up and circling again. These moments are so few and so precious, but quite definitely mine forever.

SARAH-JANE: This turning point in my life was characterized by silent self-examination and meditation, alternated with the practical business of rebuilding my life. One of the projects I invested a great deal of time and energy in was getting a higher education. My need to study was an invincible force and essential in my quest to reclaim my life, the life I felt had been snatched away from me by my parents. Before therapy I had had the sense that my future had been eradicated along with the destruction of my childhood, but suddenly I had a clear set of goals, and going back to school was a central one. It was not easy. I spent two years preparing myself and others for this major turning point.

Studying at the university was far more than I had ever expected. I worked hard but I enjoyed everything about it, and each time I entered a class for the first time, thinking, "what will I learn now?" I discovered in myself a passion for learning and loved the creaking sound of my rusty brain.

However, as I pointed out earlier, this is not a fairy tale, and even years after therapy with Sheri was over my black hole was still there waiting for me if I wanted to drop in for a visit, which I did occasionally. Yet I experienced it differently.

August 8, 2000

I thought that yesterday was the worst mood I could be in. But . . . no! Today's even worse. I can't believe how vile I feel. Everything looks bad. I'm eating unhealthy food, I'm barely working out, I was horrible to the kids (and one of them is sick!) and I'm a terrible wife. Get the picture? But the sun is shining. I'm alive and in one piece. Maybe I can still turn this day around. . . .

August 11, 2000

Woke this morning feeling 100 percent better, a different person! It seems that in spite of all the best efforts of my past to drag me back into the dark hole, the truth is that the years of therapy, and of building a positive self-image, have held me in good stead. I can no longer stay in that dark, miserable place for long. Once familiar and comfortable, the black hole has become claustrophobic and tiresome. I spread my wings long ago and have been flying for quite some time now. The cramped and oppressive conditions of the black hole make it necessary for me to fold my wings, force me to tuck them close to me, and to be honest, I just can't stay there for long anymore. The world of light and growth has become my world and that's where I want to spend most of my time. Until the next trip down . . .

Was It Worth It?

SARAH-JANE: So, how did I know I was "healed"? Well, first of all, I learned that the healing process never stops, so no real end product exists, but the kind of life I would have had if I had not gone into therapy would not have come close to the quality of life I have now. It is difficult to put my finger on this quality. I am more alive. I enjoy life more. I am not constantly terrified of getting in touch with my emotions. Before I dealt with the abuse I felt as if everything was dimmed. I did not get to experience life and other people to the full. Afraid to love. Afraid to feel.

So if I had to point to the main elements of that place of health I strived for during the healing process, it would have to be a passion for life, an embracing of all the joy, sadness, excitement, anger, and love involved in being fully alive, coupled with a hard-wearing sense of humor.

Chapter 6

Closure: Coming to Peace with the Past

Sheri Oz
Sarah-Jane Ogiers

Though no one can go back and make a brand new start, anyone
can start from now and make a brand new ending.

Carl Bard

At some point, survivors invariably wonder how to relate to the
people who abused them and to the adults who failed to protect them.
The survivor needs to decide whether or not to confront perpetrators
and/or nonprotective adults face to face or by indirect means, whether or
not to continue a relationship with them with or without confrontation,
and, of course, whether or not to forgive them. Many survivors feel that
closure will not be possible until they have confronted their abusers.

In this chapter, we will look at the survivor's subjective experiences
of these issues. Survivors, who met together as a group with the
authors to discuss various aspects of their therapy, talked about confrontations, revenge, and forgiveness, and Sarah-Jane's diary entries
tell a story of growth and change in coming to terms with the parts
played by her mother and father in her abusive childhood.

CONFRONTATIONS

Very little is written on the subject of confrontations for either
adult survivors of CSA or for the therapists working with them. Aside

Overcoming Childhood Sexual Trauma
Published by The Haworth Press, Inc., 2006, All rights reserved.
doi:10.1300/5668_06

from one study in which seventy-two survivors were interviewed about their experiences with confrontations three times over a six-year span (Cameron, 1994), and four additional studies in which twelve, eight, and nineteen female survivors (Freshwater et al., 2002; Mckinzie, 2000; Roush, 1999) and six male survivors (Fagan, 1995) were interviewed, no significant research into this topic has been done. The writers of all these anecdotal reports came to the conclusion that confrontations are an integral part of recovery from childhood sexual abuse, with those who confronted their abusers glad to have done so.

Perhaps the most comprehensive treatment of the subject to date can be found in the books *The Courage to Heal* (Bass and Davis, 1988) and *Healing the Incest Wound* (Courtois, 1988). The former, somewhat controversial, book is intended for the abuse survivor and the latter was written for the clinician. Both make useful suggestions about what should be considered when the survivor is deciding whether or not to confront. They stipulate that confrontation is something that needs to be weighed carefully and should not be undertaken by every survivor.

One topic that has not yet been researched are aspects of recovery from CSA for survivors who confronted their abusers in comparison to those who did not, so we do not know how much impact the confrontation itself has on coming to terms with childhood trauma.

Furthermore, confrontation is a particularly delicate subject given that it can lead, in many cases, to family estrangements. It is not clear whether the benefits of standing up to one's abuser outweigh or are outweighed by the excommunication of a survivor from the family. Moreover, some American therapists have been sued by incensed parents who deny the accusations of sexual abuse and accuse the therapists of turning their children against them (for example, the Ramona case, Appelbaum and Zoltek-Jick, 1996). Therefore it is understandable that many clinicians do not encourage confrontations, and perhaps may even actively discourage them.

In fact, a dynamic interconnection between clinical work and social response emerges when comparing two publications written by Christine Courtois, for whom I have special regard since her book, *Healing the Incest Wound* (1988), was one of the first I read on the topic and provided me with my basic training in the subject of treating abuse. In that book, Courtois explains the possible benefits and the potential dangers involved in survivor confrontation with the perpetrator as well as filing legal suit. She suggests that the client work through family issues using role-play, drama therapy, writing letters that will never be sent, or other nonconfrontative techniques. However, she clearly outlines issues to be considered should the client decide to confront the perpetrator or nonprotective family members or sue the perpetrator in court. In her later book, *Recollections of Sexual Abuse* (1999), Courtois is adamant that confrontation not be undertaken by the client without careful preparation with the therapist. She even has them sign a contract agreeing not to engage in an impulsive or unplanned confrontation, and she is prepared to "discontinue treatment and make a referral" (p. 173) should they not abide by this agreement. In this way, although stating that disclosure of a history of abuse to family members and confrontations are issues to be decided upon by the survivor, she warns that in the current social situation therapists need to maintain a degree of control in order to protect their professional reputation and/or license to practice. Therapists are used to helping clients understand and resolve issues concerning impulsive actions in many areas of their lives, but this is one arena that makes working clinically with abuse survivors risky for the clinician.

Interestingly, one of the authors of *The Courage to Heal* (Bass and Davis, 1988), Laura Davis, fourteen years after the first publication of that book, put out another book dealing with reconciliation in incestuous families and other high conflict situations (Davis, 2002). This endeavor follows Laura's own renewed connection with her mother after about eight years of estrangement (Laura's mother did not support her when she told her she had been sexually abused by her maternal grandfatherher). Perhaps one of the most gratifying aspects of this new work is its ever-dynamic approach to life in which Davis unabashedly continues to explore and reevaluate her values, feelings, and decisions, and to make changes when appropriate. This is an approach to life survivors could strive toward: recognition that life is change, life is dynamic, and what is appropriate now is not necessarily appropriate in the future—that what seems impossible today may not be impossible tomorrow.

Unplanned Confrontations

The issue of confrontations comes up many times over the course of therapy. As described previously, some clients work through the decision of how to deal with family members together with the therapist before actually going ahead with it, whereas others present the therapist with a fait accompli after having opened a police file or having met with the abuser or nonprotective parent(s). Most dramatically, between the first therapy session and the second, a seventeen-year-old boy who was raped by a neighbor sought him out and beat him up badly enough to hospitalize him. His masculinity thus rescued, he felt no more need for counseling. Needless to say, this is not a recommended approach to confrontation. With no follow-up available, the long-term impact of using violence to avenge rape on this youth's continued personality and social development is unknown.

In the first few weeks of therapy, Orli was already talking about wanting to confront her parents about her father's abuse of her. In spite of my advice to wait until she had progressed to a later stage of trauma resolution when we would have had the opportunity to explore all aspects of a confrontation and its meaning to her, she was impatient and disclosed the secret on impulse. The denial on the part of both parents was harsh and devastating. In examining her hasty action it became clear to Orli that she had a deep wish to get past the trauma as quickly as possible. "I guess I just imagined that if my father admitted to the abuse and my mother believed it happened," Orli explained, "then that would have made everything okay. It would have been like when a mother kisses better a scraped knee and that's enough to stop it hurting. I just wanted to stop the pain in my heart. I thought my parents would love me enough to want to do everything necessary to stop it hurting."

Cindy was not ready to confront her father with her memories of the abuse before he died. One day, however, in an argument with her mother, her mother suddenly shouted at her, seemingly out of nowhere: "You are behaving like someone who was abused!" to which she blurted out: "I was—your husband, my father, abused me." Feeling raw and exposed, Cindy told her husband about the abuse and began therapy. Her mother claimed not to have known, saying that even if she had known what could she have done? Yet they lived in a very small house and it seems unreasonable to her that her mother had had no idea about it. Furthermore, she remembers her mother as rejecting and cold toward her and servile to her father. Even today, long after his death, she will not take a stand against the abuse, saying it is a figment of Cindy's imagination. So, once more, Cindy's mother is rejecting and cold.

Dina, angry at her family for not recognizing the seriousness of the abuse she suffered, impulsively opened a police file against her uncle. This naturally led to a process that took on a life of its own, and after a long wait she faced her uncle in a court of law. Being on the witness stand gave her the opportunity to directly confront him with what he had done to her. Before the trial he called her to apologize and try to convince her not to go ahead with the case. Getting the truth out and making it public was important to her. Her parents were not supportive of this decision and, like her uncle, tried to get her to back down.

She found herself feeling sorry for her uncle at different points during the trial. He seemed so pitiful. Dina finds that until recently, even though more clearly understanding of how much damage was inflicted upon her by the abuse, she sometimes had to force herself to feel anger toward her abuser.

He was found guilty, and after he was sentenced to jail she filed a civil suit for damages. The court will probably rule in her favor. However, the process has been long and arduous for her, and particularly frustrating because he could not be tried for the entire period during which he abused her (see section on justice later in this chapter). That Dina convinced the three judges (in Israel no jury is used, but a panel of three judges on criminal cases) that she was sexually abused by her uncle did not make it easier for her family to accept the gravity of what had happened to her. Going to the police had come from a need to make those in her environment aware of how deeply damaged she was by her uncle's abuse of her. In this Dina was unsuccessful, perhaps partly because of the problematic court system in which her abuser was tried.

Partially Planned Confrontations

Anat confronted her abuser, her cousin, before leaving on an extended trip overseas, so that she could travel with a lighter heart. In order not to forget anything, she wrote down everything she wanted to say. Having arranged to meet him in his house so as not to arouse his suspicion regarding the purpose of the visit, she opened the topic of the abuse soon after having arrived. Shaking, his eyes tearing, he told her that he knew this day would come. He had not initiated a conversation on the topic, he said, from shame and fear. He hugged her and said he was sorry, claiming to have changed. At first, he tried to explain that it was "a child's game, curiosity." However, he finally admitted that his behavior was abusive. Furthermore, he confessed that when they were children, his habit of humiliating her in front of others was an attempt to assuage his guilt. In this way, he took responsibility and was willing to go to therapy on his own or with her, whatever she preferred.

Anat was pleased at the time that she had confronted him and they do keep up a family relationship. In spite of this, whenever she has difficult days memories of the abuse come flying up at her again and she feels she did not take advantage of the confrontation to get out all her anger. She is especially frustrated when she sees that he has married and is raising children—living a normal life—and she is still locked in pain. At times such as these she toys with the idea of suing him in a court of law, but not only has she already told him she forgives him, she truly does want to forgive him in order to put the abuse behind her and carry on with her life. She has not ruled out the possibility of confronting him again in the future, however.

Coincidentally, at about the time of the confrontation, her mother's previously strained relationship with her sister improved. Anat told her mother about the abuse, and her mother's response was: "What do you want me to do about it?" Apprehensive of the possibility that others in the family would find out, Anat's mother feared that the still fragile relationship with her sister would be destroyed. It seems that it is easier to ask the victim to continue to be considerate of others' needs than to take a firm stand against the abuser.

Confronting the Nonprotective Parent

Iris never confronted her father for having abused her because she knew he would just deny it. She did, however, tell her mother about the abuse. Her mother was not able to deal with the disclosure and did not support her. Although hoping for a different outcome, Iris had expected this. Nurit's mother became severely depressed and anxious when Nurit and her sister told her that their uncle had abused them. Perhaps this was a sign of guilt tearing her up inside, some kind of confession of having known.

Most survivors seem to expect that their mothers should have known, should have discovered the abuse on their own and put a stop to it. More is expectated of mothers than of abusive fathers: mothers should pick up subtle hints and signs, ask questions, make sure. In fact, survivors and many professionals seem to be "more forgiving of men who give in to their urges than of the women who do not protect children from such men" (Oz, 2002, p. 2). Perhaps this comes from an idealized picture of motherhood according to which a mother would "lay down her life" to protect her child.

Maybe because of this greater expectation for selflessness on the part of mothers a greater hope for reconciliation with them exists. In confronting the nonprotective mother rather than the abusive father, the survivor is hoping that his or her mother will overcome her selfish need for self-preservation and come to the aid of her wronged child. This does sometimes happen. In Debra's case her mother instantly rallied to her side and divorced her abusive father.

However, the experience of many survivors has been that their nonabusive parents would do anything rather than accept that they were being, or had been, abused. Parents may be angry at their children for having raised the subject, forcing them to take a stand in a paralyzing dilemma. Nonprotective parents are forced to choose between their child and a spouse or other significant family member, and between the illusion of how family life appeared to be and an ugly version of a reality they do not want to know about.

Some nonprotective parents are not brave enough to do this. They are afraid of the shame, afraid of being isolated from the family if they stand by the victim, afraid of facing their own guilt of not having known or, having known, not having protected their child(ren). Once the abuse has been disclosed, the nonabusive, nonprotective parent begins to process the information. Some will quickly close down and be unable to overcome the strong motivation to deny, whereas others will digest the disclosure over a number of years, vacillating between accepting and rejecting the disclosure (Hooper, 1992). Sarah-Jane traces the dynamics of her mother's reactions over the years.

SARAH-JANE: My mother's denial of the abuse started when I was four, when she found blood on my underpants. Even though she knew my father was a strange and frequently violent man, and that he was home with me for a good part of the day while she was out at work, she chose to ignore the possibility that he was the guilty party and confronted my part-time babysitter instead. The babysitter was astounded, the episode was never solved, and the abuse continued.

Years later, as a young teenager, I was riding home on the subway with my mother. We were having a conversation about everyday matters when I suddenly blurted out: "I'm afraid that Daddy or Grandpa will sexually assault me." My mother continued to stare out of the window and then, without a single sign that anything untoward had happened, picked up our previous conversation where we had left off.

My sister made a similar attempt to reveal the abuse by making up a story. She was sitting on the floor having her hair brushed by our mother when she started to talk about being sexually assaulted by a man on her way to school. Our mother, without blinking an eyelash, continued brushing my sister's hair as though nothing had been said.

As an adult, when I told my mother flat out about the abuse, she was at first very understanding and supportive. She never, for a moment, tried to deny that it happened. However, as time went on, she found it more and more difficult to cope with the knowledge I had faced her with, and I began to feel that she just could not deal with her own part in my traumatic childhood.

Although my therapy with Sheri was mainly focused on my father's abuse of me, little by little I began to see that by choosing to be the victim of cruel and abusive men my mother had made me a victim too. The angelic facade I had created for her started to crack, and a very different story to the one I had always told myself began to emerge.

July 25, 1994

As I lay on the bed I felt myself floating into that place between wake and sleep. That nice, warm feeling. Then a strange scene began to unfold in my head. Two young girls, sisters, they were talking about their mother, and one said to the other "She knew, but she chose to ignore it." The mother was somewhere crying. Then one of the girls sat at the feet of her father and looked up at him sitting in the armchair. There was a malevolent, sad feeling in the air.

July 29, 1994

In therapy today we talked about the scenes I remembered involving my father, and I cried a little. Then, somehow, while we were talking about this we got onto my mother. When my stepfather threatened to kill me she let me go back to my father, even though she knew he was bad news. I started to say over and over again that she knew he was evil and how could she let me live with him. As I talked I got angrier and angrier and started to pound my fists and stamp my feet. Then I remembered a time when I was about twelve, after yet another fight with my stepfather: I lay in bed, and my mother was standing looking at me through the half open door. I reached out my hand and said "Mum, please help me," and she said "Sarah-Jane, I can't help you." Then she closed the door and walked away.

Telling Sheri about this I started to cry and shout "What the fuck was wrong with her? Why did she put everything else before me? Was I such a hateful child that she couldn't help me? I would never do that to my child. Even if I was really angry, if my child reached her hand out to me and asked for help I would go to her." I got so angry and cried and sobbed. I still don't understand. As a child I had felt so deserted and humiliated. How could she do that? Why didn't she take care of me? Sheri said that it wasn't my fault. I wasn't hateful or bad. She was the mother and should have cared for me.

SARAH-JANE: My mother was living in another country at the time, but just about the time I started to think about her role in the abuse she came out for a visit. Sheri and I discussed it and decided that the time was ripe for a confrontation. I warned my mother on the phone that some difficult issues that had come up in therapy about my childhood needed to be discussed.

August 7, 1994

I called Mum, and after hearing the last time I spoke to her that she would support me and care for me during this difficult time, she had to go and spoil it. She asked if it was going to be heavy on her. To cut a long story short, I said I didn't wanted to lie to her, that it wouldn't be easy. So she told me that she was going through a nightmare and that she had her needs too. I couldn't believe it. I was so angry I almost cried. I spent the rest of the day furious and miserable. Everyone has needs, but she's *always* going through a nightmare. There's never a right time for me to be cared for. And telling me now about her needs is such bad timing. Just once it would have been nice to get her undivided attention. For years I have never asked for her support and now I know why. I guess I always knew that she would let me down. No point in trusting someone and reaching out for help if you know you're going to get a slap in the face. It was easier when I didn't expect anything, that way at least I wouldn't have been disappointed. Sheri said that there are no guarantees. Since she's coming out at a time when I am dealing with my childhood, there is a chance to change something in our relationship, but no promises. And if things don't change, well . . . that will just be another thing I'll have to deal with.

SARAH-JANE: However, in spite of my mother's fear at the thought of confrontation, she did come through for me, at least in the beginning.

August 13, 1994

Mum has taken it all quite well. We were at Sheri's and, eventually, after a lot of gentle prodding from her, I let out my anger at my mother. I hated crying in front of her. Hated being weak. And when she started to cry I hated that too. But she was shocked because she hadn't known the extent of my anger toward her. Afterward she said that now she knew what I went through with Dad she can understand how I must have felt so angry at her for not being there. However, now she is really eager to sort things out between us. She wants me to let it all out. Even if it hurts her. But now she wants to open it all up, I'm terrified.

August 15, 1994

The vacation is difficult. I had concentrated, before my mother arrived, on how she was going to deal with it. I gave no thought to the effect her presence would have on me. It has made the abuse much more vivid. Instead of following me around like a shadow, it sits on me. I feel it inside me. I look at my childhood and see this terrible, empty, lonely hole. The only thing I feel when I look at it is pain and loneliness. I drag myself through the days. I'm so depressed it's an effort just to leave the house. I told mum that I felt responsible for her holiday and she said that I should forget about it, that this was a family crisis, and if I just gave her another wonderful holiday she'd go back to England with nothing having been solved between us. I'm surprised by her reaction.

SARAH-JANE: In retrospect I realize that my mother wanted to get through this crisis as quickly as possible, as though she wanted the abuse processed during her three-week visit and then neatly packaged and stored away by the time she got on the plane back to England. But I couldn't do that. I needed to do it at my own pace. Hurrying through it was not going to help anyone, and her attempt to do that just fed my anxiety and depression.

August 22, 1994

Today we're at the pool. Mum's worried about us not getting to the bottom of things quickly enough because she won't be here for long. But it's so hard to talk about and so difficult to express my anger toward her. When I started to talk about it I had this strange feeling that the people sitting around us on the grass were sitting too close and getting inside my space, when, in fact, they weren't close at all. I felt vulnerable, as though layers of protection had been peeled off me and I was completely exposed, like an open wound that you're afraid to get infected. When I did tell her how betrayed and angry I felt she tried to explain why she had done the things she had, that she herself had felt abused by the men in her life. This made me angrier, even though she said that she wasn't justifying her behavior and accepted full responsibility for it. I told her that I had been saying for years that I'd had a shitty childhood, but that she had been in and out of nervous breakdowns and had been unable to be a real mother. Now I had reached the point, in working through her part in my childhood, where I refused to justify her behavior any longer.

SARAH-JANE: During this vacation I shed my perfect-daughter skin. I had no energy for my parental-child role. But the guilt resulting from this came out full force when my mother left.

August 31, 1994

I toyed with the idea of taking mum to the airport, but decided that getting up at three in the morning and then working a full day would probably finish me off. So, I said my good-byes and went to bed. At about half past three I woke up and realized that she had left for the airport. I started to cry and couldn't sleep, went to the kitchen for a cold drink and a cigarette. I was overcome with sadness and guilt. I was so sorry that I couldn't have been different and so sad about the hours sitting silently in a coma during her visit. I didn't know what to do with the myriad of emotions flooding through me, and I wished I could bring her back. Eventually, I just went back to bed and cried myself to sleep.

SARAH-JANE: Six months later I went to visit her in England, and I decided to travel to my hometown to try to get my old diaries stored at my father's house. My mother immediately offered to come with me and provide moral support.

January 12, 1995

Yesterday morning I called Dad. It was something I had to really work myself up to. I was almost hyperventilating when I dialed the number and when he answered the phone I could barely speak. He sounded perfectly normal, as though nothing had ever happened between us, as if the past four years of no contact had never been. I'm terrified that he might squirm his way back into my life. I'm terrified about having to say no to him, but I know that it is an important part of my healing for me to be able to stand my ground with him, even if it's just refusing to stay for a cup of coffee. I just want to get my stuff and go.

January 14, 1995

Went to see Dad yesterday. As the train drew into the station, and then as the bus drew closer to his street, my panic grew. Walking toward his flat, my feet dragged more and more slowly and it seemed as though I was going into a full-scale anxiety attack. Mum went first and knocked on the door. Strangely, my fear and panic disappeared when I saw him, and I realized that in spite of him having taken on gigantic proportions in my mind during the past couple of years of therapy, I could actually stand and face him, look him squarely in the eye and not be afraid. We went in and he offered us coffee. We refused and he made himself one. We stood about in the hall and looked at his picture gallery, as he called it. Oddly, the only two pictures of me were copies of photos taken when I was a teenager that I had shown Sheri during one of my therapy sessions, because they seemed to be inappropriately seductive and had made me feel strange.

I looked through the door of the hallway to his front room and noticed that his desk was surrounded by pictures of girls, including one of my eldest daughter when she was tiny. I felt like ripping it off the wall. Then I saw a photo of the young girl who had been abused by her father years ago. Dad had been involved in that and it all got very nasty. I don't remember the girl's name, so I'll call her Jenny for convenience. However, I do remember the chain of events quite clearly. About ten years ago my father made friends with a couple who had three young daughters. According to my father, Jenny, the eldest daughter, took to him immediately and would curl up on his lap and tell him she loved him. He became very close to her to the point where he described his feelings for her as romantic love. He stated it quite clearly, with no shame, and with an air of the unrequited lover. At the time my relationship with Avi was becoming serious, and I told my father that I loved Avi so much that I couldn't imagine life without him. My father turned to me and said "So, now you understand how I feel about Jenny." Jenny was eight years old at the time. Anyway, the story goes that when she complained that her father was sexually abusing her, my father got involved and it ended with him and her father both accusing each other of pedophilia. I looked more closely at the photo of Jenny. She must have been about eight or nine when it was taken, and in the picture she was wearing only underpants. God, how sick can you get!

When he realized I wasn't sitting down, he told me that all my stuff was in the next room. So I went to get it and saw that I had diaries there from 1973 to 1980, when I went to Israel. I was really pleased. Meanwhile, Mum had

had to sit and listen to him drone on about yet another young girl, a gymnast, whose picture he had over his desk. He said she was his inspiration. Whatever . . . I went through the stuff quickly, came back into the room, and packed everything into the bag I'd brought. I stood there for a few minutes. I could barely bring myself to say a civil word to him and couldn't wait to leave, but I wasn't afraid of him. So I told Mum we should leave and we went. She said he looked sad when we left, but he'll never be sad, lonely, or miserable enough for me. He can't pay for what he's done. There's nothing he could ever suffer that would be punishment enough.

We left and walked along the seafront, enjoying the rough, stormy sea. As we breathed in the fresh, pure, sea air, after having breathed his poisonous evil, we went over what had happened. Mum said that from the way he was talking it seemed as though he is now living in a complete fantasy world. It was only after a while we realized that he hadn't once referred to my life, or asked about my children or husband, or Mum's life. I can't believe he could have been so totally uninterested, but perhaps he just really didn't know what to say.

January 20, 1995

Mum was wonderful during the past two weeks. It's hard for me to believe that she's finally coming through for me. But she really supported me and I felt her love and caring coming through loud and clear.

SARAH-JANE: The visit to England, and meeting my father, was an important milestone in my work with Sheri, and a few months later, in August 1995, I left therapy.

Frankly, looking back today, I know I could not have faced my father after so many years without my mother's support. And however I feel about her today, nothing can erase the period in my life when she stood, unflinching, by my side.

Several years later my mother immigrated to Israel. We found her an apartment in our town and helped her settle down. At first it was wonderful. We had mother/daughter walks and shopping sprees, made dinner together, saw movies, but gradually I began to realize that although my mother had been loving and supportive when she had to deal with my father's abuse of me, talking about her part in the abuse was a completely different matter. I knew, of course, that we could not turn the clock back, but I did feel that we had the chance to build an honest relationship with each other. However, any mention of her dysfunctional behavior as a mother prompted a "poor me" reaction from her. At the same time I was waiting patiently for her to get used to being a grandmother to my two daughters, but not only did she barely notice the girls, she would take her anger out on them when we quarrelled, becoming cold and refusing to play with them. Luckily they had plenty of warmth and love from my husband's family, but each time it happened it was like a knife twisting in my heart. I just could not bear to see the bewildered looks on my daughters' faces. Their reactions were too close to home.

After a few years my mother moved to a town on the other side of Israel. She could not have got farther away from me without actually leaving the country. However, I tried valiantly to pretend it had nothing to do with her wanting to put as much distance as she could between herself and her whining, complaining daughter! She would visit us one weekend a month, but gradually started to spend most of her visits seeing her friends, paying little attention to me or my family.

Intended Purpose of Confrontations and Real Possibilities

Throughout therapy even survivors who always remembered the abuse express difficulty believing that the abuse actually did take place. "Maybe I did make this up." "Maybe it didn't really happen and I just have a wild imagination." Therefore, survivors often wish that external proof of the abuse existed. If mother says, "Yes, I know it happened," or if the perpetrator says, "Yes, I am guilty," or if a court deems that abuse occurred, this means that the survivor is not crazy or manipulative or attention-seeking; he or she really was abused.

The first CSA survivor I ever worked with, when I was a student in Canada more than twenty years ago, wrote me a letter some years later to tell me how life had gone since she went back to her native province in eastern Canada. She decided to confront the brother who abused her. Three days after the confrontation he shot himself dead. An admission of guilt, that act of suicide also suggests the extreme pain and shame that are involved when a perpetrator's denial breaks down. But he left her, his victim, alone with the guilt and shame and with the unanswered question "Why did you do those things to me?"

Survivors can never be sure how others will react when they are confronted with knowledge of the abuse. Most respond with an adamant denial (Courtois, 1988). So many survivors are torn between a need to disclose the secret and fear of the repercussions. Some fear the abuser will commit suicide, as my first client's brother did, or that an elderly or ill mother, father, grandmother, or grandfather will suffer a sudden stroke from the shock. With these fears the survivor continues to carry a heavy burden of responsibility for the well-being of all family members, putting their needs before his or her own. It is tragic that the abuser did not feel any of this same responsibility before he or she betrayed the trust of both the victim and the rest of the family.

In some cases it is possible that the survivor hopes a confrontation with the abuser and/or nonprotective parent will preclude the need to mourn the happy childhood he or she should have had, the healthy family relations that were supposed to have been, and his or her lost innocence (not to mention the lost ability to play, lost ability to concentrate, lost years that could have been devoted to study or career development, lost ability to laugh or cry, lost ability to make friends, lost right to grow into sexuality at their own pace, etc.). The pain of all these losses may seem too overwhelming to bear. "Perhaps if I confront my uncle" the survivor reasons, "he will admit to what he did, apologize, and I will forgive him—after having been sufficiently angry at him of course—and then I will be able to put this behind me and get on with my life." Unfortunately, even after confronting, even if he does admit and apologize, as Anat's cousin did, a feeling of something left unsaid, something still not closed may linger. Even after a successful confrontation or court case, an emptiness of "What now?" can persist. Going to court did not save Dina the hard work of resolving the traumatic experiences and grieving the many losses she suffered as a result of having grown up in a family that did not protect her from abuse.

The empty feeling is not filled by others saying that it did happen and it was wrong. The empty feeling is filled only by hard work of grieving all the losses while in a trusting relationship with a therapist and in other close relationships with significant others. No other way exists—it appears that closure can be reached only by the survivor within himself or herself. Sarah-Jane's diaries and reflections describe the painful path that is followed in attempting to find closure.

SARAH-JANE: Eventually, I confronted my mother about her indifference toward my children and it soon spiraled into a gigantic fight. I waited for tempers to cool and then tried to call and make peace, but she accused me of verbal abuse and refused to see me for a long time. I had broken the unspoken pact we had agreed on in my childhood. She was the victim and nobody was going to take that away from her. At about the same time, my sister told me that my mother had said it was time I put it all behind me. I was furious and pointed out that since I was the one who suffered the abuse I would be the one to decide when to "put it behind me." But my mother's message was clear: "If you want a relationship with me, you must keep this out of my sight."

March 2, 1999

For the umpteenth time I tried to get Mum to come and stay with us, but she started off again about how we needed more time. It pissed me off and ruined my evening and most of the next day. Anyway, the next morning I called her and said I thought it was probably best to leave things the way they were, the way she wanted them, and that whenever she was in the area she was welcome to come by for a visit. I'm just so tired. Tired of her always turning everything around so that she's this poor, pathetic little victim, helpless in the face of her monstrous daughter; tired of her hurtful behavior toward me and the kids; and even more tired of not being able to tell her about it, because when I do she erases me from her life for two months. The thing that gets me most is the way she is with the kids. I mean, even if she's not speaking to me, how could she not call the girls and ask how they are? After all, they are her grandchildren, but I guess that isn't the most important thing in her life. Anyway, like I said, I'm tired of being hurt all the time, tired of expecting her to make up for my appalling childhood by being the perfect mother and grandmother.

July 15, 1999

The atmosphere between Mum and I is still very strained. Ever since the time when she pissed me off big time, and I told her just to come by if she was in the area, things have been very tense. Conversation is stiff and forced, visits are awkward to say the least, and I suffer greatly from her presence. The only thing we really talk about anymore is my sister, and we have never mentioned what happened between us again.

SARAH-JANE: This stressful charade continued for a few months, reminding me more and more of the make-believe world of my childhood, until the dishonesty was too much for me to bear. Feeling that I was suffocating, I decided, once more, to reach out for help.

October 6, 1999

An eventful week, to say the least. The outcome was that I decided to open the Pandora's box of my childhood once again, at least for a short time. Not that I don't know what's in there. It's just that I keep it closed, because the contents are so horrifying. I started to feel that I was hurtling down into a black hole, gaining momentum and losing control, so I called Sheri and left her a message. By the time we spoke I was somewhat calmer, but I knew the anxiety wasn't really going anywhere. We decided I should come in for a few sessions, for what she called a booster. Apparently, many survivors have to do this. Come back, deal with different aspects of the trauma, or the same aspects but on a different level. So next Friday I have an appointment with her, and until then I'll have to hold things together. The amazing thing about this is that all the old symptoms came back. Last week, when I was sitting in my sister-in-law's house, crowded with people I hardly knew, I felt that old suffocating feeling of anxiety and restlessness. The feeling was so familiar that I almost reached out and greeted it as one would pet a family dog.

October 21, 1999

If I think about it now I never really worked on issues with my mother previously in therapy, and I always thought of her more as a partner in the healing process rather than a passive abuser. She was all I had left and I was determined to build a rosy relationship with her. But things didn't turn out that way, and when we had that terrible fight in January and she turned her back on me I was devastated. I began to realize that there wasn't going to be any rosy, perfect, mother/daughter union, that although Mum loves me and hates Dad and is sorry for what happened, she doesn't really want to dig into her own wounds and change. If she'd wanted to break the chain of abuse she would have done so years ago, before Dad abused my sister, when she was supposedly becoming a stronger woman who he couldn't hurt any more. Well, all this happened months and months ago and I think the emotional ramifications are surfacing now. And I'm pissed off big-time that I even need more therapy after my glorious rebirth.

November 17, 1999

Tomorrow, I have a session with Sheri which, oddly enough, I'm really not looking forward to. Or perhaps it's not odd. I was thinking this week: when I was in therapy before I was in terrible crisis. I couldn't get through the week without a session and sometimes I couldn't get through the day without a call to Sheri or someone from the support group. Today, I know there's a problem I have to deal with, but it's just polishing. It's like missing two fingers. I know that I'll function better once I've resolved this problem with Mum (my "two fingers"), but I just don't feel like going the extra mile. I've already learned how to function with two fingers less and although I know it's not optimal, the effort involved in acquiring the missing fingers is just too much work. But having said that, since I'm not one to leave stones unturned, I will at least try to go the extra mile.

SARAH-JANE: Sheri did her best, despite my reluctance. But in order to go that "extra mile" I had to accept that this was much more than "two fingers" and more like heavy scouring than "polishing"! It is clear to me now that I was still not ready to face the truth about my mother and our relationship. To do that I would have had to destroy the very last vestiges of our illusory, make-believe world. So I went in for only a few sessions, and I was only willing to receive what I call first-aid therapy. It gave me breathing time, but the problem was still there, and the truth was desperate to get out. So, a few months later, although I was functioning well and enjoying many aspects of my life, I was struggling with low-level depression. It continued for almost four years before I could face the underlying causes.

March 27, 2000

Life has become difficult. I wish I knew why. I mean I can point to all the symptoms but I can't seem to find the cause. I feel like I've shut down and am functioning in emergency mode. Like the doctors when they go on strike; only the minimum needs are taken care of. Well . . . at least I'm still going to the bathroom on my own.

August 10, 2000

Today wasn't good. I lost my temper with the girls and completely bounced off the walls. I've been nasty to Avi too lately. It's not surprising I find myself in introspective moods, asking myself if I'm who I want to be. I wonder why I've started to lose control recently?

SARAH-JANE: The rage I felt toward my mother simmered under the surface, occasionally exploding at inappropriate moments. It was impossible at the time to even envision bringing this anger up in a confrontation with my mother, who became weaker and older every time I saw her. So, during visits to her I kept my feelings tightly sealed, only confessing them to my diary.

May 13, 2001

Here we are at Mum's house and I've already promised myself three times that I'm never coming back. I am incredibly irritated with my mother's total alienation from the world the rest of us live in. When we arrived the fan was broken (and of course not even a remote possibility of an air conditioner, like the rest of civilization), and until Avi fixed it we were encased in an ovenlike heat. There are no kitchen utensils to speak of, and now the gas stove doesn't work so it's almost impossible to make a meal. Mum sits around like a zombie, totally unphased by anything that happens. The light broke in the middle of making dinner so I had to prepare the rest of the meal in the darkness. But this didn't seem to bother Mum! Sometimes I think the floor could just open up and swallow her and she'd still be staring vacantly at the wall.

SARAH-JANE: In spite of my anger, I went on and on and on justifying my mother's behavior.

August 30, 2001

I think Mum is just very depressed, and if I've decided to hold myself at a distance and not get involved then the least I can do is accept it. It's true that she's the antithesis of everything I've come to believe represents the matriarch, but maybe there are different aspects of womanhood that I can learn to appreciate in my mother. Haven't found any yet . . . will have to keep a lookout . . .

December 9, 2001

Discovered through my sister that my mother had spent the weekend in my town but had kept it a secret because she didn't want to see me. Needless to say, I was cut to the quick. I really don't know what to do. On the one hand I don't want to lose touch. I mean, she and my sister are the only family I've got, but on the other hand it seems pointless keeping up the charade of being a happy family when she doesn't even want to see me.

January 4, 2002

The confrontation (or rather nonconfrontation) I had with Mum was more or less resolved. After much consultation with friends and putting off the inevitable phone call, I called her, and discovered that she was just as interested as I was in avoiding a scene. Instead of the recriminations I got the last time we fell out, she pretended, as I did, that nothing had happened. Which was fine by me. Now we can all go on pretending that nothing happened.

SARAH-JANE: It started to dawn on me that although my mother accepted that what had happened to me was terrible, it had nothing to do with her. As my panic grew I became increasingly alert for "creases" in our relationship that I would immediately leap up and smooth out like an obsessively neat person who cannot bear to see a crumpled bed sheet. Except that my perfect, pure white, tightly stretched sheet hid a filthy mattress. My hypervigilance grew until it was almost unbearable, but rather than face and deal with the real problem, risking my mother's final abandonment, my anxiety surfaced in other areas.

February 18, 2002

Yesterday when I went to the doctor and told him about my early-morning awakenings he said that it was sign of depression. And it suddenly clicked. I have been feeling not exactly depressed, but as if a shadow of depression has been following me around. I guess it could be a result of Mum's indifference toward me, which always triggers my old childhood fear of abandonment.

SARAH-JANE: Even though my family doctor tried to persuade me to take antidepressants, I refused. After all, if I admitted that I was actually depressed and not just "shadowed" by depression I would have to accept what was lying behind that depression, and maybe finally face the truth about my mother and our relationship.

August 17, 2002

Had another awful night. Fell asleep okay, then woke up half an hour later (as usual!). After a restless night woke up at five. God! It's so fucking infuriating—waking up two hours before I need to and feeling exhausted instead of rested. I don't know why this is happening to me.

SARAH-JANE: My sleepless, anxious state of mind continued as my feeling of frustration and anger toward my mother grew.

December 14, 2002

My sister called me to tell me she is pregnant, and that she doesn't know what to do. How can she not know what to do?! Isn't it clear? She's got two kids already, no money, no job, no partner, and no prospects. And Mum wasn't much help. I don't know what goddamned planet those two live on! Mum said, coyly, "Well, you know I'm not very practical, you've always been the sensible one. And you know your sister, she's always getting into a mess." I hate it when she says that. What does that mean? Is it engraved in fucking stone that my sister is the daughter who makes messes and I'm the sensible daughter that cleans them up?

March 20, 2003

In one of my awful sleepless phases. Woke up this morning in the pitch-black and refused to look at the clock so I wouldn't know how much sleep I hadn't had. Lay for hours, with a headache to boot, and heard the birds start to sing! Weird. I don't know what it is that stops me sleeping.

SARAH-JANE: Looking at these entries now I feel like shaking the woman who wrote them. Today it is crystal clear that I was depressed and needed help, but the mind is a complex, wondrous thing, and I guess I was protecting myself from truths I was still unable to face. I often wonder how long I would have gone on pretending that we were one happy family, with regular happy-family ups and downs. But eventually the illusion was shattered for me.

In June 2003 my sister gave birth, and I took my family to visit for a few days to see the baby. I did my usual pathetic pleasing act. I cooked an entire buffet for a party of my sister's friends, and I gave her money for the baby, which she quickly pocketed without a "thank you" or even a smile. The next day I was told that my sister was too weak after the birth to cope with our visit, and my mother accused me flat out of only coming to enjoy myself and not helping my sister enough. Since I had been there for less than forty-eight hours, which I had spent cooking for and entertaining a bunch of my sister's friends, I was speechless for a few minutes. When I realized they were asking me to leave I burst into tears. I cried so hard I could hardly breathe, and nothing my husband and children could say would placate me. I felt ten years old, being turned away by my mother yet again. She was finally disowning me, throwing me out of her house. The ultimate abandonment.

We packed, we left, and no contact has occurred between my mother and me since. My picture-perfect fantasy had been revealed for what it really was: an elaborate net of deceit and lies. I had weaved every inch of it myself. I felt humiliated, and for a while even worthless. I had practically fallen over backward to please, and the farther my mother pulled away, the harder I tried.

And it was still not enough. In the end, the walls of my fantasy prison collapsed and I was left looking at the rubble.

REVENGE FANTASIES

Whoever said that living well was the best revenge never watched his rapist walk free. I live well today. It is not good enough, and it has to be good enough. But it is not what I thirst for. It is not vengeance. (Abraham, 1997)

For many years, Jana fantasized that when she reached the age of sixteen she would murder her father. She waited for this birthday, waited to kill him. When she was fifteen he died of complications caused by alcoholism. She met with him just before his death. His family called to tell her he was dying and that he wanted to meet her and her brother. This certainly did not fit in with her plans but she felt she had to agree to see him. She and her brother met him in a popular coffee shop that was always filled with people.

Her father came in a wheelchair. Jana struggled to think of what she would do next. She was upset that he foiled her plans, and realized it had been a mistake to agree to the meeting because his pitiful appearance vanquished her anger. In this meeting of only a few minutes she felt that he was taking her with him to the grave. Until then, her anger toward him gave her energy, it was what gave her life intensity, but this man in the wheelchair was a miserable old man, not her abusive father.

Other survivors also spoke of revenge fantasies and dreams in which they murder, or threaten to murder, the abuser, enjoying the fear they would invoke in him or her. Joel imagined telling his sick uncle that he remembered the abuse, and then watching him as his heart gave out and he died painfully on the spot. Nurit thought of ways to poison her abuser. Loren, unable to imagine actively bringing about her abuser's death, would often daydream about serious traffic accidents.

Herman (1992) suggests that revenge fantasies, such as those just noted, are actually "often a mirror image of the traumatic memory, in which the roles of perpetrator and victims are reversed" (p. 189). The imagined infliction of harm upon the abuser may be satisfying momentarily, but it perpetuates the emotional connection between abuser and abused. As long as the survivor is preoccupied with the issue of revenge, the perpetrator remains a central feature in the survivor's thoughts and dreams. In this way, the survivor does not free himself or herself from the tentacles of the abuser but, rather, ties himself or herself to the abuser indefinitely.

SARAH-JANE: My fantasies about my father are not exactly vengeful, more like corrective revisions of my childhood. For years I lived with the fear that my father would get to my children (he has never met them—I made sure of that), so occasionally I find myself wrapped up in imaginary scenes in which I save my children from him by suddenly exhibiting superhuman physical strength or extraordinary expertise with a knife to ward him off. Fantasizing about single-handedly keeping him away from my children is no doubt a way to rewrite the story of my childhood, with me as the victor rather than the victim. But I never imagined killing him and over time, as my anxiety about how to keep my children safe from him has waned, so have my fantasies. All the same, I imagine myself one day heaving a huge sigh of relief upon hearing of his death. I admit, that he is now alone in his old age is a form of punishment and does give me some satisfaction. However, when I saw him like that it did not lessen my pain, and the consequences of his abuse of me did not evaporate into thin air.

Wishing evil on others is something I try to avoid, and this extends to the people who abused me, however challenging that may be. Survivors of childhood sexual abuse have seen evil up close and personal. Refusing to allow it back into my life in the form of vengeance or revenge fantasies is, for me, breaking another link in the chain of abuse.

FORGIVENESS

Just as revenge fantasies do not free the survivor from the abuser, neither do "forgiveness fantasies" by which the survivor "imagines that she can transcend her rage and erase the impact of the trauma" (Herman, 1992, p. 189).

Carla thought that it was her duty to forgive her mother for not having protected her from her father, but she felt unable to do so, and she struggled with the issue for a long time, feeling something must be wrong with her because she was not able to let go. Nurit, on the other hand, felt sorry for her mother when she saw her collapse after being told of the abuse. Recognizing her mother's inability to cope with stress and knowing the terrible circumstances under which her mother grew up, she forgave her. She was not able to maintain this stance, however, and she directed her anger at fate for giving her a weak mother. In Barb's case, it is superfluous to speak of forgiveness—Barb feels her mother is a total stranger to her. Even though she and Barb live in the same neighborhood, they have not spoken for several years. Barb wonders how she will feel when her mother dies—will she be relieved and happy or will she cry in grief? In the meantime, she feels apathetic toward her, emotionally cut off. She would prefer to feel anger sometimes, to hate her.

Not all the professional literature on CSA contends with the subject of forgiveness toward the abuser and nonprotective adults, and those that do clearly state that it is not an essential part of resolving childhood sexual trauma (e.g., Barrett, 2003; Bass and Davis, 1988; Courtois, 1988; Herman, 1992; Mather and Debye, 1994). Forgiving abusers who do not understand the nature of the injury they caused perhaps only relieves perpetrators of any need they may otherwise have had to face up to their guilt and precludes their taking responsibility and undergoing therapy themselves (Bass and Davis, 1988; Courtois, 1988; Regehr and Gutheil, 2002). Yet when survivors wait for abusive or neglectful adults to express remorse, their recovery, rather than being in their own hands, is dependent on change in others (Herman, 1992; Regehr and Gutheil, 2002). In other words, both forgiveness and nonforgiveness exact a price from the survivor.

Psychological studies examining both sides of the issue found that, on the one hand, forgiveness can bring definite mental and physical health benefits (Coyle and Enright, 1997; Witvliet et al., 2001), but on the other hand, it may be followed by regret (Exline et al., 2001, cited in Exline et al., 2003) or the false security of trusting someone who is not trustworthy (Katz et al., 1997). In addition, research has attempted to determine whether or not certain personality traits are related to the tendency to forgive or not forgive (e.g., Exline et al., 2004). However, Exline (2005, personal communication) suggests that any unwillingness of the CSA survivor to forgive the abuser and/or nonprotective adults is probably specific to the abuse situation, and not a general attitude toward forgiveness and compassion.

Interestingly, forgiveness of wrongs committed upon nations or minorities within a nation has been treated differently than forgiveness of violent crimes against individuals. Individuals abused by family members are usually admonished to "forgive and forget." They are told that forgiveness means letting go of anger and giving up the right to get even and that this is for their own good (Enright and Coyle, 1998; Freedman, 1999; Freedman and Enright, 1996). However, wronged nations or minority groups are expected to receive a sincere apology that first and foremost involves an acknowledgement of wrongdoing, followed by compensation for injuries sustained (Auerbach, 2004; Danieli, 1998; Quinn, 2003; Regehr and Gutheil, 2002; Tutu, 1999).

If most people believe that forgiveness means either forgetting or excusing the crime (as shown by McCullough et al., 1999), and continuing the relationship as if nothing had happened (as shown by Kearns and Fincham, 2004), then a CSA survivor may feel shortchanged by the suggestion that they forgive the unrepentant abuser or nonprotective parent. Alice Miller (1994) suggests that this kind of forgiveness may even increase mental and physical health problems by forcing feelings of anger and powerlessness underground. She is adamant that forgiveness should not be a goal of childhood abuse resolution therapy. Interestingly, in the two cases of so-called forgiveness therapy presented by Freedman (1999) and Freedman and Enright (1996), one of the abusive fathers was already dead and the other died during the client's therapy. Remembering some happy times spent with an abuser who is no longer alive may make forgiving him or her much easier than forgiving the perpetrator who is still around angrily calling the survivor a liar, insisting he or she recant the tales of abuse, or frightening him or her into maintaining silence.

In fact, the common view of forgiveness does not reflect its complexity. Some people are utterly unable to forgive, some forgive prematurely, others forgive the same transgression repeatedly, and others forgive overtly while covertly remaining vengeful (Akhtar, 2002). Some individuals may exhibit one attitude toward forgiveness when under stress, and another when calm. It is likely that a change in attitude toward forgiveness occurs with experience and maturity or a change in life circumstance. For example, a woman might forgive her abuser for having abused her, but not for having abused her younger sibling or child. Time is an important factor and, as time passes, the intensity of anger toward the wrongdoer generally subsides, resulting in an increased willingness to forgive (McCullough et al., 2003). In the case of CSA, however, the passing of time (and therapy) can bring the survivor to the point of feeling the anger he or she was not able to feel as a child and, therefore, he or she may actually be less forgiving with time. In an important study, Zechmeister and Romero (2002) found that although victims' empathy for their offenders increased the chances of forgiveness, offenders who developed greater empathy for their victims' pain were actually less likely to forgive themselves.

Forgiveness has generally been considered as belonging more to the realms of religion or spirituality than to psychology (Exline et al., 2003) and, contrary to common conceptions, the religious attitude toward forgiveness may actually support the view previously expressed: that the victim need not forgive his or her abuser. It is likely that different and perhaps even contradictory interpretations of the texts can be found in all religions. Although the general impression of Christianity, for example, is that it promotes unconditional forgiveness (Auerbach, 2004; Rye et al., 1999), this is not strictly so: "Contrary to popular belief, Jesus does not insist that victims grant forgiveness. A closer look at Luke 17:3-4 reads, ` . . . and if he repents, forgive him'" (Morris, 2004). In other words, the abuser must ask forgiveness and it must be a sincere apology accompanied by a change in behavior and a promise never to repeat the abuse (Father Dr. George Khoury, 2005, personal communication). If the abuser truly repents, then the Christian is obligated to forgive. No personal choice exists here.

If, on the other hand, the abuser does not repent, then the Christian is not obligated to forgive, but he or she is strongly encouraged to do so (see Matthew 6:12-15 and Colossians 3:13 for different approaches to forgiveness of the unrepentant). The ability to forgive, however, is not easily attained, and Jesus' exhortation in the Sermon on the Mount to "turn the other cheek" does not imply a simple solution. Rather, forgiveness toward the unrepentant abuser is part of a long process of healing from the injuries of the abuse that includes several stages (Reverend Tom Ball, 2005, personal communication): letting go of the search for revenge, pursuing personal emotional healing and spiritual growth independent of the abuser, and only last praying to God to show mercy to the abuser. This last stage runs contrary to survivors' sensitivities at earlier stages of recovery and, when the approach to forgiveness is simplistic (i.e., forgive and forget), it is easy to understand why this is so.

Similarly, Judaism does not offer easy forgiveness for the perpetrator of a crime and even if the abuser provides restitution, "s/he must still ask for forgiveness" (Rambam, cited in Auerbach, 2004, p. 158). If the abuser does not publicly acknowledge wrongdoing and repent, taking steps to make sure he or she does not repeat the abuse, then forgiveness is discouraged, because to forgive without penitence minimizes the crime, belittles the victim, and perpetuates the risk of victimizing others (Rye et al., 1999).

However, in Judaism, as in Christianity, if the offender offers a sincere apology, the injured party is obligated to forgive and, failing that, is considered a sinner (1 Samuel 12:23: "Far be it from me that I should sin against God by not praying for you). What comprises a sincere apology in Judaism? According to Rambam (Hilchot Teshuva, Chapter 2:9), an offender truly repents when he or she apologizes repeatedly and sends friends to plead his or her case. This may at first sound silly, but imagine a situation in which a perpetrator acknowledges the abuse, clearly states that he or she was wrong, tells the victim that he or she was strong and brave to reveal the secret, sends other relatives who tell him or her that the perpetrator is in therapy, wants to pay for the victim's therapy, and cannot forgive himself or herself. This is not the same as asking the wronged party to "forgive and forget."

In Islam, three conditions must be fulfilled in order for an abuser to warrant forgiveness (Judge Mohammed Abu Obied, 2005, personal communication). These are: confession of wrongdoing, sincere remorse and belief that his or her actions were wrong, and performing good deeds both for the sake of the victim and for the sake of God. If these conditions are not met, then the victim has no obligation to forgive, but forgiveness is nonetheless encouraged as a charitable act in the eyes of Allah.

In Buddhism "there is a tremendous emphasis on compassion and forgiveness . . . and also on personal responsibility, i.e., Karma. The abuser will pay for the abuse by accumulating negative Karma which will be detrimental to him/her when the time is right. The abused will accumulate positive Karma by working through his/her pain and ultimately coming to a place of forgiveness" (Jeremy Safran, 2005, personal communication). Therefore, although "Buddhism places forgiveness at the top of the hierarchy of values" (Auerbach, 2004, p. 159), it is understood that the ability to forgive is the end result of a psychological/spiritual process.

Anne Salter (1995) raises some interesting points. She suggests that when a perpetrator asks for forgiveness it may be a manipulative move to minimize the abuse and/or appear repentant in the eyes of others. The survivor may be put in the position of feeling obligated to forgive. In this way, the offender reabuses his victim. Salter makes it clear that the survivor should only offer forgiveness for his or her own sake, and not to satisfy the needs of the abuser or other family members who want the crisis to be over as soon as possible.

Some crimes may be considered unforgivable. These are crimes of such great dimension that most people are disgusted to hear of them and cannot find any human qualities in the perpetrators with which to empathize (Exline et al., 2003). However, unforgivability is usually reserved for war crimes committed by "those soldiers," or serial murder by "that insane killer." In other words, it's reserved for situations of "them" versus "us." Perhaps because the parent or other relative who abuses a child is our neighbor, cousin, child's teacher, friend of the family, etc., the boundary between "them" and "us" is blurred and we seek comfort in either denial or quick forgiveness that puts things back into order and silence. However, for the individual survivor of CSA, the crime may, in fact, be unforgivable, because it shattered the child's belief in safety, trust, self-worth, self-efficacy, fairness, etc. (Flanigan, 1998).

Sometimes forgiveness is just not a realistic goal for the CSA survivor. In Sarah-Jane's case, she feels that if she said "I forgive you," the words would be as empty of meaning as her mother's "I'm sorry."

SARAH-JANE: Frankly, I'm in two minds about forgiveness. It is true that forgiving has a price, and not forgiving has a price. For me, not forgiving means that I do not release part of the trauma from the abuse, and forgiving means accepting those who haven't repented for hurting me when I was a child in their care. Words such as forgiveness, regret, and repentance are meaningless empty shells unless they truly come from the heart.

In the case of my father, the perpetrator of the abuse, I have no question in my mind. He has been out of my life (physically, that is!) for more than ten years now, and the one time I saw him he was an old man, completely alone, living with a picture gallery of little girls. So although time has passed and he is in a pitiful state, he is still living, unrepentant, in a kind of pedophilic heaven, and no forgiveness will be given to him.

As for my mother, his passive coconspirator, it is not easy to make such a cut-and-dried statement. She did believe me about the abuse, although almost immediately after the disclosure she wanted me to put it behind me so that it would be out of her sight. Not that it made any difference. Even though I hardly mentioned it, it was always there, and I believe that when she could no longer bear to look at it she sent me away. Every time I think about forgiving my mother I come to the same conclusion: no repentance there—at least not the kind of repentance that would allow me to forgive her.

Today, as far as my mother is concerned, I try to aim for compassion rather than forgiveness, and recently, I did have a moment of compassion for her. The moment crept up on me and I was suddenly filled with sadness at the waste of her life. A woman with the soul of a painter, she could have lived a full rich life but chose instead to give up, to just lie down and turn her face away. This pathetic picture is only the way I see her, of course, but, still, it was the first time in years that I had thought of her without anger.

So, all in all, the price involved in forgiveness is too high for me. But compassion? I can live with that.

JUSTICE

All other crimes go to court, are prosecuted, and punished. But crimes committed by parents toward their children are dealt with secretly and shamefully in therapy, buried with the advice to forgive, and never find justice. (Rogers, 2005)

It appears that in the Jewish and Islamic approaches to forgiveness cited previously, justice is an important element if we understand justice to mean public confession that a crime was committed, resulting in appropriate restitution or punishment. So, if religious courts did have legal standing today (in Christianity, sin is not dealt with in a legal manner and so no Christian court system exists), justice regarding CSA would be largely unattainable unless the abuser sought repentance and spiritual growth. Due to the early establishment of civil courts, the Jewish religious courts have not developed an approach to handle the circumstantial evidence (Rabbi Dr. Eli Kahn, 2005, personal communication) that comprises the main body of evidence in child abuse cases. Interestingly, Islam provides for circumstantial, medical, and expert testimony in rape cases, which fall under the crime of "hiraba" (taking of property) rather than fornication (Mazhar, 2002). These are currently applied in criminal courts in Islamic countries (Dr. Hani Jahshan, 2005, personal communication). In the Arab sector in Israel, for matters that are not decided in criminal court, a big difference often exists between the adjudication of community sheiks and judgments that would be offered by the Sharia Islamic court (Judge Abu Obied, 2005, personal communication), the former being based more upon local customs and the latter upon the religious texts.

In fact, even civil criminal courts often cannot mete out the justice the victim deserves because the rules of evidence do not always allow for all factors to be presented to the court. During legal proceedings in many jurisdictions, the victim of the crime is shunted aside and disregarded. In an attempt to strengthen the voice of the victim in trials, a victim impact report (VIR) may be requested by the court. This has some effect on sentencing in certain cases. Unfortunately, VIRs are neither consistently requested nor given sufficient weight (Erez, 1991).

Were justice more accessible to the abuse survivor, he or she would probably be less preoccupied with revenge fantasies, and the survivor would be able to move more easily toward closure (Barton, 1999). Dina, who bravely faced her abuser in court, was nonetheless shortchanged by the system. An irreversible technical error made during filing of charges (with respect to statute of limitations) reduced the period of time for which the accused was held accountable—three years instead of the nine years he actually abused her. His sentence of five years imprisonment was reduced upon appeal to two years by a judge who did not take Dina's testimony or suffering into account, because aside from the acts committed against his niece, the accused led a normal family life and held a respectable job! Had she had more of a voice in the handling of the case, had justice been primarily hers and not society's (Barton, 1999), her recovery process would probably have reflected her sense of accomplishment.

In some cases in Israel the punishment came closer to fitting the crime. For example, a father received a sentence of twenty-eight years for abusing his four daughters. However, some cases end with a plea bargain resulting in a sentence of six months community service or parole. To date, no research has been done on the impact of court proceedings and trial outcomes on the psychological health of adult CSA survivors.

RECONCILIATION

Reconciliation means finding a way to continue a relationship after an injury has been inflicted by one party upon another. Davis (2003) suggests four levels at which this can be accomplished when the injury is CSA. They are the following:

1. Both abuser and survivor undertake the effort to grow and change and the ensuing relationship is very different than before.
2. Either the abuser or the survivor (usually the survivor) lowers expectations for change on the part of the other and is willing to engage in a relationship in any case.
3. Both abuser and survivor agree to put aside the issue of whether the abuse occurred in order to form a new relationship with new rules.
4. A relationship is impossible for a variety of reasons: the abuser is unwilling to be in contact, is incapacitated by mental illness or substance abuse, or is dead. Perhaps the abuser's behavior is still toxic and the relationship is too damaging for the survivor to continue.

In these cases the survivor grieves the lost relationship and seeks a personal reconciliation with the past.

Barrett (2003) presents a three-stage model, called "the third reality," for accomplishing reconciliations when the fact of abuse remains contentious. She suggests that even if the family member accused of abuse denies having abused, it is possible to work toward a manageable relationship. In her examples, the reconciliations were sought because the CSA survivor wanted to break down the wall of alienation and be able to be present at various significant family events. She states: "Participants have usually learned through painful experience that a reasonably satisfying connection is more valuable than holding on to their righteousness or to old myths of the perfect family; ending the war has become more important than winning it" (Barrett, 2003, p. 61).

Funnily enough, it seems that the reconciliation suggested by Barrett means that the "old myth of the perfect family" is reinstated by capitulation on the part of the survivor, who needs to do so to be able to attend her sister's wedding or help take care of her sick niece. Agreeing to disagree on whether or not sexual abuse occurred seems to imply not only that the war is over but that it has indeed been won by those on the side of denial. How else do family members, other than the alleged abuser, interpret the accuser putting his or her accusation on hold?

Barrett's model, however, does seem to empower the survivor in that the survivor lays down the ground rules for renewed contact and "feeling safe" is the foundation upon which future relationships are built. Perhaps within some families this is justice enough. However, calling this a "third reality" is problematic in that it implies that doubt exists as to whether abuse really occurred. For many survivors this may be intolerable. Moreover, it provides unwelcome support for continued societal denial of the extent of child sexual victimization.

It is important to recognize that, in contrast with the promotion of reconciliation in abusive families even when the question of abuse is left unresolved, reconciliation among nations is based upon acknowledgement of past crimes and victimization (Quinn, 2003). Reconciliation between Germany and Israel and between Australia and the Aboriginal Peoples, for example, included public declaration by the offenders of their wrongdoings and compensation of the victims (see for example The Australian Declaration toward Reconciliation [Reconciliation Australia, 2004]).

From a religious perspective as well, *reconciliation* is not necessarily implied, notwithstanding that forgiveness is encouraged even when the abuser does not repent. The religious leaders consulted during preparation of this chapter clearly stated that the survivor has an obligation to protect himself or herself. How does this coincide with the religious injunction to honor one's parents? Given that, according to Christianity, God is within each human being, protecting one's safety and one's dignity is protecting the Godliness within; therefore, if the parent continues to injure one's dignity or mental or physical health then one is obligated to take self-protective steps (Fr. Dr. Khoury, 2005, personal communication). In Judaism, causing injury to one's child is against the law, a sin against the word of God. As such, the injured party is not required to cooperate with the transgressing parent (Rabbi Dr. Kahn, 2005, personal communication). In Islam, given the seriousness of the sin of the parents who hurt their child, the parent who does not confess and make restitution is a parent who continues to hurt the adult child. In this case the child will be advised to protect himself or herself (Judge Abu Obied, 2005, personal communication). This may mean that, even from the perspective of religious leaders, it may be best, in some cases, for the CSA survivor to cut off relations from the unrepentant parent—the abuser as well as the nonprotective parent who insists that the survivor maintain his or her silence and allow the family to keep up appearances.

From the types of family reconciliation listed previously by Davis (2003), we see that her definition of reconciliation includes the entire range from warm to cold peace. Perhaps, because society is not yet ready to acknowledge the extent of CSA and deal with it unreservedly, true family reconciliation (warm peace) will likely be possible in only a very small minority of families for some time to come. Therefore, the process whereby family relations can be reinstituted and/or maintained with an agreement to disagree about whether abuse occurred may be more aptly named détente. This solution should be offered, not triumphantly, but sadly, as the last option when the only other alternative is total estrangement.

FORGIVENESS AGAIN

Survivors need to learn to forgive themselves for having been helpless children dependent on the abuser, for having bodies that respond sexually even to unwanted touch, for not having been able to stop it, for all the time it took to heal, etc. It is possible that once the survivor reaches a place of being kind to himself or herself he or she is open to seeing the context in which the abuser and other adults grew up and lived and understand the factors affecting their lives—not to provide excuses for the abuse or to pretend no abuse occurred, but in order to understand. Understanding factors at play does not reduce the adults' responsibility for their choices. Abusing a child and denying to oneself that a child is being abused are both choices made by the adults in the abused child's life. Those adults, similar to the survivor, can do the psychological work of confronting the truth, and possibly come to forgive themselves. Possibly.

Sarah-Jane's continuing therapy is her struggle to find peace of mind, to come to terms with the family she grew up in, and to defuse the toxic lessons she learned.

October 3, 2003

Not doing too well. Yesterday was the peak though. I woke at half past four! and didn't fall asleep again like I sometimes do after tossing and turning. I had a terrible day, although I didn't actually burst into tears like the day before. But I was miserable, tired, and behaved irrationally.

SARAH-JANE: I was convinced that my depression was temporary, and that if I waited long enough it would evaporate just as stormy clouds dispere to reveal a calm blue sky. After all, I had had bad times with my mother in the past, and we had always moved on—after carefully sweeping the debris under the carpet. But this time was different. I did not know it yet, but something had snapped inside me and I could no longer push my head back into that suffocating, yet familiar, hole in the sand. In the meantime, I struggled through each day and cried almost constantly.

In October 2003 I started taking antidepressants, which got me functioning again. The nonstop deluge of tears dwindled to a trickle and I was able to think clearly. Although I knew deep down inside that the antidepressants were just buying me time, and that I had serious work to do, it took me another few months to decide to go back to therapy.

I had ended therapy with Sheri years ago, and we were already working together on this book. Our relationship had changed and therapy with her was not an option, but she referred me to another therapist, Sary. In spite of feeling strange at having to work with somebody else after my years of therapy with Sheri, Sary proved to be an excellent choice, and we clicked almost immediately.

March 19, 2004

Last Friday went to first therapy session with Sary. Or should I say first trial session. We've decided on three sessions and then a reevaluation and decision about continuing. I realize that the consequences of the scene with my mother last summer haven't gone anywhere, and, in fact, the depression is simmering under the surface of the antidepressants I've been taking over the last four months. Sary seems sharp and perceptive, strong and capable. During the first meeting she gave me an interesting metaphor: my dysfunctional relationship with my mother is a sword lodged in my belly, stuck there for so long that I had learned to live with it, and had learned which of my bodily movements cause most pain, which cause least. During the final awful row with my mother the sword was twisted and the pain was searing. But pulling the sword out leaves an open gash, a void, and the pain is no less frightening.

April 2, 2004

Another interesting metaphor from therapy. When asked when I would separate emotionally from my mother and if I felt my children would be able to separate from me I said that I felt that the fact that they always got plenty of love and security from me, would make it easier for them to leave. So, the metaphor is:

Imagine a man starving, really bellyaching hungry, seeing a restaurant with his favorite food, going in, and ordering what he wants. And waiting. Waiting five . . . ten . . . fifteen . . . twenty minutes, with repeated promises from the waiter that the food is on its way. How long would he wait? On the other hand, if he received the food quickly, what would he do? Eat and leave the restaurant, right?

How long will I wait? When will I say "forget this restaurant, they're never going to give me what I want"? If, as Sary tells me, I need to be my own inner mother, loving myself unconditionally, I can write the end of the previous story by leaving the useless restaurant and going home to make myself a meal. Interesting.

April 7, 2004

Had the heaviest session so far in therapy. Came to the conclusion that my mother's immaturity means that not only had she never been able to give me the love I wanted, she never would. I left feeling very strange. So now, whenever I fall back on my usual pattern of thoughts concerning my mother, where I simmer in resentment wondering when the hell she's going to realize her wrongdoing and take responsibility, I find myself pulled up short with the realization that there is no point in me thinking those thoughts. It is ridiculous to think thoughts like that about a child-mother. I was a mother-child to her child-mother for years. And it's not going to change. At least not for her. At that realization I felt emptiness. My wound, no longer filled with the cold steel of a sword, is now an echoing void. Sad . . .

May 7, 2004

Had a heavy therapy session today. Sary showed me a photo from the album I brought her last time, a photo of my father and I, with him looking at me seductively, a photo that I have looked at many times and been troubled by. I told her that I didn't come to talk about him, but rather about my mother. I just couldn't bear the thought of looking at all that shit about him again. She said that this isn't about either of my parents, but about me.

May 28, 2004

In therapy today I talked about growing up in a house with my parents, paternal grandparents, and the little boy my grandmother looked after. How crazy and weird it was, and dark and despondent, how my mother, in her childlike, narcissistic way, was the only light. How my grandmother terrorized my grandfather, who wore women's clothes and didn't bathe; the way my father brutally tormented my grandmother's ward, out of apparent jealousy at her taking him in and making him in her expertly sick way a kind of boy-lover; the way my grandmother beat the little boy with a long cane—while he glared at her with half-closed eyes full of hate—and sent him out of her room, his usual place of sleep, to spend the night in a broom cupboard just big enough for a folding camp bed. We talked about how my father's room was furnished in a way that spoke of his presence, while my mother's was bare and unlived in, as though she were just passing through. We laughed at the insanity and compared it to the Addams family. Except that now I think of it, the Addams family redeemed themselves and everyone lived happily ever after . . .

July 2, 2004

A light therapy session today. Talked about how narcissism in parents is a taboo subject. Because the most sacred idea in human history, whether it be Jewish, Muslim, Christian, or any other human experience, is parenting. And the thought that parents could not only *not* love their children, but actually want to devour or erase them, is not entertainable. A mother of a friend of mine is narcissistic, but she is the all-supportive, all-loving epitome of motherhood, the kind that inhales her children in a breath of all-consuming love and connection. My mother is the other side of the narcissism coin, unable to connect to me in even the smallest ways, and just as blind to my pain as an adult as she was oblivious to my pain as a child. Sary said that recognizing that my mother is incapable of mothering me or of changing doesn't mean I have to stop loving her. If I recognize that she has the emotional intelligence of a child then whatever relationship I choose to have with her will be easier. To my question of "who will be my mother?" she answered that I was more than capable of being my own mother, along with the other mother figures I had found throughout my life.

SARAH-JANE: This time my subconscious needed barely any prodding to cooperate. I fumbled in the dark for answers less, and my dreams became more meaningful, almost taking on a life of their own.

August 8, 2004

Had a terrible dream, well . . . nightmare really. Mum was a serial killer, who killed a man every time a woman was hurt. I was astounded, but when she told me that she'd killed her father with sleeping pills (my grandfather died in his sleep), I broke down. In the dream I kept wondering, as I drove through the streets crying hysterically, how on earth I had survived a woman who was capable of killing her family. I arrived at the house where Avi was waiting for me, together with his parents, and my mother and sister. We were all in this tiny bedroom, almost completely filled with a bed, which I lay on, crying hysterically. When my mother and sister looked at me, they had eerie, doll-like, glassy-eyed, smiling faces. My mother-in-law, sitting like a shield between my mother and me, realized I was in a bad way and took me out of the room. Then I woke up. Not sure I want to analyze this dream, which is basically an inverted version of the film *Serial Mom,* where instead of killing people who hurt your family, my mother is killing her actual family!

September 3, 2004

In last night's dream, I took four babies home from a hospital to care for. One of them was bigger, more developed than the others. She liked me and always had a joyful, pleasing smile every time she looked at me. I became very involved in looking after her, breast-feeding her, changing her, dressing her, hugging and kissing her. Suddenly, I remembered that there were other babies for me to look after. I looked around at the cots and they were still and quiet. I knew they weren't dead, but I felt they were weak. I went to the smallest and picked her up. Her eyes were shut. She was tiny, wrinkled, and feeble. Her face was half blue. I had to decide whether to breast-feed her immediately while she was asleep, or to wake her up by changing her diaper to make her eat better. But there was no time, so I brought her to my breast, gently nudging her face as she started to suck.

After analyzing this dream in therapy, it seems that the first child was my parent-child self, with a continuously smiling face, eager to please, who grew out of living with dysfunctional parents. The tiny weak baby I tried to save was the part of me that didn't get parenting and love. She is underdeveloped, and now I am bringing her back to life.

I feel like my subconscious is working overtime, but don't see yet where I'm headed.

CLOSURE

Do happy endings exist? It depends on the criteria for happy ending. It also depends on our time perspective—when do we declare that an ending? An individual's life story comes to a close only when facing the grave (and those who believe in reincarnation would say that it even extends beyond that). Until then chances exist to continue processing earlier experiences and make further changes. Laura Davis (2002) gives us evidence of that with her reemergence fourteen years after publication of her first book with the story of her reconciliation with her mother. It will be interesting to see what further developments she will disclose as time goes on.

As Hodaya's drawings and Sarah-Jane's diary illustrated in Chapter 5, and Sarah-Jane's diary shows again in this chapter, the end of therapy is not the end of the healing process. Therapy should provide tools to better handle the conflicts and problems that life throws in the survivor's way. Sometimes the survivor returns to therapy, as later stressors may send him or her back into previous trauma-based patterns of thinking, feeling, or behaving that are best resolved with professional help.

SARAH-JANE: When I went into back into therapy, this time with Sary, to work on my relationship with my mother, I was distressed at first. I mean, here I am writing a book about recovering from childhood sexual abuse while I am still recovering! But then, remembering the healing spiral Sheri and I had talked about so many times, I realized that the spiral process is best for me, because it gives me time to play in between phases of working on myself. Not that I'm trying to insinuate for a moment that therapy isn't the greatest fun. And that last remark was only partly in jest. Although it is true that quite a lot of time is spent sitting in un-fun dark places and crying un-fun tears, a lot of vibrant, energizing moments are also had.

However, this is all very well. But what about closure? What is closure anyway, apart from being yet another aspect of healing I feel ambivalent about? If it is reconciliation with the people who hurt me so badly when I was a child, then I am far from that.

Nevertheless, some form of closure is desirable, as an outcome of the healing process, and I feel that, like most facets of this process, I reach a different level of closure each time I complete a stage of my journey. However, aiming for a life that is entirely free of the consequences of the abuse is far too optimistic. For me, complete closure—if such a thing exists—is living a life that is not *permeated* with the abuse, based on choices that are not made from the point of view of a victim. Forgiving my parents will not bring me to that place. No form of reconciliation or confrontation will do it either. The only way for me to get to that place is to let go of the terrible, paralyzing shame that is left over from my childhood. Little by little I feel that shame loosen its hold on me, but I still have work to do in the area of self-forgiveness.

For most of the therapy process my clients generally see coming to peace with their past as unthinkable. However, by the time they have crossed the Wall of Fear and mourned the childhood they should have had and all the losses that entails, most feel differently. Iris, for example, says that although she is sad for the little abused girl she once was, if she had the choice to live her childhood again without the abuse she would not, because the abuse and her recovery from it contributed to making her into the person she is today. She likes who she is and would not want to be any different. Her history is part of that.

Does closure involve other people? Yes, I believe it does—in a positive as well as a negative sense. Survivors cannot control how others will respond to their growing strength, assertiveness, and ability to be emotionally intimate with others. Hopefully, the tools they acquire in therapy will help them decide how to interact with those in their lives who support them and with those who do not. In addition, they need to decide what, if anything, they believe their abusers and nonprotective parents still owe them, such as being willing to continue to talk about the abuse, for example, or being willing to continue apologizing (Coleman, 1998, p. 93).

I think that those survivors whose parents and other family members are not prepared to accept responsibility for their actions of the past and are not willing to sustain the survivor's anger until it has extinguished itself are left with a little bit of emptiness in their hearts that will never be filled regardless of whatever else is right in their lives. I think this is true even for those who have managed the type of reconciliation suggested by Barrett (2003).

In an ideal situation, the perpetrator would call together the entire extended family and read out a declaration such as the following:

> I hereby declare that I, _____'s father [for example], did willfully and cruelly sexually abuse my son/daughter [for example] from the ages of ___ to ___.
>
> This was my fault and my fault alone. S/he did nothing to initiate or encourage my behavior. S/he did not deserve this abuse.
>
> It was my responsibility to care for and educate my child/niece/nephew/pupil etc. while respecting his/her absolute and unquestioning dependence on me. I exploited my position in his/her life.
>
> I am deeply sorry that I so seriously harmed you when you were a child. I do not expect my apology to be accepted.
>
> I commit myself to get psychological help to understand where this behavior came from and to ensure that children are not at risk in my presence.
>
> I commit myself never to be alone with a child for the rest of my life. I commend myself to accept whatever punishment this family deems I merit.

This would be followed by similar declarations by the nonprotective adults in the family. Then everyone would eat a sumptuous meal to celebrate the victory of truth and conscience.

In the song "Imagine," John Lennon sings, "You may say I'm a dreamer." Yes. You may say we're dreamers.

Chapter 7

How I Get Through Therapy in One Piece

Sarah-Jane Ogiers

If you are going through hell, keep going.

Winston Churchill

Healing from childhood abuse is an ongoing process. I never really stop working on it. However, I have times in my life when I need to work on it more intensively. At those times I turn to therapy to anchor me, and my therapist is always an ally in my journey. Therapy is a place where I can expose my deepest flaws and my darkest moments. When the path on my journey is paved with glass and my feet are bare, when all I can see at the tip of my nose is a thick, dense wall of thorns, my therapist must be there. That is what we have therapists for: to hold us up when we can barely put one foot in front of the other. Your therapist cannot take the journey for you, but he or she has to cheer you on from the sidelines. He or she has to be ready to jump in at critical moments to break your fall, pick you up, dust you off, or whatever it is you need.

However, therapy is not always critical moments and we are not always stranded helplessly on a heap of glass (even though sometimes it feels that way!) Most of the time it is about just getting through the day, painting a smile on your face as you go out into the world, putting something edible on the table for your children, or simply getting a decent night's sleep. It's about steering through the obstacles of the day, whether that be dealing with difficult people around you or avoiding the triggers that bring up feelings from the past. All the tire-

Overcoming Childhood Sexual Trauma
Published by The Haworth Press, Inc., 2006, All rights reserved.
doi:10.1300/5668_07

some, everyday irritations with which everyone has to deal do not go away during therapy. Not only that, but when you are in therapy, pain and anxiety are close to the surface, psychic wounds are open, and the barrier between your conscious and subconscious is more fragile, with information hurtling back and forth between the two. In other words, you are hypersensitive. The daily annoyances so tiresome to everyone else take on gargantuan proportions for the survivor in therapy and are like salt in his or her open wounds.

So life is tough in therapy. Making any change that is worth holding on to always is. My therapist cannot shadow me from morning till night, and putting my life on hold until I next speak to her is not feasible. So I found alternative ways to get me through the days and nights, which I can group into two categories: "support network" and "coping alone."

SUPPORT NETWORK

Ideally, we would be surrounded by supportive people. Our family of origin would believe us and be the first to sign up for the healing crusade. Our partners would give us emotional support and not balk at the horror of our past, while taking care of all those tiresome everyday chores. Our friends would stick by us through thick and thin, accepting any odd behavior on our part; our employers and teachers would tell us to take off as much time as we need to heal; our children would bring home a string of good grades, accompanied by idyllically happy tales from their lives that would redeem human nature in our eyes. Unfortunately, life is not ideal, and you might just have to settle for a little less.

When I was in therapy with Sheri and I was practically crawling through my life, I had several "helpers," some of whom came and went, and some who are still with me today. At work my principal helper was Tal, a male friend, who would listen to me and not freak out at the increasingly frightening intensity of my reactions to the gruesome memories I had to work through. He would convince me to push on through therapy toward the light at the end of the tunnel, and perhaps most important, would write with me. Over a period of several months we got together once a week or two after work, and some of my most powerful writing about my childhood came out of these evenings. It was an activity that also offered light relief, because sometimes we would just write amusing sketches about work, because we had a similar sense of humor.

At home, I had my best friend and neighbor, Mazi. When I could not bear to stay in the house a moment longer I would cross the hallway to her apartment and, as a stay-at-home mum, she was usually there. Mazi's compassion, unwavering belief in me and quirky sense of humor were just what I needed. Of course, I had to deal with the insecurities and fears of abandonment I bring to every relationship, and Mazi was by no means a paragon of virtue, so she had her moments of impatience with me. But most of the time she listened, hugged me when I cried, and laughed with me when things got so bad that the only thing left to do was laugh. I did not reveal the gruesome details of the abuse to her, for I didn't need to. As my friend, Mazi just wanted to ease my pain, and she could hold me in her arms without knowing exactly what was causing that pain.

Now I am in therapy with Sary, where I have advanced from crawling to walking, and Mazi is still here holding my hand. She lives in a different neighborhood now, but we still do a lot of talking and listening and laughing, and even when our friendship is strained (what relationship doesn't have those moments?) we still find ways to stay connected. In short, I am eternally grateful to her. I have no idea what going through this healing process would have been like without her. I know that it could not have been better.

Tal, my work helper from the days of therapy with Sheri has become someone to whom I nod and smile whenever we bump into each other, and we sometimes exchange a few friendly words. I have a warm place for him in my heart, and I believe that we came into each other's lives at a specific time for a specific purpose. Today, I have a different helper at work: a young woman, Anna, intelligent and wise for her years. Apart from her warmth and compassion, she has—yes, you guessed it—a great sense of humor. We were already friends when I decided to go back into therapy, and Anna told me, without hesitation, that she would be there for me during the difficult moments. And she is.

Nevertheless, do not imagine for a moment that my helpers just fell into my lap. Just like the rest of the coping techniques described in this chapter, I had to work at these friendships. And so will you. I know that it will sometimes seem impossible to reach out to others, and occasionally you will be disappointed, but it is all part of reclaiming your life. Make no mistake about it, one of the most important steps we can take in our healing journey is take back what should have been ours to begin with. However terrifying it is, the subsequent feeling of empowerment and joy is well worth the risk. I can promise you that, although you may feel shame about your history of abuse, others usually just feel compassion. Of course some people cannot cope and withdraw from us. I have lost friends over the years, but not because they thought anything was shameful about me, either they just did not know what to do with the idea of child abuse and the intensity of my feelings, or they could not come to terms with the "new" person I was becoming. In general, though, my experience of "coming out of the closet" was that most people do not recoil. Good-hearted people are out there. Start reaching out and you will see for yourself.

Having said that, let me give you a word of caution: Beware of the unhelpful "helpers." Remarks such as *"but you were already sixteen. I mean . . . you were old enough to say no. I don't understand,"* or *"You've been in therapy for two years. Are you sure it should take this long? I was sexually abused by my uncle as a teenager and my therapy only took six months,"* are, needless to say, *not* helpful. I am not good with boundaries, and I tend to open up to people too quickly, so sometimes by the time I recognize the false helpers I've already been burned. I am getting better at this, but I still have to be careful.

Really good helpers like Tal, Mazi, and Anna are like islands, places you can climb onto to get your breath back and find your bearings before plunging back into a sea of intense emotions. I was lucky to have these islands, and they made all the difference in my life between unbearable and tolerable. But sometimes islands are more than places to catch your breath. One particular island of mine was both a sanctuary and a place for painful therapeutic work. It was really a collection of islands.

When I was in therapy with Sheri I joined a weekly therapy group for survivors of childhood sexual abuse. This group of women was run by two trained therapists, and each session lasted two hours. The atmosphere was always emotionally charged and often full of rage and sadness for wrongs inflicted by our abusers, so basically I was spending at least three hours a week dealing with the abuse (not including the time I spent talking, thinking, dreaming, and writing about it outside the formal framework of therapy). Needless to say, having the group in my therapy process made the journey through the pain of my past far more intense.

December 11, 1993

Today I arrived to the third meeting of the therapy group in a pretty good mood. I had been shopping beforehand, had found some lovely shoes, and then bought a really good sandwich, stuffed with all sorts of delicious things, and ate it on my way up to the rape crisis center. I sat on the wall outside to finish my meal and had a quick cigarette. I saw the sisters arrive and figured it was time to join the group. I threw away my half-smoked cigarette with reluctance and made my way up the stairs. I felt an inexplicable tiredness run through my body, and, as I sat down in the room where the group met every week, recognized it as similar to the way I feel lately in therapy with Sheri, where we search my past for answers. As the meeting progressed I felt more and more exhausted until it became an effort to keep my eyes open.

We began the meeting with each woman describing how she was feeling and what she had brought with her to the meeting emotionally. As each one went into long tirades, I began to go inside myself. The strangest feeling . . . again I felt an imposter. What was I doing there? They could say this to me, and quite justifiably, in my opinion, for I felt that I remembered nothing, that the memories I've always had were not evidence of abuse. "How do you know anything even happened?" they could ask me. The women continued to speak, some, in fact, asking this same question of themselves later on.

The sensation of turning inward and wanting nothing to touch me or relate to me was mixed with resentment and anger toward myself and the others. What was I doing here, wasting my own and other's time? I planned to say when my turn came that I had nothing to say. I suddenly realized with a flicker of self-knowledge that, along with the feeling of not wanting to make the effort and the fear of being found out as an imposter, was a childish need to grab attention, to make them notice me and say "But why don't you have anything to say? We want to hear you." So I sat, sulkily, and when my turn came, said that I had nothing to say, which, disappointingly, was immediately accepted, in keeping with the noncoercive atmosphere of the group.

The group leaders had prepared material on ways sexual abuse victims deal with their traumas. It was fascinating and woke me up briefly. I discovered, much to my dismay, that I had used, and was still using, most of the methods they described. God, how dismal! What is the right way to deal with it all? Is there a right way? Is there a wrong way?

Lily told her story. A strange warped tale. When she was twenty-three years old she hunted down and met her father for the first time—a father who had abused and deserted her mother before she was born. The story was confusing but I tried to follow. She wanted, on the one hand, to get the love from her father that she had missed for so many years, and on the other hand, she wanted him to admit to his abuse of her mother. She began to meet with him regularly, and, in her desperation to win his love, ignored the fact that the hugs and fondling she received from him became less and less fatherly. Eventually, he used her need for his affection against her and manipulated her into spending days and nights with him. The nightmare continued for months, until finally she tried to escape him and he beat her up, the whole affair ending with her in hospital. This strange story ended only two months ago and now Lily is in therapy.

I found myself, and felt it in the others too, disbelieving of her helplessness. At twenty-three, she didn't have to continue meeting him. After pondering this for a few days I felt overwhelmed with guilt at my automatically blaming her. How can one judge another person? Isn't using a grown-up daughter's desperate need for fatherly love against her as bad as abusing the same need in a young child?

We had come to the end of the session, so we closed our eyes and began a guided fantasy. But because some women couldn't find their safe place, we were instructed to explore a box of tools we could use to get us through our crises. This only served to enhance my irritation since I already had a safe place, which had taken me a long time to build, and an even longer time to enter. But I very nearly fell asleep and after coming out of this relaxed state, trudged to the bus stop in a foul mood. Funnily enough, when I got home, I stayed up reading for a while, no longer exhausted. Go figure.

Today, I see that my momentary disbelief of Lily's story was directly related to my ambivalence at the time toward my own story. This perhaps explains why I would get so upset at the unhelpful remarks I mentioned in the previous section, which bring into question how helpless I really was as a teenager. Did I really believe myself?

February 1, 1994

Yesterday I went to the group straight from work and had a very intense experience there. The focus was on me and the other participants were asked if they could think of anything to ask me that would help me piece together the puzzle of the abuse. From their questions about my father I began to relate an experience I'd had with him and my school friend when I was fourteen and he had fondled us sexually. While I related this story I became overwhelmed by a now familiar pressure: a weight on my chest, difficulty breathing, a feeling of wanting to break free from my body. Remembering the feeling of his hands on my body, which at the time hadn't invoked more than a slight discomfort (or maybe more but I've forgotten?), now overwhelmed me with disgust and my skin crawled. I looked down into my lap, at my fingers frantically twisting a pen, and knew that everyone was looking at me. The leaders were watching me carefully and the women asked occasional questions. I felt as if I was glowing, radiating my panic, and the pressure was so intense that I thought I would explode. The group was asked if they thought that occurrences like this in my childhood are enough to explain the way I feel, and they all answered in one voice that they were. Since then, I have been overwhelmed with the knowledge of my father's wrongdoing, his abuse of my trust in him as a father. Once I used to believe that he was just a nonconformist who acted differently from other parents. But no more. Now I know that there are guidelines for behavior with children that every parent should respect.

In spite of the intensity, one of the most important aspects of the therapy group was realizing that I was not alone, that others had gone through the same nightmare that I had, and were now experiencing the same loneliness, rage, sadness, and despair that I was. Also, meeting women who exhibited strength and a dogged determination to build something worthwhile out of their lives was an uplifting experience and gave me the energy I badly needed to lift myself up and out of the swamp of misery my parents had bequeathed me.

May 22, 1994

At the group Moran was in a very bad way and we focused on her. We asked her to tell us about the last memory that she had: the terrible beating and violent rape by her brother when she was sixteen. It was very moving and I cried. She was afraid to tell us, afraid we wouldn't want to know her afterward. How strange! We always think our own story will estrange and repel those close to us, yet when we hear another's nightmare tale we feel compassion and understanding. She looked so much better after she had told us. She realized, as we all do, that the world doesn't cave in when we reveal the shame that our abusers dumped on us.

July 10, 1994

Today I went with the rest of the group to a t-shirt painting evening at the "Haifa Women's Coalition," a local feminist organization. Women, who had experienced violent trauma, whether physical, emotional or sexual, sat on the roof of the building, surrounded by brushes and colors, and painted t-shirts to wear in a demonstration. I saw some very moving pictures and words. While I was there I went into the kitchen to make myself a coffee. It was all so colorful and cozy. As I came out of the kitchen a sudden smile came to my face. It took me completely by surprise, for it was nothing like the forced smile I give these days. I had a warm feeling of being completely at home and safe.

October 4, 1994

I feel sick, sick to my stomach with this whole abuse thing. I have written something terrible, and I cannot believe that it could possibly have happened. But if it didn't happen then that makes me sick and perverted. I'm so angry and miserable that I just don't know what to do with myself. What I wrote opened me up and made me vulnerable, and now, however much I try to stay in control, I can't subdue the rage that rolls around inside me like tidal waves. I sat with the knowledge of what I wrote all day yesterday and came to the therapy group feeling restless and fired up. One of the girls read out a letter she'd written to her abuser, and I was overwhelmed with the hate and anger that poured out of the letter. It caused a panic in me that I didn't know what to do with. So, of course, I dissociated, froze completely. I felt paralyzed, my muscles tensed, and I couldn't move or speak. After about half an hour, it finally passed, but not before my arms started to hurt. When I came out of it my anger, rage, and impatience just got worse. I rushed out at the end of the group session without saying good-bye and slammed the door. Angry, I drove home, terrified that I'd cause an accident. At home, my rage slowly evaporated, leaving a sick feeling in my gut. I dreamed about my father, and although he wasn't doing anything menacing in the dream I was terrified. I could feel his evil in the air. I must have cried out in my sleep, because I half awoke to find Avi comforting me. Now, I walk around sick and miserable, and the rage sits just under the surface. I don't know whether I'll go to the group next week and I even contemplated canceling my session with Sheri.

Paradoxically, the more I trusted the group the more emotionally loaded my experiences there became. A direct correlation existed between my increasing feeling of safety there and the amount of fear, anger, and empty sadness I was prepared to show. My emotional numbness thawed and my walls of defense crumbled one by one. The situation came to a head when I had to leave the group to study for an exam, my first step toward being accepted at University. It was a difficult parting to say the least.

February 27, 1995

I had a terrible last session with the group. After I had been promised enough time to finalize things there I was left with the last thirty minutes. I was furious because I knew that this wasn't enough time to go into anything heavy and come out of it. I felt betrayed and hurt, so I walked out without allowing anyone to say anything about me leaving, telling them that I wouldn't believe them anyway. Later, my anger dissolved into an overwhelming sadness at the chance I'd lost with the group, the one chance I'd had to make things right, to try and express my terrible rage without hurting anyone and explain to the women that the anger didn't belong to them, that it was just the eleven-year-old Sarah-Jane feeling rejected and suspicious of everyone. Although I even wanted to cancel my next session with Sheri, because I knew she would try to convince me to try again with the group, I decided to go in the end. And of course she did just what I thought she would, because after talking to her about it I did manage to sort it out with the group leaders. They were very sad that they hadn't read me well enough to realize that thirty minutes wasn't enough. We agreed to try again.

March 6, 1995

At the group today while talking about how unfair it was that my life had been stolen from me, I broke down and cried uncontrollably. One of the group leaders hugged me. I was embarrassed at how contorted my face must have been. I felt vulnerable and there were danger signs flashing all over the place, a result of me having let down the aggressive, hard, angry wall and shown my weakness. Smadar hugged me and I had her and Hadas on either side of me holding my hands.

So, finally, I had opened my heart and shown my pain, in the best place I could have chosen to do so. With two therapists who could contain my intense emotions and a group of survivors who understood where my anger came from, the group was a safe place to let down my guard. My rage was so overwhelming that I had been unable to envision unleashing it without annihilating myself and everyone around me. But in the group I did. And we all survived.

If you find it hard to open up to people about the nightmare you went through, then a therapy or support group is a good place to start. You will find a place where you can talk about what happened to you. Only if you want to though. The people there will understand the rage and pain and shame in your heart, even if you do not open up.

COPING ALONE

My husband once said to me, "If someone told you that there were special tomatoes that can help you heal from the abuse, you'd go straight out and buy them." He was exasperated, but he was right, and I told him so. During my healing process I did try everything I could find. I went to healers, palm readers, Reiki masters; I meditated in the desert; I took long walks in nature; I exercised on a daily basis; and I practiced deep relaxation. I wrote, drew, and painted, and I read every self-help book I could find. Some of the techniques I tried and discarded. Some were quick first-aid solutions that provided temporary relief. A few are still with me today. For instance, an ability to laugh at my own dysfunctional behavior is a tool I consider invaluable. During my childhood, experiencing the abuse in real time, I couldn't use humor to get me through the days. The days were too terrible and I was too frightened. Instead, I froze, shutting down my ability to feel. As an adult reliving the memories of that abuse and the feelings that accompanied it, my sense of humor often keeps that paralysis at bay. As a child, with limited emotional resources, paralysis was a defense mechanism, a way to prevent me feeling the pain that I could not have felt without going insane. I think that, over the years, my subconscious came to the conclusion that a sense of humor was a better defense mechanism. If nothing else, it is a mechanism that leaves me with the ability to light a cigarette while trying to cope!

In short, freezing up was once vital to *not* feel the pain. Today, a sense of humor offers me one way to look at my childhood and feel that pain without losing my mind. For, even now, I still have moments when that pain is so thick and black that I have to find a humoristic angle so as not to suffocate. I can still become petrified with the emergence of a particularly horrific memory, but in general, when it comes to defense mechanisms, I'll take humor over paralysis any time. As I am fond of saying to myself, "whatever you do, don't mislay your sense of humor. It'll stand you in good stead when you're wading through the shit."

In this section I will talk about other techniques that worked for me. I hope that they will be as useful to you, or that they will at least motivate you to find your own ways of coping. Before I talk about that, though, I want to point out a fundamental necessity in this healing journey: sleep.

December 20, 1993

Today must have been one of the worst days of my life. I was exhausted after coming home at two in the morning and getting very little sleep. When I'm tired the black always looks blacker, the gray darker, and the white is nowhere. So I spent a day of misery, unable to concentrate, tired and unhappy, holding back the tears and anger. I went home and of course everything exploded. It was like everything just poured out, all the emotion trapped inside for so long just overflowed.

I cannot stress strongly enough how important it was for me to look after myself physically during those difficult years. It seems like a trivial matter, barely worth thinking about when one is going through extreme emotional pain. Who cares about sleep? But sleeping properly contributed significantly to my ability to deal with the anxiety and depression brought on by dealing with painful issues. Sometimes the therapy process is like a war, a battle with old ghosts, with all the pain involved in working on memories of abuse. If you do not rest your body it cannot fight the fight. However, although it is true that sleep is an essential tool in any battle, at times my recommendation will seem pretty useless, precisely because the ghosts you wrestle with during waking hours have followed you to bed. I know. All I am saying is that when you do get the chance for a good night's sleep, grab it.

If I already know that it's going to be a hard night, I find bedtime rituals to be very soothing. Books, in this respect (as in many others), are my greatest friends. From the moment I learned how to read, books have always been a part of my bedtime ritual. Today I usually opt for light reading, which, in my case, is both a way to balance the heavier reading I do as a literature student and a kind of transition from the noise of the day into the silence of sleep. That noise could be just the regular stuff of living, or the more stressful stuff of healing. Either way, I recommend it—unless you are like a friend of mine who has great difficulty putting down a book and usually ends up going to sleep at three in the morning. In that case it would be counterproductive, the object of the exercise being "getting a good night's sleep." If reading is not an option, watching television seems to be good for falling asleep. Again, the emphasis is on light. Sitcoms are effective as they are particularly mind-numbing; scary, violent horror movies will not do the trick.

If I am going through a exceptionally rough time, and I know that bedtime reading will not be enough, I put my book aside, turn off the light, and move on to another part of my ritual. This involves lying on my back and trying to reach a state of deep relaxation, usually by focusing on each part of my body, starting from my toes up to my scalp, and consciously relaxing the muscles. Nine times out of ten I fall asleep in the middle of the exercise. However, sometimes nothing works. When that happens, rather than toss and turn with frustration, or try in vain to banish scenes of the abuse from my mind, I get out of bed, make myself a hot drink, read, watch some television, and try again an hour later.

Suppose you have fallen asleep, all is well and good, and you suddenly find yourself sitting bolt upright in the middle of the night, drenched in sweat, after a nightmare about the abuse. In my case, as luck would have it, one of my cosurvivors from the therapy group worked night shifts, so if I woke up from a nightmare about the abuse and was afraid to go back to sleep I could call her and talk it over, or just hear the reassuring voice of someone who understands exactly what kind of a nightmare I just had. Also, I would often write about the dream after it woke me, which served two purposes: I would get it out of my system and, if I thought it significant, bring it to my next therapy session, another safe place for me to talk about it.

Since we are back on the subject of writing, if you asked me what, out of all my self-coping techniques, was the most helpful, I would have to say it was keeping a diary. Writing is, and always has been, a cathartic activity for me. I officially started keeping a diary at age thirteen, which was useful when it came to writing Chapter 2 of this book since it documents my journey through a sad adolescence. Apart from my diary, I wrote long diatribes about whatever happened to be annoying me about the world at the time. In my late teens, filled with existential questions, I wrote about the futility of life. In my early twenties I was furious about the oppression of women and held forth at length, with my pen and paper, on equal rights. Nobody else ever saw my mini essays, but I still look at them fondly from time to time.

When I went into therapy with Sheri and quickly found myself entangled in painful memories, my diary/essay writing habit became, just as quickly, my most crucial self-therapy tool. The feelings of sadness, terror, and rage were sometimes so huge and dark that they would cut the breath out of my mouth and leave me staring up at them, amazed that for so many years they could have fit so compactly inside me without ripping me apart. Writing about them named them, made them less nightmarish and bizarre, and more like what they were: natural responses to a desolate childhood.

If you already have a way to express yourself creatively, then this is the time to use it. If not, you might consider developing one for the duration of therapy. I did not always write; sometimes I drew. Drawing wasn't something I did before therapy and I abandoned it immediately afterward, so, similar to other coping techniques, this was something that came into my life when I needed it and left when I didn't. I used pictures when I had no words, when the pain I was feeling was too deep and indefinable to express in writing. At these times I would sit down with a sheet of paper and draw, using pens, pencils, paints, charcoal—whatever was available, depending on where I was. I would draw without thinking, letting my hand move over the paper, a kind of "free association" drawing. Similar shapes and images, in black and red, would come up, which I would usually bring to the next therapy session. Sometimes the drawings, even the more abstract among them, would depict an abuse scene; sometimes they were just a way to articulate anger and sadness that I could not express any other way.

Another technique I found useful was guided fantasy, something I used a great deal in therapy with Sheri. Once I had mastered the knack and created an imaginary safe place, I used this technique on my own, outside therapy sessions, when the abuse of the past was so tangible that it threatened to spill over into the present. My safe place was idyllic: a beautiful garden carpeted in lush green and hundreds of vibrant, colorful flowers growing wild, with a magical stream running through it. The garden was protected by a tall wall with an octopus that patrolled its length (yes, I know octopuses can't live out of water, but in imaginary safe places anything is possible and everything is allowed). Inside the garden, lying by the stream, was a kind and serene lion—Aslan, named after the lion of Narnia from my favorite childhood books. He was both protector and healer. On really bad days I would find a quiet spot at home or at work, close my eyes, and enter this garden. I would lie in the stream and let its healing water wash over me, and then nestle close to the lion, hugging his soft fur. Here, in my imagination, the monsters from my childhood could not reach me.

As I mentioned earlier, I worked intensively in therapy. So there were times when I did not want to do anything remotely therapeutic. I just wanted to numb my mind and escape from the twenty-four hours a day, seven days a week absorption in the abuse and its consequences. I did not want to talk about it, think about it, write about it, or draw it. I wanted it to *go away*. When this happened I would watch recorded tapes of my favorite sitcom or go to a movie—but only comedies, no tearjerkers. Sometimes I read—fiction only, no self-help books, since the idea was to escape, not read more about the abuse. Even the therapeutic drawing I talked about earlier was not always heavy and painful. Occasionally, I would set aside my blacks and reds and draw scenes from nature in soothing blues and greens. And then, of course, finding someone with a problem they needed to talk about is always a good escape from self-absorption, for it is a paradoxical, if somewhat overstated, truth that one of the most effective ways to forget one's problems is to focus on someone else's.

But, you may be asking, "what's the point?" You cannot really escape the depression and anger, you cannot actually make the abuse go away. It's true. But you can make it go away *for a while*. Even if you know that it is still going to be there when you leave the movie theater or put down your book, you have given your mind a well-earned break. You know that the moment you turn the television off or hang up the phone after talking to a friend you will find that the shadow of the abuse has been sitting patiently next to you all the time, but you will face it with renewed energy.

A final word of advice: Remember what life was like before therapy? Remember those activities you loved to do? Did you love to dance, walk your dog, windsurf, collect stamps? Whatever it was, do it now. Even if it seems like a complete waste of time, and you feel like you are faking it, do it. Force yourself to get up and go through the motions. If you cannot hold on to anything else, hold on to the things that once gave you pleasure.

If you never had any pleasure in life, never had a hobby or an activity that gave you relaxation or fun, then part of your job now is to find something. Be stubborn. I can hear you grumble now, saying that nothing can make you feel better, that the best you can hope for is to survive the next moment, if only for those to whom you feel committed: your therapist whose life you are reluctant to complicate by committing suicide, or your children whom you would never want to hurt in any way. I know that some of you are just hoping that the Angel of Death will find an elegant way to whisk you off so you can be relieved of your torment. However, I do hope you will be willing to try something to "help the medicine go down" while you are waiting. Give yourself a break.

EPILOGUE

Recently, as our deadline for sending this book to the publisher grew closer, I had a bad setback in my journey. I managed to manipulate myself into a situation in which I had to literally disconnect from my body to get through it. I did this through choice, but was pushed from behind by my history of abusive relationships and my inexplicable pull toward the role of the victim. I slipped into this role so easily it was frightening. Once more I ignored my own needs to meet someone else's. Again I erased myself (albeit temporarily) to please another, and it was such a plainly brutal act of self-inflicted violence that it left me reeling. With my usual melodramatic air, I looked around me at the debris my trip back into hell had left in its wake, and thought "Oh, my life is in pieces again. How original I am!"

The point of this story, apart from emphasizing that setbacks and new challenges will always occur in the healing process, is to show you a recent example of the way the support network and other coping techniques work for me. Today, I am far more assertive about reaching out and asking for help, and during this period, Sary, Mazi, and Anna provided what I can only describe as round-the-clock support. Sary and I increased the frequency of our meetings for a few weeks. We spoke on the phone between sessions, and when we couldn't she sent encouraging text messages to my cell phone. Mazi called me several times a day, and provided coffee and a shoulder to cry on several times a week. Anna kept an eye on me at work and hugged me as I cried during cigarette breaks.

One day during this crisis Mazi and I spoke for a long time on our mobile phones. When we had to break off because our ears were burning, I told her that now I had to go back to my less-than-satisfactory reality and suddenly remembered what I had written at the end of this section: "give yourself a break." That is exactly what I had done by talking with her! So after having refilled my batteries I sat down and started writing this epilogue. Taking myself out of my misery for an hour, with Mazi's help, made it possible for me to go on to another coping technique: "write about it."

So it went on for a while, the storm of tears and self-recriminations, sprinkled with panic attacks and even a touch of hopelessness. I wailed a great deal. I even railed a little at the universe for testing me again. After a couple of weeks I began to see something comical in the image of me shaking my fist at the sky. A sense of humor returned to my conversations with my support network. I let out the breath I'd been holding in. What a relief! For a while there I thought I had lost the ability to laugh at myself.

I pushed forward with writing this book, and used the breaks in between to either write in my diary or watch escapist films—starring undercover spies of extraordinary intelligence, who outwitted everyone, never got caught, and walked along a dusty road into the sunset at the end (talk about wishful thinking!). Most of my coping techniques came into play during this crisis, and they enabled me to continue being a good-enough mother, go to work each day, and attend classes at the university. Occasionally, wrapped up in myself as I was, I even managed to ask my friends how *they* were.

Now the storm shows signs of wearing itself out, and I have the time and energy to look at this last episode, to see what I can learn from it. For it is a life lesson, and life lessons, as I already know, are not to be missed. I would like nothing more than to share with you what I have learned from this particular lesson; unfortunately, at the time of writing, I still do not know. But I am working on it.

PART III:
COMPANIONS ON THE JOURNEY

Chapter 8

Children of Survivors:
Growing Up in the Shadow of Trauma

Sheri Oz

Children are the living messages we send to a time we will
not see.

John W. Whitehead

A parent's unresolved childhood sexual trauma casts a long shadow
over the crib of his or her infant. What is it like for a parent to raise a
child when weighed down by such a shadow? This was explored to
some extent in Chapter 2 and will be discussed in greater depth here
from the perspective of research conducted on parenting in traumatized populations.

What is it like to grow up with this shadow hiding the person your
mother or father could have been had he or she not been sexually
abused? In this chapter, the subjective experience of second-generation
childhood sexual abuse (CSA) survivors is heard for the first time.

WHAT THE RESEARCH SAYS

The impact of parents' trauma history on their offspring is referred
to as the "intergenerational transmission of trauma." This phenomenon has been researched with respect to children of war veterans and
survivors of wars or other mass tragedies, but most of all with respect
to second-generation Holocaust survivors. Parents who suffered CSA
have been studied to a much lesser degree, and the research studies

Overcoming Childhood Sexual Trauma
Published by The Haworth Press, Inc., 2006, All rights reserved.
doi:10.1300/5668_08

have had a more narrow focus. For this reason, the impact of the parent's CSA history on the next generation will be examined against the background of our understanding of intergenerational traumatization gained from families ravaged by the Holocaust.

Transmission of Holocaust Trauma

Children of Holocaust survivors are more vulnerable to developing post-traumatic stress disorder (PTSD) than their peers when confronted with stressful life situations (Baider et al., 2000; Yehuda et al., 1998). In addition, many reportedly suffer from identity problems (Adelman, 1995; Grubrich-Simitis, 1984; Hogman, 1998), preoccupation with themes of death and destruction (Bar-On et al., 1998; Pines, 1992; Sorscher and Cohen, 1997), depression (Felsen, 1998; Grubrich-Simitis, 1981; Kellerman, 2001a), inability to tolerate intense emotions (Adelman, 1995; Felsen, 1998), and difficulties in achieving autonomy (Felsen, 1998; Hogman, 1998; Kellerman, 2001a; Pines, 1992; Ruedenberg-Wright, 1997). Four different avenues have been suggested to explain the impact of the Holocaust trauma on the next generation. They are explained in the following sections.

Biological Predisposition to PTSD

Trauma causes neurological and hormonal changes in individuals (van der Kolk, 1989), regardless of whether the trauma occurred in childhood or adulthood. Changes occurring in childhood have been found to persist into and throughout adulthood, and the offspring of these individuals, more than children of nontraumatized parents, are biologically more likely to develop PTSD in situations of extreme stress (Nader, 1998; Yehuda et al., 2001), such as after a cancer diagnosis (Baider et al., 2000).

Inadequate Parenting Skills and Dysfunctional Family Dynamics

The direct psychological damage of having been in hiding or in concentration camps, the loss of a family in which to grow up and learn family-life skills (for the survivor who was a child at the time), and the overwhelming trauma of the destruction of home and family (for survivors of all ages) all contribute to the various degrees to which the parenting abilities of Holocaust survivors were impaired (Adelman, 1995; Weiss and Weiss, 2000). Difficulties in applying consistent discipline (e.g., Kellerman, 2001b), in allowing children autonomy (e.g., Ruedenberg-Wright, 1997), and in adequately responding to the emotional needs of their children (e.g., Bar-On et al., 1998) are all evidence of impaired parenting skills. Furthermore, in their efforts to rebuild their lives and provide for their families, many parents put in long hours at work and the children were left on their own (Bar-On et al., 1998).

Living in the Shadow of Overwhelming Grief

The incomplete mourning over the loss of home and family members, and the continuing depression, anxiety, and other symptoms experienced by Holocaust survivor parents contribute to a family environment that may provide a compromised developmental space for their children (Auerhahn and Laub, 1998; Kellerman, 2001b; Prince, 1975; Sorscher and Cohen, 1997; Weiss and Weiss, 2000). For example, second-generation Holocaust survivors tend to put their parents' psychological needs before their own so as not to drain the emotional reserves of their parents (e.g., Tauber, 1998). Some offspring may feel that their parents do not love them for themselves but for the dead relatives whom they were intended to replace (e.g., Kogan, 1992).

A Kind of Unconscious, Unspoken Transmission of Trauma

Children have been known to dream about the Holocaust or have trauma symptoms as if they had gone through it themselves (Auerhahn and Laub, 1998; Grubrich-Simitis, 1984; Herzog, 1981; Kellerman, 2001b; Rowland-Klein and Dunlop, 1998; Sorscher and Cohen, 1997; Tauber, 1998; Weiss and Weiss, 2000). When a child born after World War II is troubled with flashbacks of war experiences he or she clearly could not have experienced firsthand, it is safe to assume that the child is suffering from the parent's trauma.* Reports exist of second-generation Holocaust survivors whose psychological difficulties

---

*It is possible that some children growing up in Israel, whose parents are not Holocaust survivors, would experience such dreams at some time as a result of the saturation of Holocaust films, memorial ceremonies, and other reminders in the media of this difficult period in Jewish history (Ruti Gavish, 2005, personal communication).

seem to reflect their parents' unspoken memories of close relatives killed during the war. Pines (1992), for example, writes about a young woman whose strange behaviors indicated that she was confused and unable to distinguish between her own inner world and her father's repressed memories of his dead sister.

Weiss and Weiss (2000) suggest that the term *transmission of trauma* is inaccurate. By focusing on the parents' Holocaust experiences, as if the parents' trauma is somehow injected into the offsprings' psyche, the children's emotional experiences are shunted aside. Rather, they suggest, one should pay attention to "*subjective experience* concerning [the children's own] *traumatic childhood experiences*" (p. 380, italics in original) since "the tragedy of the second generation" (p. 381) is that they grow up under a cloud of overwhelming pain and grief. Also, one must wonder what it is like to know that your parent, someone who is supposed to protect you from danger, was subject to persecution, rape, internment, torture, etc. (Tauber, 1998, 2005, personal communication). In short, the effect of the trauma on each individual is the main point, not the trauma itself!

Furthermore, because of the individual differences among their children, parents interact differently with each of their offspring (Fine and Norris, 1989). In this way, not all children in the same family, being raised by Holocaust survivors, are similarly affected; some suffer severe psychological impairment and some do not (Mook et al., 1997; Wardi, 1992).

Transmission of CSA Trauma

In the concluding remarks to their study on second-generation daughters of Holocaust-survivor mothers, Sagi-Schwartz et al. (2003) suggest that "Holocaust survivors are in a better position to avoid transmitting their traumatic experiences than child abuse victims," because of the impersonal nature of the former and the very personal nature of the latter trauma (p. 1090). The Holocaust was perpetrated on masses of people who suffered openly and together, whereas the CSA victim is a lone child suffering a secret trauma while having to pretend that everything is okay (and who sometimes feels the need to go on pretending throughout adulthood).

What does all this mean for the children of men and women who suffered CSA? No research has been done exploring their subjective experiences, beyond the possibility that they, like their parents, fell victim to abuse. The term commonly used to refer to transmission of the trauma of abuse to the next generation is "the cycle of abuse." Not only does that oversimplify the issue, but, as we will see in the following sections, leads to research into the parenting behaviors of CSA survivors that is very degrading. Most of the studies examine parenting deficits, and if one does not know, either clinically or personally, a CSA-survivor parent, then this leaves the impression that "these people" should not be raising children. That is a damning indictment.*

Exploration of the impact of a CSA history on parenting and consequently, on the second generation, should be multifaceted, just as research into Holocaust survivor parenting is. The biological, psychological, family, and social aspects need to be considered to fully understand the challenges facing the CSA survivor who wants to break the transgenerational transmission chain.

Research on the coping skills and resilience of CSA-survivor parents is sorely lacking, research that would explore how so many of them manage to do a better job (even if in some cases only marginally so) than the parents who raised them (some of whom, of course, may also be CSA survivors). Therefore, the likelihood of positive parenting skills ought to be kept in mind when reading the next section. After the description of the research on CSA survivors as parents, parents will voice their thoughts about telling their children about the abuse, and the second generation will share thoughts and feelings about growing up with parents who were betrayed by those who were supposed to love and care for them most.

---

*When preparing for this chapter I put a notice on my Web site asking CSA-survivor mothers to notify me if they were interested in having their children meet in a group situation with other children aged thirteen and older for the purposes of discussing their subjective experiences of growing up knowing their mother was sexually abused. This was not intended to be a therapy group (even though I, a trained clinician, would be conducting the sessions), and only one or two meetings were planned: I anticipated that participation would be calming for the children who would feel less alone with their experiences. Instead, I was contacted by two sources who informed me that they thought it was unethical of me to so advertise because "CSA-survivor mothers are unable to be protective enough of their children to accurately evaluate whether or not participation in such a gathering would be harmful for them"! One of these individuals is an advocate for abused children and the other is a therapist-researcher working with abused women. Jan Willems (2005, personal communication) wonders if it is not unethical to deny these children "a helping witness to their plight" that meeting with me would have entailed.

CSA Survivors As Parents

The research on CSA survivors as parents has looked almost exclusively at mothers and not at fathers. In the one study including fathers, Newcomb and Locke (2001) found that men who suffered CSA are very rejecting toward their children, whereas women are aggressive. Now that sexual victimization of boys is beginning to be openly acknowledged, further studies will likely be conducted. It will be interesting to note if the gender difference found in the previous study will be replicated by later research. Given the focus of the research to date, the remainder of this chapter will refer to mothers only.

Although some CSA-survivor mothers may sexually or otherwise abuse their own children, apparently most do not (Buchanan, 1998; Kluft, 1987; Oliver, 1993). However, discussion of the intergenerational transmission of trauma for this population emphasizes the possibility of, and thereby seems to imply the certainty of, an unrelenting chain of abused children who in adulthood either abuse or do not prevent the abuse of their own children (Kluft, 1987; Leifer et al., 2004; Oates et al., 1998) and so on through the generations—an inevitable cycle of abuse that Buchanan (1998) repudiates by critically examining the contradictory research.

Unfortunately, even if the children of CSA survivors are not abused themselves, it does not mean that they do not suffer, to varying degrees, the aftershocks of their mothers' abuse histories (Scharff and Scharff, 1994). This is partly due to their mothers' parenting behaviors and partly due to the children witnessing, in the privacy of the home, the PTSD, depression, anxiety, and dissociation from which their mothers suffer. In other words, just as therapists can be vicariously traumatized by working with CSA survivors (see Chapter 9) and partners by living with them (see Chapter 3), children too can be vicariously traumatized by growing up with them (Danieli, 1998).

CSA survivors seem to anticipate having difficulties in parenting (see also Chapter 2). Survivor mothers in a unique study (Douglas, 2000) were anxious about their ability to sensitively and safely attend to the hygienic care of their infants, an activity that involves cleaning of the genital and anal areas. A mother's intimate ministry to the needs of her child can be an opportunity for closeness and tenderness; however, if she is anxious about touching in a hurtful way, she may convey discomfort, or even disgust, to the child. The study showed that these mothers were more comfortable with their second child, evidence of flexibility and an ability to learn and improve parenting behaviors.

Other studies suggest that mothers who were sexually abused as children or teenagers are more likely to be harsh disciplinarians than mothers who had no history of sexual trauma (Banyard, 1997; Banyard et al., 2003; DiLillo and Damashek, 2003; Dubowitz et al., 2001). Some are outright physically abusive (DiLillo et al., 2000). Perhaps this is because CSA-survivor mothers seem to be angrier (DiLillo et al., 2000; Newcomb and Locke, 2001) or more anxious (Roberts et al., 2004) than their nonabused peers. Other studies have shown that some survivor mothers are more depressed (Banyard et al., 2003) or more dissociative (Collin-Vezina and Cyr, 2003) than mothers who were not abused. This is thought to explain the high degree of emotional neglect of survivors' children sometimes reported. A depressed mother may not have the energy to look after her children (Cole et al., 1992; Ruscio, 2001), and some dissociative mothers might not be able to identify their children's emotional states or needs (Kluft, 1987).

These research studies seem to support the idea of polarity discussed in Chapters 2 and 3 in that some CSA survivors do not seem to be able to find a balance, but rather they exhibit extremes of a given form of behavior. In the case of parenting, rather than falling midway along the "discipline gradient," able to modulate between a degree of permissiveness and adequate limit setting, the CSA-survivor mother may at times be inattentive (neglectful) and at other times overly controlling (physically punitive, verbally aggressive, or examining every action of their children "under a microscope").

Aside from the painful loneliness of the child whose mother is emotionally and/or physically neglectful is the sad fact that he or she may be easier prey for perpetrators of abuse in the environment than the offspring of more alert mothers. Furthermore, finding out that her daughter or son was abused may plunge the mother into deep distress, either because this triggers memories of her own abuse or because of her overwhelming guilt at not being able to protect her child. Sometimes she resolves this guilt by denial, which on the surface seems to be easier for her, as a defense against the blame she expects from others (Hooper, 1992; Oz, 2002) while on all levels it is devastating for her child.

Of course, some sexually abused children have mothers who are not CSA survivors. The mother who was not abused herself may be able to cope better with the family crisis and emotionally support her child (Hiebert-Murphy, 1998) perhaps because she has a supportive spousal relationship and/or a better relationship with her own parents and siblings. It seems intuitively correct to assume that a mother who is supportive of her children was probably told about the abuse sooner than a mother who is not emotionally available. Leifer et al. (2004) found that daughters of supportive mothers (and many supportive CSA-survivor mothers exist) recover more quickly and completely than daughters of unsupportive mothers. The daughter who is supported, then, is less likely to be left with a trauma response that threatens to infect yet another generation of children. Similar studies remain to be conducted regarding the abused son.

The CSA-survivor mother is often the daughter of a CSA-survivor mother. Alexander and (2000) talk about the two-pronged impact of this upon her parenting behaviors: (1) It is likely that she was neglected as a child and took care of her own mother's emotional needs, therefore her behavior as a parent is modeled on the parenting with which she grew up; and (2) as a trauma victim, her ability to calm herself when under stress has been impaired, and she will look to people around her for relief and care. Often the only people available are her own children (Liotti, 1992). A mother who is unable to either calm herself or find other adults for emotional support, and often reacts to situations in an exaggerated or incongruous manner, communicates to her child that the environment is dangerous. Sometimes the child even fears his or her own mother or demonstrates symptoms of trauma when the only trauma he or she has experienced is that of having a mother who was traumatized (Schore, 2002).

In an interesting study (Grocke et al., 1995), the mother's CSA history was found to lead to more open communication between child and mother on subjects related to sexuality. Although the children of CSA-survivor mothers did not necessarily know more about sex than their peers whose mothers had not suffered sexual trauma, the former more often regarded their mothers as a source of information. Is this because the survivor mother is more conscientious about providing sex education? Or is it possibly because some survivor mothers may regard their daughters as their best friends (Burkett, 1991), therefore engaging them in conversations that could actually be regarded less as healthy open communication and more as inappropriate boundary crossings on topics that should be reserved for discussion with agemates?

When asked to report on their children's behaviors, CSA-survivor mothers saw their offspring as either more aggressive or more withdrawn than did mothers with no history of victimization (Dubowitz et al., 2001). Note how these two designations are polar opposites (the midpoint would be: friendliness and ability to make contact with other people while able to assert oneself and protect one's boundaries). It is not clear if this is indicative merely of the different ways in which the mothers see their children or if the children are, in fact, different. Getzler-Yosef (2005) found that survivors may perceive their children's character according to some internal schema of their own; yet, in the same study, she found evidence implying that, in some ways, children of survivors are different.

Studies that videotape mother-child interactions rather than relying on self-reports may provide more objective information regarding the children's behaviors and the parent-child interactions. In fact, such research seems to point to a tendency of mothers with an abuse history to be more self-centered and less emotionally available to their children than mothers who were not abused (Burkett, 1991). More recently, Koren-Karie and colleagues (2004) found that the young children of CSA survivors in their study generally adjust their behavior to fit their mothers' perception of them, and this role-playing for their mothers' sake keeps the mother involved with them. In other words, instead of the mother being emotionally receptive to the child's needs, these children had to be emotionally responsive to their mother's needs, in effect, parenting their mothers (Alexander et al., 2000). Getzler-Yosef (2005) reports that this clearly negative effect of a CSA history on parenting is ameliorated by therapy and trauma resolution work. This is the one optimistic note in the rather distressing series of studies pointing out the terrible legacy of intergenerational transmission of pathology, if not of outright abuse.

According to survivor mothers' self-reports, they want to provide the kind of mothering for their children that they, themselves, did not have (Cole et al., 1992). Nothing should leave one to believe this is not so. It is difficult to achieve, however, given that many survivors are unable to maintain supportive partner relationships and so raise their children alone (Alexander et al., 2000; Roberts et al., 2004).

Given the demands of single parenthood (or a conflictual marriage), the absence of support from an estranged family of origin together with the stress of their own unresolved traumatic backgrounds, and the lack of functional family models from childhood to guide them, it is not surprising that many mothers do not do as well as they could have.

Most research has focused on the early childhood years and, as described previously, many mothers may be unable to set aside their own stresses and be consistently empathic toward their children. However, many influences on children outside the home exist and children who participate in school or community activities may find a balance to some of the more difficult aspects of their relationship with their CSA-survivor parent.

One study that looked at survivor mothers' ability to promote autonomy and prepare their children for the tasks of adulthood (Cole et al., 1992) indicated that this is a troublesome arena. The mothers in the study, perhaps not knowing how to sensitively provide consistent, firm boundaries, or not having the emotional strength to do so, seemed to want their children to grow up quickly. It may just be easier to have the children become self-sufficient a little earlier than would otherwise naturally happen. However, this self-sufficiency is not always the mature, confident autonomy these mothers want for their children. On the other hand, perhaps these mothers are astute in preparing their offspring to deal effectively with a truly unsafe world with which the CSA survivor is, unfortunately, too familiar.

A Caveat

To date, a relatively small number of research reports of the parenting behaviors of CSA survivors exist. Moreover, this small number of studies provides an inconsistent picture of parenthood for this population. Zuravin and Fontanella (1999), for example, do not agree with Banyard's (1997) conclusions that CSA survivors are more physically abusive than nonsurvivor mothers. However, both statistical and anecdotal reports do seem to indicate that CSA survivors may be more anxious about parenting and less satisfied with their performance as parents than are other mothers (Cohen, 1995; Cole et al., 1992; Herman, 1981; also Chapter 2 of this book); on the other hand, aspects of childhood other than the sexual abuse may have at least as much impact on parenting competence (Buchanan, 1998; Danieli, 1998; Zuravin and Fontanella, 1999).

The research literature studying mothers, but not yet fathers, who survived CSA, paints a very dismal picture of the future. It mainly addresses the inability of the CSA-survivor mother to protect her children from abuse, if she does not physically or emotionally abuse them herself (not enough awareness of mothers sexually abusing their sons and daughters exists; they are usually accused of being accomplices to the sexual abuse of their children by men). Studies point to mother survivors who are self-centered and unable to attend to the emotional needs of their children. They generally cannot establish and maintain healthy couple relationships. They conscript their children, albeit with no malicious intent, into role reversals so that the child becomes the parent of the mother. By emphasizing parental deficits, however, society points an accusing finger at parents and is thereby relieved of taking a deeper look into the social factors that hinder parental efforts to release their children from that tragic fate.

Moreover, researchers' conclusions of parental inadequacy are only part of the story. Included in these same research samples are survivor mothers who are emotionally supportive and able to provide a healthy environment within which to raise their children. Somehow, in looking for differences between survivor and nonsurvivor mothers, more attention is paid to the greater proportion of survivor mothers who have the negative qualities than do nonsurvivor mothers. Perhaps more survivor mothers demonstrate faulty mothering than nonsurvivor mothers. I am not denying that possibility. What I would like to point out, however, is that it is no less significant that a proportion of survivor mothers do manage to overcome the negative impact of their abuse and raise healthy children. These "nonpathological" women somehow seem to become invisible in the research reports (Warner, 1996). One way for them to be invisible is when statistical trends are the only information provided in research reports and the raw data is not available for readers to assess independently (Schuetze and Eiden, 2005). A discussion of how this happens follows.

Kluft (1987) conducted an empirical study on the parenting behaviors of mothers with dissociative identity disorder (DID), a condition reported as resulting from CSA in most cases. Although not all CSA survivors are DID, they all suffer from some degree of dissociation, so Kluft's results are, to some extent, applicable to CSA-survivor mothers. However, more central to our discussion is how he explains his results and how his findings are used in later research.

In his introduction to the study, Kluft claims that the women interviewed being of childbearing age was cause for concern, because "victims of child abuse often become abusers" (p. 273). However, this is something that is not borne out by other research (including his own study!). In his conclusions he states that "the children of [DID] mothers are, as a whole a population at risk" (p. 278). In illustrating mothering behaviors, he presented one case each for the categories of exceptional, competent, and compromised mothers, and three cases of abusive mothers. (Are abuse cases more interesting?) He found that nearly 40 percent of the mothers in this study were classified as adequate to exceptional mothers. Only 16 percent were classified as actively abusive (the remainder were "compromised"). Furthermore, nearly half of the abusive mothers later become competent parents as a result of therapy.

Nine years after this study, Benjamin et al. (1996) characterized Kluft's findings as "startling" (p. 933) and went on to claim that the results of his study showed that "individual treatment of the dissociative mother was not enough to stem developmental disruption to her children" (p. 934), something Kluft only suggested as a possibility. In their own study they found what they expected to find—that dissociative mothers had more problems in parenting than nondissociative mothers. Using a nonstandardized questionnaire to measure parenting, they included such factors as parenting ability thwarted by her symptoms, being less affectionate, having inappropriate expectations of her children, support from relatives (if the mother was abused as a child, we would not expect family of origin support, and this should not be held against her as an indication of inadequate parenting), etc. However, the reader is not given any indication of how the questions were worded, and this limits the report's usefulness. Most important, they state that they "would agree with Kluft that poor parenting may be a key etiological factor in the transmission of DID" (p. 940). What happened to the almost 40 percent of Kluft's sample who demonstrated adequate to excellent parenting?

Perhaps, when parenting is particularly stressful, the CSA-survivor mother is more at risk for impairment than her nonabused peers. It is also possible that the research situation itself is experienced by mothers as stressful. In some studies she is filmed in interaction with her child and perhaps she is afraid her "performance" is being judged (it is). How much, then, does the research situation reflect regular daily life and how much does it reflect situations of stress?

A most important question yet to be examined is what allows some survivor mothers to do a better job of parenting than other survivor mothers, including their own? First, when the mother has a truly supportive and satisfying marital relationship, her parenting behavior, as well as other aspects of her life, is often healthier (Alexander et al., 2000). Why do some survivors make a better choice of partner than others? Is it luck? Is it something else? Second, mothers who were less self-centered and who pulled their children into role reversals to a lesser degree are mothers who have had or are in therapy (Getzler-Yosef, 2005; Kluft, 1987).

If we assume that both the specific sexual abuse events, as well as the family and/or community environment in which they occur, are traumatic, then it may be instructive to compare the parenting behaviors of CSA survivors with Holocaust survivors, who also suffered specific and environmental traumas. These are now discussed in view of the four areas of impact noted at the beginning of this chapter.

Biological Predisposition to PTSD

In contrast to studies on second-generation Holocaust survivors, no evaluation of the possibility that second-generation CSA survivors have a higher inborn vulnerability to PTSD when faced with a current traumatic event has been done. However, given that CSA affects the neurological and hormonal systems in the same way as other traumatic events (Schore, 2002; van der Kolk, 1994), it seems logical to hypothesize that the same vulnerability observed in offspring of Holocaust survivors would appear in the offspring of CSA survivors.

Inadequate Parenting Skills and Dysfunctional Family Dynamics

The impact on both populations of not having grown up in a healthy family environment can be expressed differently in some areas and similarly in others. For example, Holocaust-survivor parents, afraid that independence on the part of their children may mean their permanent loss, do not easily allow them autonomy. On the other hand, CSA-survivor parents, feeling overwhelmed and unable to define appropriate boundaries for the children's behaviors, or in view of their own early autonomy, may encourage their offsprings' precocious independence. In contrast to this difference, some CSA- and Holocaust-survivor parents seem to have similar difficulties in being sensitive and responsive to their children's emotional needs, and parentified children are common in the second generation in both cases. Furthermore, in their anxiety to provide a safe environment for their children, the Holocaust survivor "frequently provided messages of extreme and imminent danger" (Bar-On et al., 1998, p. 325). My clinical experience shows that this is often true for the CSA survivor as well.

Living in the Shadow of Overwhelming Grief

Survivors of CSA and of the Holocaust both suffer enormous grief, and the children cannot escape their parents' sadness and anxiety. Whereas the second-generation Holocaust survivor is, perhaps, intended as a replacement for members of the parent's family who were killed, for the CSA survivor the child is perhaps a representation of the child the parent wishes he or she could have been himself or herself. Therefore, both second-generation populations may be confused between past and present: the child of the Holocaust survivor is caught between present reality and the parent's idealized prewar past, and the child of the CSA survivor is caught between present reality and the parent's fantasy of the past that should have been. It is possible that some survivor parents are even jealous of their own children for having parents or a childhood that they wish they, themselves, had had. Furthermore, were the parents to truly mourn their losses, the Holocaust-survivor parent would have to face a past that will never return (Gampel, 1992), and the CSA-survivor parent would have to face a past that will never be.

A Kind of Unconscious, Unspoken Transmission of Trauma

It seems to be commonly accepted that the inner world of some second-generation Holocaust survivors has qualities similar to those of survivors who were actually there. This raises the question of whether CSA trauma can be transmitted to offspring in the same way. When an individual has dreams, flashbacks, or sensations of having been sexually abused in the absence of clear memories, is it possible that in some cases these represent the vicariously experienced sexual trauma of a parent?

When parents can acknowledge their traumas and recover from the injuries, either through therapy and/or within healthy adult relationships, they open up new possibilities for their children. Many CSA-survivor parents surely provide their children with a safer and more reliable parent-child relationship than they had while growing up. Hopefully, if each generation can improve, even slightly, on the model provided by the preceding generation, these are steps in the right direction. However, it is not right to regard this as the sole responsibility of the individual parent; communities need to develop strategies that involve educational, social welfare, health, and political sectors in finding a solution to the traumatization of their young (Buchanan, 1998).

SHOULD I TELL MY CHILDREN I WAS ABUSED?

Scharff and Scharff (1994) present a case study in which two children both displayed symptoms of the vicarious traumatization discussed previously, seemingly as a direct result of their mother's still unresolved secret CSA trauma. Both the son and the daughter exhibited difficulties in autonomy and sexuality. The husband knew of the abuse the mother suffered, but not its full impact upon her. The Scharffs encouraged the mother to tell her teenage children she was sexually abused by their grandfather and to share information with her family that would help them understand the significance of the abuse to her psychological state. The children's knowledge of their mother's sexual traumatization and the ensuing "working through" released them from the insidious effects of the secret.

During my early family therapy training I became aware of the possible impact of secrets on future generations. A young husband was unable to commit himself to his marriage or to any career direction. His family did not talk about their life in Europe before WWII, but he was led to believe that he was of Dutch origin. With my encouragement, he prodded his grandmother until she told him about the family. She informed him that they were really German and had given themselves a Dutch name upon arrival in North America. With this information, he understood that his inability to settle down was a result of the lie behind the facade his family presented, not only to the outside world, but to themselves as well.

Given the impact of both trauma and secrets, I believe it is important for children to know about any sexual abuse that occurred in older generations of their family. The questions are how and when to tell them. The following are some examples of how mothers related to these questions:

I told my children I was in therapy because I had had a difficult childhood and there were some things I needed to talk over with someone professional. That was all I could think of to say at the time. They were ten and fourteen. Some time later they asked me if I was feeling better (because they could see I wasn't). They wanted to know more about what had happened. It took me quite some time until I was able to say I was sexually abused and even longer to tell them it was my father. That was enough for them. They didn't seem to want to know any more than that. We live on the other side of the ocean from my family and only see them once every few years. My kids don't seem to miss having contact with them so that's where it stands now.

How do you tell your children that their mother was raped and that it was their uncle who did it? I still can't figure that one out.

I think all the time about telling my teenage kids about the abuse. But I just don't think I can handle it. They know I'm in therapy and they probably know it has to do with my uncle because I can't stand him being near me at family affairs. They have asked why I'm in therapy and all I can say is that bad things happened to me when I was a kid. I just can't get it together to tell them and they seem to want to know more.

My kids know that my father put me and my brothers down all the time and that my mother hit us. I tell them a lot about what it was like growing up with parents who didn't take care of me. So when I told them I was also sexually abused by my grandfather, they weren't surprised. They don't want to speak to my family at all.

My kids seemed to appreciate that I told them I was abused. I told them when they were ten and thirteen and I was in a really bad state. After I started therapy I was sick all the time and even more obsessive about the house being clean than I had been before. I seemed to be yelling at them more. When I told them they took it well. It explained all my strange behavior. It also helped them understand why their father doesn't want anything more to do with my brother after they had been friends for so many years.

I'm afraid maybe I told my kids a bit too soon. They were aged eight, ten, and twelve. But they noticed so many weird things about my family it just seemed inappropriate not to tell them everything. I don't know how to tell if they have been hurt by knowing at this age.

My kids love their grandparents and they can't connect what they know about my mother abusing me with these elderly people who give them gifts and money. But they accept the fact that I never let them visit my parents alone.

THE VOICES OF THE CHILDREN

In my clinic I sometimes meet the children of women who are in therapy with me for CSA. In some cases it is important for the children to meet their mother's therapist in person so that later, at home, they can see me in their mind's eye and remember that, even if their mother is having a particularly hard time, I am helping her get through it, and they are relieved of taking care of her emotional needs. Of course, my clients are frequently adult children of CSA survivors—in other words, the great majority of my clients are not only CSA survivors but also second-generation (or more) CSA survivors.

In preparation for this chapter I met with a small group of clients' adolescent and adult children, individually interviewed others, and a colleague in Canada conducted two interviews there for me. I will present the material here by combining all of the material into three conglomerates. Gali will represent the teenage girls, none of whom were sexually abused themselves. Linda will represent the adult women interviewed, about thirty years of age, who were not abused, and Molly will represent the adult women who were themselves abused.

Gali (About Sixteen Years Old, Was Not Abused Herself)

When I was thirteen my mother sat me down and told me she was abused as a child. I didn't understand, really, what that meant until a year or so later. Then I grew very curious. I don't know very much about what happened. I want to know more, but my mother will tell me what she thinks is okay for me to know. At first I was shocked. It took me awhile until I was able to digest it. She told my younger brother and sister also, but neither of them seems to want to hear anything more about it. They try to pretend nothing happened.

I hadn't understood a lot about my mother—why she was so hard on us, why she always seemed to get into bad moods, why she yelled so much. After I knew about it I was more considerate of her. I stopped asking why her mother doesn't come to visit and why she didn't cry when her father died. At first it was hard to think I wouldn't see my grandmother anymore. I couldn't seem to connect this quiet old woman with someone who hadn't protected my mother when she was my age. Not that we had a great relationship. She isn't a warm person; she isn't like the grandmothers my friends talk about. So it isn't a great loss. But I think I feel bad knowing that I'll never have a grandmother like theirs. I think I used to wait for my grandmother to turn into the kind that bakes cakes and gets excited about your grades. Now when I talk with her on the phone I notice all kinds of behaviors or things she says that are strange, things I didn't notice before. And I'm actually glad my grandfather's dead. That's not nice to say, but I'm afraid if he was alive that maybe he would abuse me too.

My father takes care of me when my mother is feeling too bad. I can see he's sad sometimes when my mother is having a hard time, but he's good to us kids. He came to talk with me to see how I felt knowing about my mother's abuse. I'm glad he came to ask and I have gotten closer to him since then. I talk with him a lot, even though I still talk with my mother more. She's the kind of person you can talk to about anything. I can ask her anything I want about boys and sex and she'll try to answer as honestly as she can. I know that I can talk with my mother about things like that more openly than many of my friends with their mothers.

But she is very sensitive about how I dress and where I go and who I'm with and when I come home. She's stricter about these things than my friends' parents. Now I understand why. But it still bothers me. She's afraid something will happen to me. And so I have to try to push it out of my mind, not to think about it because otherwise I may be afraid too and I don't want to be afraid.

I can see a difference in my mother now that she's been in therapy. There are longer periods of quiet between her explosions. She used to be mad all the time. Now it happens less. Sometimes I even forget how mad she used to get. She's also alone in her room a lot. And she has a look that lets us kids know we should just keep out of her way—she needs peace and quiet. But it takes her less time to come out of her room now. I'm proud of her for being so strong.

I think children should know about things like this. I don't think it can hurt to tell even if the child is too young because if they don't know how to relate to the information then they'll just ignore it, like my brother and sister. But children should be allowed to understand why their parents sometimes seem so troubled. Knowing has made me grow up a bit faster, I think. My classmates seem to me a bit naive and too trusting of everyone. I am always on the lookout for warning signs. But that's not a bad thing after all. The newspaper has stories every day of kids being sexually abused.

Linda (About Thirty Years Old, Was Not Abused Herself)

My mother was always having fits of either anger or crying. It was so distressing to see her lose control, and when my father was around he would try to calm her down. Sometimes it would work and sometimes even he wasn't able to help her. I felt something was going on that I couldn't quite understand. Sometimes I was very angry at her and sometimes I was worried about her. I always knew her relationship with her parents wasn't good. I couldn't understand why my friends had more contact with their grandparents than we did. So when I was twenty-five and she finally told me about how her father sexually abused her I wasn't surprised at all.

Knowing about the abuse explained things to me I hadn't understood about my mother until then, such as why she dropped out of school and married a man she didn't love when she was only seventeen and why she hated alcohol and wouldn't allow any into our house. Having wine at Passover was almost more than she could handle. My mother told me that her father was always drunk when he abused her. But she explained that drinking isn't the reason, just the excuse people use for doing things they may not have the guts to do sober.

Also, I now understand that all her anger was not because we kids made her angry. I have always found her rages distressing. Now that she's worked through her childhood traumas she's much calmer and doesn't get into rages anymore. But I do. I wish that she had told me earlier, because for so long I took her anger personally and perhaps that is part of what made me into an angry person. I also thought the anger was genetic. After learning that it was in response to her trauma, it gives me hope that I can learn to calm down as well.

I feel lucky that in spite of what my mother went through she was able to protect me and my brothers and sister. I never had to experience anything like what she went through, not even with a stranger, let alone a family member. But, even though I didn't know about the abuse when I was growing up, I was still somewhat distrustful of people. My mother was very protective of me and wanted to know where I was and who I was with. She was always telling me how to be careful. She told me to always trust my gut feelings when I'm with a guy and not be afraid to walk away from someone.

She was very friendly with my friends and preferred me to bring friends home rather than go out. She liked to know I was in the house, but then she would leave me and my friends alone and it seemed she liked having me there, busy but not bothering her.

I find it hard to get close to men. I have trouble trusting them. It might also have something to do with my parents' relationship. Now, after my mother has really worked on herself and she is calmer, and my father stuck with her even though he didn't really understand what she was going through and so couldn't really be supportive, they are starting to enjoy each other. They spend more time together—also, perhaps, because we kids are all out of the house—and they are better friends. It gives me hope to see how they are working on their relationship. My mother has told me about other survivors she has met who have had worse luck than her, marrying men who are emotionally or physically abusive of them.

I am very proud of my mother. She tackled her problems and stuck it out. She was in therapy and in a support group. I'm sad she had to go through all of that. I hate my grandfather and stopped calling him "grandpa" the day I found out what he did to my mother. I don't understand how my grandmother let it go on for so long. I know she had her problems as well, but how can a mother let something like that happen to her child? I'll never understand that. But I love my grandmother and have to accept that nobody is perfect.

While my mother was in therapy, the abuse was always "there" in the house. She talked about it a lot, but not when my younger brother was around because he doesn't know yet. The fact that my father stood by her stoically helped her get through it as well. And she had me and my sister to talk to. Now, it feels like she has definitely moved on. She is happier, doesn't get angry so much, and if she does she doesn't explode anymore but can talk about it. She is proud of herself, I can tell. It is much more pleasant to be around her. She is more affectionate now, and my younger brother grew up with a very different mother than I had. Also, she can drink a glass of wine now and is not so obsessive about how clean or messy the house is.

I definitely think children should be told about the abuse. They are aware when something is not right. I don't think age twelve or thirteen is too young. Although they are not sexually active, they understand enough about sex. So at this age they know about sexual attraction and understand the difference between the sickness of sexual attraction toward children versus healthy attraction toward other adults.

Molly (About Thirty Years Old, Was Abused Herself)

I found out my mother was abused by her father when I told her my uncle had abused me. She was horrified to learn that I was abused, but she was more absorbed in her own story than she was open to hearing about me. So I know there's not much point in trying to talk to her. My older sister and younger brother were also abused, and our whole childhood all we wanted was for our abuse to stop. Now, knowing about her abuse (even though I did suspect it when I was growing up), I can understand that she probably felt helpless to change anything about our family. She didn't have any skills to protect her children. It has made me feel less guilty for not telling her about it when it was still going on. Perhaps if I hadn't been abused myself I might feel more compassion toward her. But she didn't take care of me like she should have.

Knowing that she was abused explains why she was blind to our suffering. As a child I thought all families were the same but nobody talked about it. Even though I slept over at friends' houses a lot and so should have been able to compare other families with my own, I just didn't notice the differences that much. I remember feeling strange at friends' houses, not knowing how to act. Now, thinking back, I see how cold our family was. There were no hugs or kisses, little praise was given from either parent. We were three sad children trying to look out for one another with no adult protection. I didn't know if my parents loved me or not. Now, my mother sometimes tells me she loves me and it just irritates me.

My mother was both overly permissive and overly controlling. She would let me do whatever I wanted—there were no rules for when to come home or who I could or couldn't go out with, but if I did something she didn't like she would report it to my father and he would beat me. I couldn't consult with her on anything. She didn't listen. And when I was sad she didn't notice. Everything was always about her, about who had insulted her, who had argued with her, who didn't obey her, who disappointed her. But on the other hand, she would go through my desk and my papers and after the first time I discovered she had read my diary I stopped keeping one.

When I should have been given information about puberty and menstruation and given some guidance about dating and relationships, it was my father who gave me the basic data. And then he told me about his sexual problems with my mother. My mother did try to explain things to me better but I could see that it was too difficult for her. The message I absorbed from her was a confusing one. On the one hand, she tried to tell me that sex is beautiful in a loving relationship, but the underlying message was that sex is all that men want from us, and it makes me anxious.

My mother never confronted her father and she never told her mother she had been abused. I don't know if my grandmother knew or suspected. The relationships in the entire family were distant and formal. I would visit my grandparents and not feel any special warmth or affection, but theirs was a quiet house to be in. When I see how there were no real relationships in my extended family it makes me sad to see how everyone wasted their lives. If my mother had gone to therapy maybe she would have been able to be a parent to me. I see in her what I could have become if I had not decided to take control of my life and resolve the trauma of my abuse. She is still denying that anything is wrong, and the face she shows to the public is very different from the mother we grew up with.

I believe that if children are told about their mother's abuse it should only be after she has done a great deal of therapy and it is no longer a heavy issue for her. The question is: why tell the children? If it is to make excuses for her own behavior, then it is only traumatizing for the child. If the children are told in order to help protect them, then it can be done slowly, in degrees. Why do children need to know of any horrors that have been experienced? In order to understand their mother better? To know that things like this happen? It should be determined first how this will help the children.

A FINAL WORD TO SURVIVOR PARENTS

Telling your child about your traumatic past seems to be important for his or her psychological well-being. Children are quick to blame themselves for their parents' stresses. It is common knowledge that divorcing parents need to reassure their children that the divorce is not their fault. Similarly, openness about the origin of your trauma symptoms helps them recognize that it is not their fault that mother is angry (well, not always), depressed, frightened, etc. When you are upset, open communication can help your child understand whether you are distressed over what happened in your past or about something he or she has done or said.

The age of the child when they are told does not seem to be a crucial factor. Children who are not yet able to relate to the information may just not "get it." It will not be relevant to them. It is also possible that other, more pressing, problems exist in their lives at the time that to them are more significant than your history. When they are reminded at a later age, it may seem as if they are being told for the first time.

More important than the age at which children are told is the manner in which they are told. They do not need to know the details of the abuse. Graphic examples will likely be traumatizing for them. That you were sexually abused, the impact of the abuse upon you, and that you are working at overcoming your traumatic background are the important factors for your children to know. It is also helpful if you explain to your children the kind of relationship you expect them to have with those who abused you. If they are still minors, will you allow them to be alone with your abusers or would that put them at risk? Are you open to them loving your abusers, visiting them when older, and talking with them, or would this feel like betrayal to you? Even if you do feel betrayed, you need to decide how you want to respond to your children if they feel it is important for them to have a relationship with your abusers.

If you have no clear memories of having been sexually abused, then it would be confusing to the child and inappropriate to talk about your suspicions of having been abused. People who suspect they were sexually abused by a family member are people who have probably grown up in toxic families. Enough clear memories of emotional abuse or neglect may exist that you can discuss with your children to help them understand your symptoms and strained family relationships.

A quality I suggest you learn is the quality of calm curiosity. Your children will have an experience of you that is not necessarily consistent with the parenting you wanted to provide. Perhaps while growing up they perceived you in some ways that seem to mirror your perception of your own parent(s). This is devastating to hear. However, for the purpose of promoting a truly open relationship rather than one based on duty alone it is important that you listen nondefensively to your children talk about their experiences of you as a parent. This is the best way to reverse the pattern of the parentified child. That means that you will accept your children's perception of you as a parent as a legitimate reality, and you will not try to convince them that you were not the way they say you were. To survive this, you will need support from other adults: your partner, friends, and/or a therapist. My clinical experience has shown me that children are anxious for their parents to learn how to be healthy parents, even if the "child" is already over the age of seventy and the parent over ninety.

Chapter 9

Being a Therapist:
Notes on Working with CSA Survivors

Sheri Oz

The greatest good you can do for another is not just share your riches, but to reveal to him his own.

Benjamin Disraeli

Being a therapist is a privilege and a responsibility. To me it is awesome to be allowed into the intimate inner world of another human being. To think that the person before me is trusting enough to share with me things that have perhaps never been revealed to another human soul takes my breath away. However, it is also a serious responsibility. The psychotherapist, similar to the doctor, is instructed to "do no harm." I am aware that the potential for harm exists. Witnessing how a phrase to which I may have attached no particular weight can carry a client through periods of crisis, I know that another phrase, gesture, or facial expression can be hurtful and damaging. Yet, if I think that only I can "rescue" this person, or if I think that I have the power to destroy this person, then I am arrogant and disrespectful.

I must find a fine balance between respecting my clients' vulnerabilities and respecting their strengths. This chapter is dedicated to the people who have come to me for help and who have helped me, in turn, learn so much about respect, trust, human resilience, and more.

Overcoming Childhood Sexual Trauma
Published by The Haworth Press, Inc., 2006, All rights reserved.
doi:10.1300/5668_09

STARTING OUT

I did not set out with the intention of working with child sexual abuse (CSA) survivors. It just seems to have happened. I was barely aware the phenomenon existed until, in my second year of family therapy training in Guelph, Canada, I began work with a young woman who was already an alcoholic at the age of twenty-one. I knew nothing about substance abuse, had no preconceived notions about the subject, and was intrigued that none of my fellow students wanted to work with her. Near the end of the first session I found out that her older brother fooled around with her starting when she was ten years old. That moment in 1985 was my entrance into the field of childhood sexual abuse. At that time, no university courses were offered on the subject of sexual trauma, and the main source of training was by way of lectures and workshops presented at professional conferences. I made a point of attending meetings and seminars that addressed this topic and began to devour articles in the professional literature in the hope of learning enough to be of help to her. She exerted such a pull on me because she introduced me to two topics (alcoholism and child sexual abuse) that seemed to be odious to others, both of which were apparently interrelated in my client's case and neither of which anyone else in the clinic wanted to touch.

At the same time, while gathering data for my MSc thesis on adolescent mothers, I found that a large majority of the teen mothers, as opposed to their nonmother peers, were CSA survivors (Oz and Fine, 1988). This drew me further into an exploration of the factors affecting women who suffered sexual abuse during their childhoods and the clinical approaches to working with them.

I moved to Israel in 1986, and again I did not seek out this population. One of my first clients, however, was a CSA survivor, referred by a family doctor who knew of my research in Canada. The field of treating CSA survivors at that time in Israel was very lonely. Few therapists worked with this population, and my main source of support was the staff at the Haifa Rape Crisis Center. They referred clients to me, and over time I slowly built up an expertise, partly due to my insatiable thirst for reading the professional literature. The library at Haifa University was well stocked with the journals that served as my ad hoc textbooks on the subject.

One of the most important books for my professional development was Tilman Furniss's *Multiprofessional Handbook of Child Sexual Abuse* (1991). His recommendation to professionals to sit with a colleague over a cup of coffee and discuss the information currently available regarding a child and his or her family before going into action stands in sharp contrast to the hasty emergency responses that seem to be the most natural reaction when faced with new reports of suspected sexual abuse. The message I got from the pages of his book was: listen, ponder, consult, understand, then act. Furthermore, his model of the "interactional aspects of secrecy" (p. 24), what I refer to as the "nature of the trauma," formed the basis for my growing understanding of the intrinsic qualities of clinical work with adult survivors, as described in Chapter 5 of this book.

In addition to Furniss I had four other very reliable "consultants." Surfing the book sites on the Internet now reveals that a number of publications on the topic of CSA were available during the 1980s and early 1990s. At the time I found Dolan (1991), Courtois (1988), Finkelhor (1984), and Blume (1990). Through their works, these authors played the role of the colleagues I did not yet have.

Over the past years the cadre of psychologists, social workers, and expressive arts therapists in Israel experienced in working with issues involving the sexual abuse of children has been growing. Quite a community is growing and, no longer isolated from one another, therapists meet and consult with peers. It is enriching and comforting to be part of this community of therapists. Much still needs to be learned, and it is much more rewarding to learn together, sharing thoughts and feelings with others who understand the territory.

WHAT THE LITERATURE SAYS
ABOUT BEING A CSA THERAPIST

Professional reports talk about two major aspects of working with CSA survivors: countertransference and vicarious traumatization. According to the literature, the basic difference between work with CSA survivors and work with other clinical populations lies in the intensity of the countertransference and the potential for therapist burnout. The following discussion can only briefly touch on these topics since they are complex issues that have been the subject of numerous books and articles; however, it is important to lay the groundwork for the later description of my own personal experience.

Transference and Countertransference

Families in which abuse continues over time include at least one victim, a perpetrator, and an unseeing (or tacitly avoidant) bystander parent and/or sibling (based upon the original Drama Triangle model of Karpman [1968], and the bystander role described by Clarkson [1987]). Sometimes a "rescuer" also participates in this configuration, when someone (perhaps a sibling or someone outside the nuclear family) tries to save the victim. The CSA victim internalizes all of these roles and later plays them out in some adult relationships. In the vicious rectangle, the survivor may be victimized by others, an abuser of others, "blind" when someone else is being mistreated, or perhaps tries to rescue other individuals in distress. In addition, the victim has learned that love and affection can be confused with sexual behavior, and so the survivor may feel loveable only when seductive or compliant sexually.

The vicious rectangle also appear in the therapeutic dyad. For example, a client may find the therapist's questions intrusive and threatening, or a comment may be experienced as a menacing exposure of client vulnerability. The client may thus feel victimized by the therapist, who may be seen as taking advantage, for some reason, of his or her greater status and power over the client (Elliot and Briere, 1995). At other times clients may feel that they, themselves, are abusive, perhaps by making excessive and escalating demands of the therapist's time or by being rude and dismissive. Therapists who are unable to kindly yet soundly define limits can be seen as weak and easily manipulated (Davies and Frawley, 1994). Both patterns can be exhibited alternatively within the same therapeutic pair, and both conditions can exert a negative impact upon the client's sense of safety and the therapist's sense of competence.

That, as a child, the survivor fell victim to a sexual predator means that the child's normal developmental needs were not seen or respected by the abuser. In addition, unless someone became aware of the abuse immediately and stopped it, the child's distress was not seen by other adults in the child's life. This sense of being unseen continues into adulthood and is certain to play itself out in clinical sessions (Davies and Frawley, 1994; Seligman, 2004). At times clients may feel that the therapist does not appreciate the depth of their distress. Therapists are supposed to know that behind the mask (Winnicott, 1960) clients present to the world they are scared, hurt, angry inner children waiting to be seen while simultaneously dreading that very moment. If the therapist is fooled by smiles and jokes or always interprets silence as resistance, he or she may not perceive the true emotional turmoil within the client and the conflict aroused by the attempt to verbalize thoughts and feelings, just as adults in the abused child's life did not see.

Alternatively, many clients do not take notice of their own distress or needs (Elliot and Briere, 1995). Their history of abuse and neglect trained them to be attuned to the needs of others since satisfying these needs was often the only way for them to maintain relationships with the adults in their lives. These clients, then, will pick up on subtle signs of fatigue, illness, emotional stress, or anger in their therapists. Therefore, rather than use the therapy hour for themselves, they may act in ways that either take into account what they feel the therapist needs or that serve to protect themselves from what they believe is the therapist's imminent abandonment of them. Clinicians, in turn, may experience their clients' lack of attention to their own needs as a kind of disengagement from the therapist, leading the therapist to daydream or to feel sleepy or emotionally deadened (Davies and Frawley, 1994).

If, as Dalenberg (2000) and Davies and Frawley (1994) suggest, the countertransferential pressure experienced by the therapist is greater when working with CSA survivors than with other clients, then it is not surprising that clinical work with this population is full of drama. The drama of this work is sometimes remarkable for its exact opposite—the emotional deadness noted previously. For, if the CSA survivor is known for polarized behaviors (see Chapters 2 and 3), then it is not surprising that the therapist experiences this polarization as well. Therefore, the therapy, itself, can have what can be "affectionately" referred to as borderline qualities. In other words, we may be overwhelmed with the overly dramatic and emotive state of one client and so totally disconnected from another that we find it hard to stay awake. Sometimes we are on this roller coaster from one session to another with the same client, or even within a single session.

Erotic feelings can sometimes play havoc with the therapeutic relationship. Clients, sometimes confusing affection with sexual arousal, may experience their growing attachment to the therapist as romantic or sexual attraction, regardless of gender and sexual orientation. On the other hand, they may think that in order to be special to the therapist they have to provide sexual favors as they did as children. Therapists may feel sexually attracted to or become romantically interested in their clients, sometimes in contradiction to their usual sexual orientation. The professional literature includes serious discourse on the problem of erotic countertransference of the therapist, viewing sexual exploitation of clients by therapists as the most extreme boundary violation (e.g., Celenza and Gabbard, 2003; Norris et al., 2003). This is perhaps the most researched subject in countertransference and boundary issues for this client population. On the other hand, the erotic transference/countertransference may open up opportunities for understanding underlying dynamics when discussed rather than acted upon (Davies, 1994, 1998; Fonagy and Target, 2004; Yahav and Oz, 2006).

Another form of countertransference discussed in the professional literature is the compulsion to rescue clients—from abusive families or partners, from themselves when they are suicidal or self-mutilating, from poverty, etc., and, in fact, clients may see the therapist as someone who will make up for all that was missing in childhood, as someone who will be the perfect parent the client never had (Elliot and Briere, 1995; Neumann and Gamble, 1995). Although the therapist understands that this is impossible, the emotional pull of the client's projection that puts the therapist into the position of omnipotent savior ("You're the only one who can help me") can be very seductive.

Both therapist and client actually begin to form a relationship even before the first session. Their voices on the telephone when making the first appointment already give them some information upon which they begin to build a picture of the person they will soon meet face to face. However, even before this point therapists have a relationship to the subject matter itself. Tauber (1998) called this "a priori countertransference." Therapists may view the subject of sexual abuse as an issue that challenges their therapeutic skills. Some anticipate that they will function quite well with their current knowledge base, whereas others feel a need for continuing education. The topic may arouse disgust, anger, curiosity, helplessness, or other emotional responses. A priori countertransference affects many aspects of the clinical work before the client even walks through the door, such as the therapist's approach to traumatic memory resolution (Haaken and Schlaps, 1991; Oz, 2005), openness or resistance to hearing about the trauma, attitudes toward confrontations with abusers and nonprotective adults from the survivors' childhood, and more (Dalenberg, 2000). Similarly, clients have preconceived notions regarding the therapeutic process and the particular therapist with whom they chose to work, which together with the impression made during the initial phone call constitute a priori transference (Birnbaum and Birnbaum, 2005).

Vicarious Traumatization

Hearing horrific stories of the betrayal of a child's trust and vulnerability, regardless of the actual details of the abuse, has to have an effect on the therapist. Some writings point to the possibility that therapists "catch" post-traumatic stress disorder (PTSD) from their clients (Elliot and Briere, 1995; McCann and Pearlman, 1990a). This may show up in various symptoms, such as sleeplessness, nightmares, hypervigilance, depression, emotional numbness, depersonalization, changes in world view, decreased self-esteem, and relationship problems (Brady et al., 1999; Courtois, 1988; Davies and Frawley, 1994; Elliot and Briere, 1995; Neumann and Gamble, 1995; Stevens and Higgins, 2002). It can bring therapists, who previously may not have personally dealt with such issues, face to face with social injustices, causing them to confront issues of lack of safety and powerlessness in their own lives (Pearlman and Saakvitne, 1995; Regehr and Cadell, 1999). Clinicians may find themselves grieving when their assumptions and beliefs about parents, families, and humanity are shattered (Cunningham, 1999). Ultimately, it may lead to burnout, with the therapist needing to take a break from clinical work. Some may even leave the profession entirely. Interestingly, however, Way et al. (2004) found that less experienced clinicians suffered higher levels of vicarious traumatization than their more experienced peers.

Personal Background of the Therapist

In addition to discussing the therapist's countertransferential responses to the CSA-survivor client and his or her projections and vicarious traumatization, the literature also addresses the personal issues that therapists bring to the therapeutic encounter. The therapist's life history is, of course, central to his or her approach to interpersonal relations both in professional and personal spheres. The therapist's personal history affects her or his ability to trust others (McCann and Pearlman, 1990a), capacity for empathy (Davies and Frawley, 1994), emotional lability or stability (Davies and Frawley, 1994; Neumann and Gamble, 1995), coping style (Haaken and Schlaps, 1991; Stevens and Higgins, 2002), need for control, values, and other aspects of self that impact functioning in the clinical setting. In the sexual-abuse field, the aspects of self-of-the-therapist that have been explored are gender, age, and theoretical orientation, but mostly their own history of having been abused.

Some controversy exists regarding the ability of therapists who are themselves survivors of child abuse to work effectively with this population of clients. If 10 to 30 percent of the general population have experienced some form of unwanted sexual attention by the age of eighteen (Briere and Elliot, 2003; Finkelhor et al., 1990), then it is safe to assume that among therapists the proportions would be the same. In fact, research shows that childhood abuse is found in the histories of therapists to the same degree as the general population (Feldman-Summers and Pope, 1994; Follette et al., 1994; Little and Hamby, 1996; Nuttall and Jackson, 1994).

On the one hand, we can point to the advantage survivor therapists may have in their ability to "empathize with the terror, rage, and loss encapsulated in childhood sexual abuse at levels nonabused clinicians may never reach" (Davies and Frawley, 1994, p. 166). Furthermore, given the fine-tuned antennae CSA survivors have developed, they are highly sensitive to emotional states in others and highly invested in being receptive. This can be a particularly useful skill for the clinician to posses (Saakvitne, 1991).

On the other hand, it has been suggested that CSA-survivor therapists may overidentify with their clients. They have been said to be prone to experiencing countertransference blind spots to a greater degree than nonsurvivor therapists (Follette et al., 1994; Pearlman and Saakvitne, 1995). This may lead them to fall, more easily than those without a history of abuse, into the patterns of victim, abuser, unseeing parent, or rescuer to which all therapists are susceptible (Davies and Frawley, 1994; Haaken and Schlaps, 1991). However, both survivor and nonsurvivor therapists may be distinctly but equally threatened by the highly emotionally charged material that emerges in sessions or that is alternatively suppressed by clients, and each is likely to cope using different natural defense mechanisms.

It would be interesting to see if empirical studies could be designed to explore these important issues, which at present remain hypothetical conjecture. Studies concerning the impact of the therapist's abuse/trauma history on clinical work should be explored within the context of research into therapist history regarding other areas of practice as well, such as the impact of having been adopted or in foster care on family therapists, parental or personal divorce and the marital therapist, or early parental loss and the bereavement therapist.

Survivor therapists have been thought to fall prey to vicarious PTSD and burnout more than other therapists, and these variables are much easier to research using empirical methods than the issues just discussed. The results are not unequivocal. Stevens and Higgins (2002) and Follette and colleagues (1994) found that therapists with a history of abuse (emotional, physical, sexual abuse, or witnessing family violence) had a higher level of PTSD symptoms than therapists who were not maltreated in childhood. The results of Schauben and Frazier (1995), Paulus (1997), Benatar (2000), and Way et al. (2004) do not substantiate this. In any event, increased distress does not necessarily lead to increased burnout for the survivor therapists (Stevens and Higgins, 2002). Before deciding that PTSD results from the therapist's clinical work, it is important to consider the existence of possible concurrent personal crises, coping styles, and other plausible factors.

Perhaps what is most pernicious is the shame felt by survivor therapists. It seems that they need to maintain "secrecy in their professional lives because of the danger of stigmatization and pathologizing. The message is that to be seen as a survivor means to be seen as somehow damaged, devalued, and inadequate as a therapist" (Saakvitne, 1991, p. 7). This is counterproductive to the field as a whole because those working in the field want CSA survivors to be able to lift their heads high and not be ashamed to say "I was sexually abused," although the same openness to accept this from their fellow therapists does not seem to exist.

MY OWN EXPERIENCES AS A CSA THERAPIST

My Relationship with the Field

I must admit that I do not easily volunteer the nature of the work I do to casual inquirers. To other professionals, I have no problem identifying myself as a therapist who works with survivors of sexual trauma. However, when I am asked in casual social conversation what I do for a living, I sometimes answer, "I'm a family therapist," and at other times I say, "I run a clinic for trauma survivors," leaving off the "sexual" part. If they insist I tell them more—since 9/11 everyone is interested in trauma—I admit to working with sexual abuse, but I cringe within as I say this. Why? Have I been contaminated with the shame of sexual abuse that society projects onto the victims?

Perhaps another reason I avoid talking about my occupation is because everyone has an opinion about it (and often an emotionally loaded one at that) and I do not necessarily want to get into social conversations about how hard it must be to work in this area day after day (do you have to remind me on my time off?), how the laws concerning this issue aren't good enough (true, but I'm not at work now, thank you), or about how some women seduce men and then cry rape (HELP, get me outta this conversation!).

I am glad that a greater openness to discussing sexual trauma seems to be occurring in the media. More movies and television programs have sex crimes themes, and a higher number of reports of sexual abuse against minors are given to the authorities than ever before; however, the field is still struggling under a veil of controversy and contention. It is not easy to watch peers overseas (United States) operate in an atmosphere of apprehension and caution, wary of legal action should a former client or irate parent challenge their professionalism in a malpractice suit. Clinicians have learned the lessons of overenthusiasm, and practice with greater restraint, taking care not to jump two steps ahead of the client by waiting for clients who begin therapy with few or vague memories to come to their own conclusions about whether or not they were abused. I think we have benefited from the reality check that was provided, making us less sure of ourselves. However, I hope we have not gone a bit too far. In our search for evidence-based therapies that statistically evaluate treatment success, are we, perhaps, losing some of the artistry of therapy?

I am troubled that some of the techniques offered in the literature as methods for helping clients stabilize and modulate overwhelming emotions and flashbacks do not work for me as well as they "should." In addition, when asking for help with complex issues, I may be offered another tool that others swear by. I have pondered on the possibility that some of our CSA clients, trained from a young age to deny themselves and please those upon whom they depend, may pretend that a technique works in order to please their therapist (Haaken and Schlaps, 1991) or because they believe that it works for others and should work for them as well. They may view their difficulty as further proof of their "badness" rather than a lack of fit between the client and the technique. Perhaps what works more than the technique itself is the attention and safety provided by the therapist while teaching them what to do, and some clients are more honest in reporting the impact, or lack thereof, of a clinical tool than are others. Indeed, some clients may feign recovery in order to leave a therapy they feel is not helping them rather than disappoint the therapist. If these points are true for some clients (and this also happens in treatment for non-CSA clients), then are we getting an accurate report of treatment successes in the case study or empirical literature?

The literature suggests that clinicians' caseloads should be balanced, with only a proportion of them being sexual trauma clients (Regehr and Cadell, 1999; Schauben and Frazier, 1995). For many years my entire caseload has been survivors of CSA. Occasionally, I will get a referral for couples therapy from a professional who knew me when that was the bulk of my practice. I do like the chance to take a break with an "easy case"—easy cases such as marital affairs, for example!

I do not agree that seeing only sexual trauma cases is problematic. Looking back, I think I took my work home with me emotionally to a greater extent when I was seeing a more varied client population. Then, the sexual trauma cases were prominent, demanding attention, and I could not stop thinking about them. Now, perhaps both because I have a rather homogenous caseload as well as having more experience and feeling more confident of my professional skills, I find it easier to leave my work at the office. Oops! I should qualify that statement since here I am writing a book about sexual abuse, spending most of my spare time reading and writing about sexual abuse. Don't take my work home with me? I guess I actually do. Only now, I realize, it is not that I am usually thinking about any particular client—I must admit, I do that too—but to a larger degree it is struggling with the general area of sexual abuse. I find myself thinking about developing better ways of working with CSA survivors and training other clinicians as well as exploring how to bridge the gap between academic research and applied clinical practice.

Is my professional writing a way to cope with the onslaught of this work on my psyche? Well, if I was a financial advisor and invested the same amount of time and energy reading the financial pages of the newspaper and whatever books it is financial advisors read, and poring over international reports on the Internet, would that be a sign of anything other than single-minded ambition to do my job as well as I can and perhaps being a workaholic? I, personally, would probably be a single-minded workaholic regardless of the profession I found myself in!

A couple of years ago, I asked a colleague who does not know me personally to read a chapter I had written for a book. Among other comments, she told me she thought from my writing that I was suffering from burnout. At first I disagreed with her intensely, but later thought that she may be right. I continue to explore with colleagues what it means to be suffering from burnout while working in this most difficult field.

Whether or not I am actually suffering from compassion fatigue, I am acutely aware that sexual abuse victims are everywhere. I see them in school photos, at the playground, in the mall. Does that mean I am burned out? Does a hairstylist look at women on the street without examining their tresses? What does this immersion in one's professional material mean other than simply immersion in one's professional material? Does it have to mean burnout in the case of trauma therapists? Or does this question have less to do with sexual trauma professionals themselves and more to do with society that would rather we not constantly point out this underside of life?

Interestingly, in their study of vicarious trauma, Brady et al. (1999) found that clinicians who work with a large number of abuse survivors seem to subjectively experience life as more "spiritually satisfying" (p. 391) than therapists with fewer CSA clients in their caseload. They suggest that this work "may force therapists to challenge their own constructs of meaning and traditions of faith . . . [and this] may strengthen psychotherapists' spirituality" (pp. 391-392). Pearlman and Saakvitne (1995), on the other hand, report that therapists may find their optimism and faith in humanity severely challenged by the nature of this work. I know that over the years I have explored different spiritual paths and reevaluated my approach to life and relationships. I don't know if my explorations have been related so much to my daily confrontation with the evil acts some adults can perpetrate on innocent children, or to my personal encounter with a near-death experience in 1998, or to the difficulties of raising two daughters as a single mother in a country I was not born in, or any number of positive as well as difficult personal experiences that have made me into the person I am today. Without comparing more versus less spiritually satisfied therapists with other professionals, I don't think one can say much about this.

I do think one clear "occupational hazard" exists in being a mental health professional in general and working with abuse survivors in particular, and that is the constant need for self-examination. I do not believe therapists can be helpful to their clients if they do not continue to explore themselves and grow. That means that one is constantly working on oneself. My CSA clients touch me in ways that simple social interactions cannot. To make sure that my responses to them and my work with them remain as pure as possible I need to examine and reexamine my thoughts, feelings, automatic responses, values, attitudes, etc. I am not without supervision regardless of how experienced I get. And sometimes I return to therapy for a time. My most important clinical tool is my "self"—my personality, my behavior, my way of being in this world. I am a tool that needs constant honing.

It can get tiring after a while. Sometimes I wonder what it would be like to work in business or politics, or to be a mathematician or carpenter or a cashier in the supermarket and not have to constantly delve into the recesses of my past and my mind and soul as part of my continuing professional development. Is this a sign of burnout? However, I cannot imagine many professional activities that are more fulfilling and exciting than international psychology conferences with my peers or the thrill of seeing clients do things they never thought they would be able to accomplish.

My Relationship with my Clients

I have always been aware of the difficulty clients experience in coming forward and asking for help in overcoming their traumatic pasts. Not only were they sexually abused, but generally no one paid attention to their distress. Because their early relationships were so fraught with danger, and they basically had only themselves to rely on, no reason on Earth exists for them to really open up to me, to trust me with their secrets, to depend on me to help them. Therefore, I do not assume that just because someone has come to me for a first appointment, they will return. As a matter of fact, I have learned that sometimes actually getting from the phone call to the first appointment is not to be taken for granted. Most of those who do not turn up for the first session do not call to cancel. Sometimes I can predict, during the initial phone call, those who will be no-shows. If they called me in dire straits and I made complicated arrangements to be available for them I will be peeved, of course, but I try to take it in stride. Although the client has the right not to come even after having made an appointment, I may call them back and tell them that I understand it was not possible to come in and that when they are ready we can reschedule. Some come back and some do not. Since I am aware that CSA survivors are generally burdened with guilt and shame about the abuse and frightened about beginning therapy, my call to them is intended to remove the no-show from their personal list of "misdemeanors."

I recognize that I am not the only person in the world who can "save" this client. He or she had a life before meeting me, and will have a life after leaving me. With this in mind, I have come to regard therapy as something similar to a bus stop. When clients come in for a first session, I do not know how long they will stay at this stop. Maybe all they can do at the moment is alight from the bus, take a look around, and see what therapy feels like. I try to make their stay at this stop as helpful as possible. A typical first session may include a drawing or simple collage exercise that most clients find unthreatening (see Appendix A). I would like them to leave the first session with the feeling of "I can do this!" or "Therapy's not too bad." Even if they do not return to me, I would like to think that I have helped them realize that therapy is something they may be able to do in the future either with me or with another clinician.

I do not necessarily expect clients to complete the entire therapy process with me. What is the entire therapy process, anyway? Dynamic individuals continue to develop emotionally and psychologically until their last breath on this planet (and according to some beliefs, even after that in future incarnations or other forms of being*), and for some therapy is just one of the ways they sometimes do that. If I look at my own life, I can see that I do therapy in spurts, and in the past I have rarely returned to the same therapist. Each clinician I have seen has had something to contribute to my development.

I have clients who stay with me for years, and others who come for weeks or months. I have clients who leave therapy and come back again the next day, a week later, or months later. Sarah-Jane was one of these clients. She succeeded in making the changes she had set out to make, i.e., learning to control her anger, and she left therapy. I already knew she had been abused to some degree, because during this first therapeutic encounter she told me about her father putting his hand up her dress and photographing her half nude. She was not yet ready to understand these behaviors as abusive, and I certainly did not know the extent of his exploitation of her. I had to respect her pace and let her end therapy. She had been brave enough to ask for help in order not to hurt her children. I felt sure she would continue to work on herself when she felt the need.

Perhaps part of what is behind this approach is not just a clear understanding of the individual pace of each client, but also my self-doubt. I am quite adept at "beginnings" and very good in emergencies. I see myself as a "firefighter"—the adrenaline flows when high tension exists, and I feel myself most alive professionally in crisis situations. Correspondingly, I do not fear the emotional intensity of traumatic memory synthesis. This may be part of what makes trauma therapy so suited to my character.

Dealing with long periods of inertia, on the other hand, does not seem to come to me naturally. When therapy is slow and less dramatic, with little change exhibited on the part of the client, I sometimes wonder, "What is it about me that makes me think I can help?" So perhaps when a client wants to leave I am too quick to let them go. I do try to explore with them their reasons for wanting to leave, and hope to help them make a choice that is right for them, including helping them to stay when appropriate. I struggle against my natural tendency to say "Okay, go!" This is one of the issues that I continue to work on in supervision and my own therapy. Regehr and Cadell (1999) suggest that self-doubt and de-skilling can result from projective identification

---

*Many CSA survivors I have worked with have expressed a great deal of interest in spiritual pursuits that have included a belief in reincarnation, holistic medicine, etc.

whereby survivors project their own helplessness and shame onto the therapist. With this in mind, I try to distinguish between my own issues and those that arise as a result of my client's traumatic transference. So, in some cases, I may be responding to a client's projected fears of abandonment, for example; however, in other cases, what happens to me may have nothing to do with my client, but, rather, with something within me that pulls me back and draws me into disconnecting from the client or the situation. Perhaps my clients sometimes mirror for me situations that uncomfortably reflect upon a still unresolved position from my family of origin, when I was emotionally abandoned, alone, and feeling empty. However, as a therapist, I need to be present for my clients in every situation, and not just in those that are comfortable for me. For that reason I continue with my own therapy.

Aside from my own personal issues with what may be considered premature termination of therapy, the question exists concerning for whom the termination is premature (Cohen, 2003). Is the client leaving therapy as a form of running away from a difficult situation instead of coping with it? Is the client leaving because it is appropriate to take a break and "recharge batteries" at this stage? Or, is the termination considered premature by the therapist "because of the therapist's preconception of what constitutes a complete therapy?" (Cohen, 2003, p. 199).

Some clients have taught me patience. I always thought of myself as a patient person, but I did not know what patience really was until some of my survivor clients challenged me intensely in this realm. One example was a young woman with a clear case of obsessive-compulsive disorder (OCD) rather than "just" obsession-compulsive symptoms. She was trying on my nerves, and *she* had to be patient with *me* as I learned to relax and slow down to her pace of work. We were never totally in sync with each other, but we had moments, some of them quite long moments, when I felt like we were riding a wave together.

However, after three years of work I made what appears to have been a "fatal" mistake, an empathic failure, and she left me. I got word from the referring psychiatrist that she suffered quite a setback, and as much as I tried to get her to come in and talk to me about her anger, whether that would enable her to continue working with me or not, I was unsuccessful. In three years of therapy this was certainly not the first empathic failure on my part, but for some reason it was irreparable this time. It saddens me a great deal, especially in light of the incredible progress she had made until then. I do not know what really happened and probably never will. This kind of uncertainty is one of the issues we have to live with as therapists—was the failure my own error or was it something that resides within the client or the client's environment? Being left without a way to definitively answer this is frustrating.

One of the difficulties CSA survivors have is trusting their own senses. It is absolutely imperative that we confirm their perceptions and interpretations when correct regardless of how uncomfortable it may make us feel. This is partly related to the issue of therapist countertransference self-disclosure to the client (which I will discuss further in the section on dilemmas). However, if a client sees our eyes closing (as I did more than once with one of my therapists) and asks if we are tired because our eyes are heavy (as I finally asked him), and we say that we are not tired and are with the client (as he did), then we are not living up to our responsibility of helping the client learn to correctly assess his or her environment and make decisions based on that assessment. (I think this kind of situation does not necessarily fall into the category of therapist countertransference self-disclosure.) Many situations like this are far less obvious, and, therefore, are far more difficult for the client to assess. Our CSA-survivor clients are not always able to challenge their therapists, even for something as conspicuous as drooping eyelids.

It is imperative that any therapist who is not in individual supervision at least be in a peer supervision group while engaged in clinical work with CSA survivors. This applies to the most experienced therapists as well (Maroda, 1999; Norris et al., 2003). Furthermore, anyone who is not sharing with their supervisor or supervision group their errors or almost-errors, their fantasies about their clients, and their ethical dilemmas should not be in clinical practice with this client population.

This work demands purity of intent. We are working with people who carry tremendous feelings of guilt and shame, and if we cannot face our own feelings of guilt and shame then how can we help our clients with theirs? In fact, this, to me, is the crux of this work: working with CSA survivors forces us—no, I will take personal responsibility for this comment—working with CSA survivors compels me to continually face myself without rose-colored glasses. I am brutal with myself (brutal = brutally honest, not abusive) in that I do not leave any stone unturned in the effort to understand my part in the therapeutic relationship. I want to understand my clients' transferences and projections, but I do not use these phenomena as an excuse for my behavior. If I can be said to exploit my clients, it is that I exploit the opportunities they present me with to improve my "self."

I consider myself fortunate in having supervisors and colleague-friends who are able to get into the trenches with me, bravely and supportively. I have found it most fruitful to have friends who work with CSA and supervisors who do not typically work in this area. I get the benefit of support and identification from my friends and the benefit of support and a fresh perspective from my supervisors. Perfect!

BOUNDARY ISSUES IN THE LITERATURE

I think this is the issue I struggle with most. Boundaries provide the safety within which therapeutic work can take place with all clients, not just with CSA survivors. However, it is important to question the kind of safety different boundaries provide (and to whom, client or therapist).

Strict boundaries are said to define the controlled treatment environment within which the transference plays itself out in a way that can be used therapeutically. Some authors suggest that even innocuous modifications to the traditional boundary frame can be the first step down the slippery slope leading to sexual abuse of the client by the therapist (e.g., Gutheil and Gabbard, 1993; Walker and Clark, 1999). Both of these are important points; however, it is equally important not to be alarmist and to give reasoned consideration to the issue of boundaries and the possibility of modifying some of them when this would be of benefit to the client (Brown, 1994; Duhl, 1999; Kiselica, 2003; Malone et al., 2004; Maroda, 1999; Moleski and Kiselica, 2005; Rubin, 2000).

According to classic psychotherapy, the therapist is supposed to be anonymous in that the client is not to know anything about the therapist's personal life or feelings toward the client. The rationale here is that, knowing nothing about the clinician, the client is free to project onto the therapy relationship patterns and expectations of others from his or her past, which can then be identified and discussed. Herein lies the "cure." In my experience, projection of expectations and learned patterns occurs regardless of how much the client knows about the therapist (just as it does in friendships and marriage and every other interpersonal relationship). Indeed, the therapist also has a past, which may or may not include trauma, and the therapist also projects onto the client partially unconscious relationship patterns and expectations. This means that the therapeutic relationship includes mutual projections, and the therapist is responsible for teasing out which responses are due to client projections and which are due to the therapist's own unresolved issues.

It is a mistake to think that the client knows about the therapist only if the therapist imparts that information. For one thing, the CSA survivor's well-honed antennae capture nuances of voice, gesture, and facial expression that reveal emotions, states of mind, and opinions that the therapist may think are adeptly hidden. At the same time, it is important to remember that what the client may think he or she is sensing from the therapist may actually be a projection from himself or herself onto the therapist. Being aware of both possibilities allows verification and discussion, which will help the client keep better track of sensations that originate outside himself or herself versus those that are products of his or her inner world.

Furthermore, in a small country such as Israel, as in small communities elsewhere in the world, therapist anonymity is almost impossible to maintain. In support groups run by rape crisis centers and in online survivor support forums, participants share with each other the ins and outs of some of their therapy sessions. Therefore, in the case of clinicians who specialize in survivor treatment, some clients are likely to have more knowledge of the therapist to whom they turn for help than they would have had in the past. It is also possible, after therapy has proceeded for some time, for the therapist to suddenly discover that her client's cousin is her best friend's next-door neighbor, for example, or for the client to suddenly realize that his child's teacher is his therapist's spouse!

The idea, in Israel, of therapist anonymity is absurd when another clinician seeks therapy. A strong likelihood exists that many opportunities will occur for therapist and therapist-client to find themselves teaching in the same program, attending the same workshops, or being part of the same circle of colleagues.

Therapist self-disclosure to the client is another aspect of boundaries that requires careful consideration. Some clients want to know if the therapist is married, has children, was abused, loves them, is angry at them, etc. It has been suggested that purposeful self-disclosure can serve to normalize certain problems, instill hope, provide role-modeling for problem solving, increase trust and enhance the therapeutic relationship, etc. (Barrett and Berman, 2001; Knight, 1997; Maroda, 1999; Olarte, 2003; Group for the Advancement of Psychiatry, 2001). Other writers (e.g., Curtis, 1981; Harper and Steadman, 2003; Norris et al., 2003) reject the possibility that purposeful self-disclosure can benefit the therapy, citing problems with maintaining focus on the client, the possibility that the therapist may use the self-disclosure to unburden himself or herself, or that the client may doubt the therapist's competence.

Those who support the use of therapist self-disclosure recognize the possible pitfalls and suggest that these are not reasons to reject self-disclosure as a therapeutic tool, but that therapists should be guided in using it appropriately. Mallow (1998), writing about substance abuse therapists, suggests that clinicians should be open about their concern and emotional responses to the client, but should not reveal facts about their personal life even when that is relevant to the client, in this case whether or not the substance abuse therapist was himself or herself previously a substance abuser. In an empirical study, Barrett and Berman (2001) found that when therapists shared personal information in response to client self-disclosures of a similar kind (such as forgetfulness) this lowered symptomology and a better therapist-client relationship ensued than when therapists merely explored the meaning behind the client's request for information.

However, self-disclosures of personal histories of substance abuse or childhood sexual trauma are very different from personal information related to forgetfulness or problems with children. It is possible that clients will feel threatened knowing that their therapist was also traumatized (perhaps having had a parent who was?). On the other hand, the client who knows the therapist was abused may feel this is a therapist who can really understand (Knight, 1997). In other words, as in every other realm of therapy, the decision whether or not to self-disclose must be made in the context of the particular therapist-client interaction.

In today's reality this issue is complicated even further. For example, some members of an Internet support group may be seeing the same therapist. If that therapist shared personal data with one client, that data may be shared on the forum, meaning that clients who perhaps would be better off not knowing certain personal information about the therapist would, in fact, have access to it. Therapists need to keep in mind the fact that confidentiality works one way only.

In certain cases, it is possible that strict boundaries are more for giving the therapist peace of mind than they are for protecting the client (Maroda, 1999). If boundaries are clear, then no questions need to be asked only rules need to be followed. Kroll (2001) asks who drew up the guidelines, and where was the professional debate that formed the basis for them? He claims that the guidelines offered in the literature are "politically correct" (my terminology) for a given period of time and therefore should be open for hearty discussion. Commentators on his paper say that Kroll is stating the obvious: Gabbard (2001) claims that "professional boundaries in psychotherapy are fluid and largely a matter of clinical judgment and context . . . and [b]oundary crossings are much more usefully thought of as a way of monitoring one's countertransference" (p. 285). Simon (2001) argues that the current guidelines are meant to inspire therapist reflection, and he agrees with Kroll that "inflexible, rigid treatment boundaries are inimical to good clinical care" (p. 287). Blatt (2001) contends that the controversies surrounding the issue will not be resolved by debate but by "systematic research that identifies and understands the mechanisms through which dimensions of the treatment process [rather than specific techniques] contribute to, or interfere with, constructive therapeutic change" (p. 290). In spite of this flexibility, however, discussion in the field still seems to take the general form of prescription and warnings rather than opening up ways to think about boundaries and their salience to the wide variety of clients (for discussion, see Gutheil and Gabbard, 2003; Pope, 2003; Zur, 2001).

For example, Younggren (2002) reports that a presenter at an ethics workshop declared that all dual relationships are unethical (he strongly disagrees with this claim), and in a lecture to psychiatrists on the issue of dual relationships, Somer (2003) made the same claim. He gave the example of a hypothetical therapist who risked the therapeutic gains of her client by giving in to the temptation to become friends. An otherwise possibly appropriate out-of-clinic cognitive-behavioral intervention for phobia was the vehicle for facilitating the anticipated posttherapy friendship. Instead of categorically rejecting the idea of dual relationships, it is important to question motivation of the therapist (which in the case presented was highly suspect a priori), possible countertransferential urges and transferential impact, and examine the overall framework of the therapeutic modality employed by the therapist when considering dual relationships (Gottlieb, 1993; Moleski and Kiselica, 2005; Rubin, 2000) as well as other boundary modifications (Maroda, 1999).

It is also questionable whether out-of-office phobia interventions such as that presented by Somer (2003) even fall under the classification of dual relationships. Further complicating the issue is that, at least in private practice, all client-therapist relationships constitute a dual relationship in that the client is at the same time the employer of the therapist (Rubin, 2000).

Clinicians are discouraged from seriously challenging themselves and their colleagues about boundary issues when a knee-jerk, "no-no-no" attitude cries out that anything out of the ordinary (meaning the psychodynamic approach to boundaries) will bring the risk of serious violation (usually meaning sexual exploitation) and/or set the clinician up for possible litigation. Some authors have suggested that when fear of litigation determines ethical standards, clinical judgement may be clouded (e.g., Williams, 1997; Zur, 2002) sometimes resulting in resistance to unconventional but sound therapy approaches (Aron, 2000; Orchin, 2004). Moreover, when rigidity is the prevailing overt attitude, therapists may be apprehensive about sharing with peers and supervisors their ideas about modifying (or having modified) certain boundaries with a particular client. This can lead to therapist isolation instead of participation in a supportive community so essential for working with traumatized clients. As early as 1988, Pope and Bajt proclaimed the need for open consideration of ethical issues and serious debate. Pope (2003) continues to encourage unbridled debate in his writing and on his Web site (www.kspope.com). Along these same lines, Cohen (2003) provides us with an enthralling picture of how, over a number of years, She maintained an inner dialogue exploring the subject of boundaries and their relevance to the traumatized adolescents with whom she worked. She was willing to change her approach to therapeutic boundaries in accordance to her clients' needs.

Does having had unclear boundaries in the incestuous family (Boszormenyi-Nagy and Spark, 1984) mean that the CSA-survivor client requires stricter therapeutic boundaries than clients with other issues? More flexible boundaries? Stricter in one area and more flexible in another? I am not sure, and the professional literature is only beginning to explore this area (e.g., Davies and Frawley, 1994; Harper and Steadman, 2003; McCann and Pearlman, 1990b). Interestingly, I have not found myself in a position of having to question conventional boundaries with clients who did not have abusive childhoods.* I wonder if herein lies the answer to a question I have been asking myself since I started to write this book: What is the difference between therapy with CSA survivors and therapy with other client populations? Could one possibility be related to the issue of boundaries? Could it be that boundary issues are less problematic for clients who were not abused as children? Could it be that clients who were not abused or neglected during childhood have greater emotional/psychological resources that make the psychotherapeutic adventure one for which fifty minute sessions are sufficient? Or could it be that in working with survivor clients projective identification produces pressure upon the therapist that can lead to boundary crossings (Yahav and Oz, 2005)? Or that survivor clients have needs that are more appropriately addressed in situations that may not absolutely fit with the conventional approach to boundaries?

Perhaps boundaries are more a state of mind or of being than anything else (Levine, 1999). Bonnie Simone (2005, personal communication) doubts that the issue is one of concrete place or time, stating that one therapist can exhibit more ethical behavior meeting with a client at a grave site or going for a walk with the client outside the office than another therapist who meets clients only in the clinic. Zur (2001) writes about some of the considerations behind his decisions to begin therapy in a cafe or in a client's machine shop, for example.

---

*I write this with full knowledge that many instances of unethical behaviors of different sorts occur on the part of clinicians working with a wide variety of clients and problem areas, some of which come to the attention of professional ethics committees. Although studies have examined the qualities of offending therapists (e.g., Katsavdakis et al., 2004), it seems that, aside from the important but methodologically problematic study by Pope and Vetter (1991) nobody has yet done research exploring whether or not it is possible to identify factors common to clients who fall victim to exploitive therapist behaviors. I suggest here the hypothesis that these clients were neglected or emotionally, physically, or sexually abused.

This allowed for ethical therapy as "part of a clearly articulated treatment plan . . . constitut[ing] the most effective intervention for the specific situation" (p. 98) rather than refusing to see the client because of the therapist's need to play it safe.

Respectful boundaries and assertiveness to defend personal autonomy is something that grows within a respectful family environment (Rubin, 2002). Some families promote this kind of learning, and others do not. Overcoming a traumatic childhood should lead to the acquisition of internalized boundaries, respect for the boundaries of others, and an ability to defend one's own and others' autonomy.

Therapists are no exception to this. Is it possible that a *therapist* who was abused (not necessarily sexually), neglected, or abandoned during childhood has not internalized boundaries and does not respect boundaries to the same extent as a nonsurvivor therapist or survivor therapist who has sufficiently worked through the childhood traumas? What about the therapist who was overprotected throughout childhood in an extremely enmeshed family? What then can we say about the specific therapist's need for boundaries? Moreover, what is the nature of the interaction between professionals' and clients' needs for boundaries or for boundary flexibility? It is important for professionals to find a way to discuss this issue openly and without defensiveness.

What the codes of ethics of the various professional organizations are trying to ensure is that clients' needs are uppermost in the therapist's mind. This does not necessarily have anything to do with time or place. It is just as easy to sexually abuse (or otherwise exploit) a client who is paying full fees and is seen in the middle of the day in the office for exactly fifty minutes as it is to practice ethically and morally sound therapy for a reduced-fee client seen in a cafe.

PERSONAL EXPERIENCE
WITH BOUNDARY DILEMMAS

Let's start with the most obvious boundary dilemma: this book. I am not the first therapist to collaborate with a former client on a book (other examples are Axelsen and Bakke, 1991; Barnes and Berke, 2002; Bergman and Sarah, 1998; Bryant and Kessler, 1996; Cleese and Skynner, 1996; Watkins and Johnson, 1982; Yalom and Elkin, 1990), and I probably will not be the last. This can be regarded as a dual relationship and, as discussed previously, dual relationships, either during or after therapy, is a subject of much controversy (e.g., Simon and Williams, 1999; Zur, 2001), and no consensus has yet been reached.

Sometime during 2002, more than two years after our last brief contact as therapist and client (see Chapter 6), Sarah-Jane called me, saying she wanted to use her experience with having recovered from CSA to help others who were still suffering. As we talked about different things she might do, I told her about an idea I had for writing a book and wondered if she wanted to collaborate with me on this project, making use of the diaries she kept. According to the codes of ethics in effect at the time, two years is quite a satisfactory time lapse from the termination of therapy to embark upon a different kind of relationship. I brought up the subject of possible future therapy and how working together on this project might mean that we would not be able to return to a therapist-client relationship. After further consideration, Sarah-Jane said she was interested in joining me in this project.

In late 2003, after we had already begun work on the book, Sarah-Jane asked me for a referral to another therapist. This made me wonder how pure hearted I was when Sarah-Jane came to me for a few sessions in 1999. Did I already have this book in mind? Possibly. I knew about Sarah-Jane's diary entries throughout our therapeutic relationship (1990-1996). During her treatment, although impressed with the writing and the powerful descriptions she produced, I was not thinking about any personal benefit I may get from them. But is it possible that, as early as 1999, the idea for this book was beginning to take form in my imagination? Sarah-Jane writes that she was not really ready to return to therapy in 1999. I wonder if that was partly due to a possible underlying reluctance on my part to reengage her?

As it turns out, she is happy with her current therapist and benefiting from the perspective the new clinician is providing. However, how much is her not continuing therapy with me because I wanted to write this book? Did I delve deeply enough with her in our discussions of the implications of changing our relationship? I know that she has said that her work on this project has brought issues up that perhaps would not have arisen otherwise, or at least not yet. So did my part in our new collaboration have a positive or negative impact upon Sarah-Jane?

The issue can be looked at another way if we regard this book as a case study. Case studies abound in the literature as a means for providing illustrations of clinical theory and technique. Aron (2000) suggests that case studies are perhaps more ethically written in consultation and coordination with the clients involved. A therapist who writes for professional journals is a therapist who is already involved in a dual relationship with his or her clients, both providing therapy and using their case material without their direct input—in other words, using clients, often without their knowledge. Aron (2000) discusses how direct involvement of clients in the writing up of their cases can contribute to their therapy. In fact, we can see that for Sarah-Jane, this project has served as an impetus for her continuing effort to heal, just not with me. Does our collaboration on this book really mean that at some time in the future she cannot return to me for further clinical work?

Other than for in vivo cognitive-behavioral phobia therapy, out-of-office contact with clients has not received much attention (for an example, see Orchin, 2004). I have made the decision to take clients outside on the basis of my understanding of the problem survivors have with the therapy room itself. In Chapter 1, we looked at the nature of the CSA trauma and described the World of Trauma. Reflection on the qualities of the clinical situation reveals parallels with the World of Trauma. Both situations (usually) consist of two individuals of different status, an entrance ritual, and exit ritual, and a door is closed shutting off the interaction with the rest of the world as if the two individuals are encapsulated within a bubble. The subject of the interaction is secret or confidential, and the relevant content of the situation is trauma, in one case ongoing actual trauma and in the other talking about memories of trauma. When attempting to speak about the trauma, just as during the actual traumatic event itself, Broca's area (the region of the brain that plays a part in the ability to speak and understand speech) shuts down (van der Kolk, 1994). Clients find, to their distress, that subjects they wanted to discuss in the session become inaccessible to them once alone in the clinic facing the therapist. Some find that it helps them concentrate if they write down beforehand what they want to say. For others, this does not improve their ability to put their thoughts into words.

One client, let's call her Sivan, was going through a particularly difficult time with me. I had disappointed her and she was paralyzed by her anger and her inability to express it. I understood that before entering my office she was able to find the words in her mind to tell me what she needed to, but once the door closed and we sat down she lost all powers of speech. Facing me while feeling angry at me was a trigger to traumatic memories (something she was only able to discuss after we had worked through the anger to some degree). We tried to talk about her difficulty verbalizing her inner experience and to look for ways to help her explore these. Yet, she remained speechless. I was afraid we would find no way around this impasse. Rather than wait ad infinitum (keeping me in the role of abuser and her in the role of victim frozen in fear so both of us were suffering), I suggested we go outside the clinic for a walk around the block, explaining to her the reasoning behind this break from tradition. After a few moments, Sivan got her powers of speech back, and within a relatively short time we were talking. Sitting on a bench in a park nearby, she was able to discuss being angry with me. After one more session outside we returned to the clinic, and she was able to continue talking about her anger and disappointment with me.

The parallel between the therapy room and the World of Trauma affect the client in other ways as well. Remember, one of the characteristics of the World of Trauma is the "dark cloud" that covers the world during the abuse event. I have had clients who asked to be seen after nightfall because it was too jarring for them to leave the "darkness" of the session into the light of day. Other clients prefer to have their sessions during daylight hours because the transition from darkness to light helps them "turn off" the trauma at the end of the session. Other requests, such as being the first client in the day ("I want to come into a "fresh" room") or the last ("No one should sit in my seat after I have been here") can just as easily have transferential meaning having to do with object relations as to do with the World of Trauma phenomena. When clients express special needs regarding the treatment frame or setting, I would suggest looking from both perspectives—psychodynamic as well as World-of-Trauma based—before deciding whether to respond to the request concretely or discuss the meaning behind the request without intending to act upon it.

I am in a constant state of flux with regard to boundary issues. The more I learn, the more complicated the issues seem. What I know for sure is that I will never have sexual relations with a client or former client. Other than that, my understanding of boundaries has undergone some interesting transformations. When I began practicing therapy, I was a family therapist trained within a community systems approach. In my training program, for example, it was not viewed askance when I accompanied a client to a reunification meeting with her estranged nuclear family at her parents' home after she left her violent husband. At the same time, I ran a support group for adolescent mothers, a position involving overlapping roles of teacher, big sister, cheerleader, crisis-intervention worker, suicide rescue worker, marital counselor, and more. Therefore, it is perhaps natural for me, in contrast with many other individual therapists, to work in a variety of roles and in coordination with a variety of community bodies, such as child protection workers, school personnel, extended families, alternative therapists, etc.

The first time a client revealed to me that she had been sexually abused by a previous therapist it shook me up and compelled me to reexamine my understanding of boundaries. I handled this shock by researching the issue of therapeutic boundaries and writing an article with a colleague (Oz and Yahav, 2002). In my sudden insecurity, some situations existed with which I did not cope well. For example, following a life-threatening incident, one longtime client asked to visit me after I was home and out of danger. In earlier days, I would have allowed the visit, understanding it as both her desire to show her caring for me as a fellow human being and as a need to reestablish contact and a sense of safety in view of my extended absence from the clinic. Worrying that this may constitute unclear boundaries, I denied her the visit. Now, looking back on that time, I think I was perhaps too hasty in deciding. Today, I would consult with a colleague and reflect on the situation with respect to that particular client (the only one who had made such a request), open to the possibility of responding in the affirmative.

As a family therapist by training I find it natural to have many people in the therapy room. In my earlier work with CSA clients I did not hesitate to have my clients' spouses come in for a session to help them understand the therapeutic process undertaken by their partners and assess the level of their own coping with changes in the client and in their relationship, perhaps suggesting options for taking care of themselves when they were not doing well. I would typically check with the client if it was appropriate for him or her to have me meet with the spouse. However, I learned that even when we discussed the issue beforehand, they were not always fully aware of how they would later feel working with me after I had met privately with their spouses or how they would feel in the therapy room knowing that their spouse sat in this or that chair. It is important for the couples relationship to have the partner meet with a professional who can explain what to expect as the spouse works through his or her traumatic childhood. I have resolved the related boundary problems by opening a clinic staffed by colleagues who share my philosophy and who can share the work with family members without harming the safety and privacy of the primary therapeutic relationship.

Two boundary issues that were inadequately handled both in my early family therapy training and in my later psychotherapy training are those concerning touch and money. Regarding the former, it was always forbidden, except for a polite handshake; regarding the latter, nothing was ever said. I still struggle with money issues and am not as comfortable as I would like to be regarding use of a sliding scale, handling the very infrequent nonpayment of fees, and notifying clients when fees are scheduled to increase. I was quite impressed with a psychologist I saw who, with enviable ease, charged me for a session I was unable to attend and for which I could not give adequate notice. I am still unable to follow her example, and when I am confronted with a client after a no-show I am afraid my discomfort is too evident.

I do not know what it is about money that makes it such a difficult topic. Is it because money seems to represent power? If so, then difficulties regarding money may really reflect difficulties regarding issues of power. Yet, in my attempts to deal with this uncomfortable issue I learned that money can mean other things as well. One client was seeing me not because she was motivated to work on her CSA traumas but because her husband insisted she do so. One day she did not show up for a session. When I called her to make sure she was okay, she told me she was upset about something and did not feel strong enough to come. I told her that was exactly the time she should come so we could talk about what upset her. I did not charge her for the session. A few weeks later, this happened again. At her next session, I informed her that I was charging her for half the fee of the missed session (and even that was difficult for me!). She was furious, but she paid and no more unannounced no-shows occurred. Sometime later she told me that when I charged her for the missed session she understood that I was serious about what I do, and from that moment on she committed herself to the therapy.

In my opinion, touch is, with some clients, an integral part of the therapy relationship. The general impression among clinicians is that touch is taboo, especially in recent years because of discussion of the slippery slope to sexual abuse; however, perusal of the ethics codes (e.g., American Psychological Association, 2002) indicates that no contraindication to touch is listed, only to sex. Because sexual and nonsexual touch are often confused by the CSA survivor and perhaps others as well, it is considered good risk management not to touch clients in any way except for a handshake (as discussed in Zur and Nordmarken, 2004). Leeway, of course, is made for the specific body-oriented therapies (e.g., traumatic touch therapy, reflexology, shiatsu, etc.). However, even a handshake can, for some clients, be experienced as intrusive and unwanted.

Reflecting on my clinical work, I realize that, although I do maintain that holding a client's hand or putting an arm around his or her shoulder is one way to show compassion and caring, I have actually done so with few of my female clients and even fewer of my male clients. With one client, for example, I asked if it was okay to hold her hands for a moment in response to her feelings of great disgust toward herself. She sighed in relief and told me she felt safe with her hands held by mine. With another client, I hold her hands and squeeze them gently, or even hug her when she cannot stop a flashback. This helps her feel connected with me in the present as she finds it difficult to bear in mind that the somatic experiences in the flashbacks are memories and not actually occurring. When a client asks me to hold his or her hand, I do.

In cases such as these I feel that actual physical touch has therapeutic value above and beyond the metaphoric "holding" of verbalizations. This is in contrast with Casement's (1995) well-known discussion of how his refusal to allow a client to hold his hand allowed her to revisit her trauma and truly resolve it. We must remember that Casement's client was in analysis, that is, she was seeing him four or five times a week, and this provided an actual holding that the once-a-week client does not have. Furthermore, it is possible that touch for Casement's client had a different significance than for the CSA client for whom sexual and nonsexual touch are usually confused. Moreover, later discussion of his paper has suggested that he was wrong in not holding her hand, and that his refusal was based less on ethical considerations than on his own difficulties with touch (Breckenridge, 2000; Fossage, 2000). I am glad to see that the subject of physical touch in therapy is beginning to be more openly discussed in the literature (e.g., Zur and Nordmarken, 2004; Pinson, 2002).

The Clinic

The space into which we invite our clients has an impact upon their sense of comfort and safety. In my opinion, a waiting room is an important feature for the CSA client (and perhaps some others as well) who may find it stressful to have to knock on a closed door, not certain that the previous session has ended or that the therapist is ready to see him or her. Given that CSA survivors may either be overly sensitive or overly insensitive to boundaries, a waiting room, a space in which the client waits for the therapist invitation may be comforting. This is also a space in which the client can rest after sessions when extra time is needed before facing the outside world.

The seating arrangement also has significance. In public places, such as restaurants, it is usual for CSA survivors to sit with their backs to the wall so that no surprise approaches them from behind. We respect that need when we position the chairs such that our client faces the door. Distance between the chairs is also important. Even though what is considered by most a suitable distance exists between the chairs, some of my clients push their chair against the wall as if the wall had wheels and they were trying to move it farther back. The chairs, themselves, are comfortable, with enough room to accommodate curling up.

The room is decorated with subtle use of colors, curtains on the windows, a rug on the floor for warmth, pictures on the walls that can draw attention when a need for backing away from the heavy content of the session occurs, and potted plants that symbolize nature and life.

SPECIAL CHALLENGES IN CLINICAL WORK

Clients Who Seem Unable to Do Therapy

I have a small number of clients who, for the longest time, seemed unable to make use of what I have to offer. During the initial intake sessions they were able to give me general information regarding family and personal history, however, once we got beyond that and a relationship began to develop they seemed to stop cooperating. Some would not answer questions, or would answer with: "I don't know." Over and over again, "I don't know." One client would be triggered into flashbacks in every session, something I later understood to be a distancing mechanism that temporarily arrested her growing dependence on me. Another told me I was an anchor, keeping her alive from week to week. Beyond appearing in my office, she did not seem to be doing any psychotherapeutic work. Clients such as these are very different from Sarah-Jane.

For a long time I felt quite de-skilled by these clients. I only stuck with them because once, when I tried to refer a similar client to someone else, I was witness to such a serious narcissistic injury that I vowed never to do it again. I vowed to learn how to help even those who seemed unable to take my help. Toward that end, I enrolled in a three-year program in psychodynamic psychotherapy.

Since then I have found that these silent clients have wounds that are extremely deep, from very early childhood, and that therapy in these cases is essentially holding. I am there, accepting them as they are, not demanding they be anything but what they are able to be in session, regardless of how useless I feel, and regardless of how hard it is. It is possible that the distress I experience in these sessions is a projection of the client's inner world—this is the way he or she teaches me how it feels inside to be him or her: disconnected, alone, scared, confused, unable to think.

After years—two, three, five years—the client begins to make perceptible progress. We start to have conversations, but it is not steady progress. One session may feel the way therapy usually feels, and then we may have many sessions in which we are back to silence and confusion.

Of course, it is important to distinguish between a situation in which the client cannot do anything else but be present physically in the room and a situation in which the therapy or the therapist is not suited to that particular client. Consultation or supervision should be pursued to determine which it is. When it is the former, I wish you fortitude and patience.

When I Am All the Client Has

The ideal situation for working through traumatic material is when the client has a natural support system. Whether they be family or friends, members of the support network help sustain the client, caring for his or her children when energy or patience is low, cooking nutritious meals, or making sure the individual is not isolated from other human beings (Sarah-Jane's husband and her neighbor filled this role). When the client has other people to talk with in addition to the therapist, changes are easier and depression or suicidality are more likely to be manageable.

Regardless of how many people surround our CSA-survivor clients, they are often without a real support system. Their family members are often not people to whom the survivor can turn. These may be the very people who abused them and/or did not protect them; therefore, the survivor cannot trust them. In some cases the survivor has moved thousands of miles away from the childhood home, often to another country. Spouses and friends, usually expected to provide assistance, may be abusive and exploitive of the client or may be unwilling or unable to provide emotional support (perhaps threatened by the idea and the ramifications of sexual abuse). Even when the potential for partners and/or friends to be supportive exists, the survivor may not feel safe enough to accept this help, particularly during early stages of therapy.

Some survivors, in an attempt to break their isolation, and perhaps upon recommendation of their therapists, join CSA survivor therapy groups as an adjunct to their therapy. Other survivors are afraid of exposure and therefore avoid groups until further along in their recovery.

Thus the therapist may be the only individual in the client's life he or she dares to trust. This is a serious responsibility. It is not helpful to fight the client's need for us to be more available than would be required when a working support network exists. When the client can, he or she will make friends and rely on other people. This may happen only toward the end of therapy.

Having been the sole support for a number of CSA-survivor clients, I am well aware of the difficulty involved in remaining balanced. I sometimes wish I could do more than is permitted by the constraints of the therapist-client relationship, even when boundaries are modified to make some accommodation to client needs. At other times I feel I am not up to the task of supporting my client until he or she is able to people his or her life with others. I despair of my ability to help when all I have to offer is an hour or two a week. How can that be enough, I ask myself, when my client is overwhelmed almost all the time with intense emotions previously unknown to him or her? How can that be enough when the client must deal with the arduous pressures of work, family, children, loneliness (sometimes with no help and limited consideration from the environment), all the while fearing that he or she is about to explode or disintegrate into an insane mass?

More than once I have despaired and my clients have sensed it. In some cases they have been angry at me—"How dare you give up on me! You're supposed to know that I need to complain and moan. If I can't release my distress with you, then where can I?" At that moment, I take a few slow, deep breaths and again open myself up to being with their pain. Other clients, sensing my despair, have felt guilty for having burdened me and distanced themselves from me. The angry ones are easier to help because they clearly let me know what is wrong.

One day, a client, full of trepidation, told me she thought she was bad for me. She felt I was upset and was sure she had caused it. She was afraid that the only way to protect me would be to leave therapy. It is possible to approach this kind of situation by exploring the origin of her deep sense of guilt and belief in her innate toxicity and look at the way she attempted to resolve the problem by leaving. However, because she did pick up on a feeling I was having even though she misinterpreted it, I considered it more appropriate to share with her where she was right and where she was wrong. I *was* upset; about that she was not mistaken, but she was wrong in thinking I was in distress because she was bad and had a bad effect on me. I felt her great need for my assistance and was aware of how little beyond moral support I could offer her within the difficult reality of her daily life. I was sorry I could not do more to help her, and I was upset because my rescue fantasies were not realizable. This was something she had never before considered. She was used to being blamed both by herself and others for anything that went wrong.

Suicidal Clients

At any one time I have a number of clients struggling actively with suicidal wishes. This is the most frightening aspect of CSA therapy. It is important for us to remember that suicidal ideation and suicide attempts are more common for adolescents and adults who were maltreated during childhood (Osvath et al., 2004; Swanston et al., 1997), especially when the abuse was sexual (Brown et al., 1999), than for those who did not suffer childhood trauma. Research has shown that survivor depression, low self-esteem, hopelessness and lack of social support networks are related to suicidality (Yang and Clum, 1996). Unfortunately, I have found that none of these variables improve significantly before the survivor crosses the Wall of Fear. This means that the clinician is contending with self-harm behaviors and urges until the final stage of therapy. Packman et al. (2004) suggest a thorough risk assessment by the clinician, and I recommend that the less-experienced therapist seek consultation and guidance through this process.

Actually, suicidal thoughts tend to increase as the client approaches the Wall of Fear. They are most intense and frightening while the survivor struggles with the knowledge that he or she must cross the Wall of Fear, feeling that doing so will result in death or insanity (see Chapter 5). The pain is excruciating, and the therapist may lose hope along with his or her client.

Indeed, taking into account the projective identification discussed earlier in this chapter, a client's suicidal feelings can be contagious, and I have even found myself wondering if my own life is worth the effort, or if a particular client may not be better off just giving up. In these situations my friends snap me out of my despondency. They are for me what I am for my clients—an intimate human connection that gives one a reason for living—and my supervisor helps me understand the specific dynamics involved with that client. At some points in therapy even the survivor's children may not exert a strong enough hold on them (they may feel they are a bad parent) and the most effective lever is the client-therapist relationship. When I despair most for a particular client, I remember those former clients who are now living proof of the ability of even some of the most sadistically abused individuals to emerge from the ruins of their childhood and adolescent histories into more happy and productive adult lives.

I remind my clients that we have a contract for life and not for death. I do not have them sign a no-harm contract as I have found it is sufficient to talk about the fact that in therapy we are working toward life. We discuss their fantasies of death and about how much they want to kill the pain and the fear, and I assure them that they do not have to kill their bodies to do so. Of course, they do not believe me at this point, but if the therapeutic relationship is strong enough for me to laugh at myself together with my client, I tell them I know that they don't believe me and that I can cope with not being believed! I tell them that it is enough that I hold the belief for both of us until they can claim it for themselves, however long that may take.

I have had clients beg me to release them from the contract. I simply say "no, no deal." They look at me with pain-filled eyes and beg to be allowed to kill themselves. I feel like a monster telling them no. At moments like that I feel like I am the one causing them pain, so I call to mind their other voice—the one that has, under different circumstances, told me "please don't lose hope for me, please don't give up on me." And that keeps me strong.

One day a client announced that today was her last session; she was leaving therapy. I sensed that she was so dispirited that she was a serious suicide risk and her leaving therapy was a means to be released from our contract. I told her that if she wants to quit life, I really can't stop her, and that, ultimately, it is the one thing she can control. She couldn't control having been abused, she couldn't control her mother's indifference, but she can control whether or not to take her next breath. I told her that she will still have that control tomorrow, next week, or next month; I can't take that away from her. Perhaps she'd be willing to wait awhile to see if, by any chance, I am right that one day she may feel differently—after all, suicide is not like taking a trip to Africa with a return ticket. I was afraid for her when she left my office and I promptly called her husband to tell him I thought she may harm herself and that he should watch her. She came back a few weeks later, upset that I called her husband yet understanding why I did. He told her if she wanted to kill herself she should just go ahead and do it and stop talking about it. She never spoke of suicide again and continued therapy for another two years. That was six years ago. She called recently to share some happy news about her children and to tell me she is doing well.

Clients have fantasized about committing suicide with me at their side, holding their hand. I tell them to forget that idea, and they are often astounded when I make it clear that if they commit suicide, I will be furious and would seriously consider not going to the funeral. As I said, we have a contract for life and not for death. So my clients stumble along, hoping they will be struck with cancer, that a truck will run them over, or that a piano will fall on them as they walk alongside a tall building.

For some clients, suicide is seen to be a natural progression from the soul murder committed by their abusers. But one day, taking them completely by surprise, they wake up in the morning and notice that they feel happy to be alive. The next day they may be in pain again, but they have finally had an inkling of what awaits them. I totally expect my CSA-survivor clients to be suicidal for much of the therapy, and I totally expect them to get over it. Of course, suicidal thoughts could arise at times of severe stress throughout their lives, but by then survivors will have learned to ride the wave until it passes, understanding it to be a sign that some aspect of their lives needs to be attended to.

Making Mistakes

I hate making mistakes. I guess that makes me like most other people. More than that I hate making mistakes that hurt someone. I also do not like being unable to help. This means that saying "no" is difficult for me—not impossible, but difficult. For example, I have had times when, for some reason, I could not respond positively to a request from one of my daughters and I found myself quite upset with her, angry that she "put me in the position" of being unable to satisfy a need of hers. I am more reserved with my clients, but I am aware of needing to be careful not to respond to every expressed need in the positive. I am learning. But my clients know I have this difficulty. They can see it on my face when they ask for something, such as a reduction in the fee. This can be regarded as "accidental self-disclosure." It is unavoidable.

A therapist can err in many ways. Through acts of commission, such as an inappropriate self-disclosure (guilty), or acts of omission, such as forgetting to return a call or to bring something to a session as promised (guilty), these errors have meaning either within the relationship with this particular client or for this particular therapist at this particular time of his or her life. Some errors are the result of faulty thinking (guilty) and those that result from not thinking at all (guilty). Some errors are not errors at all, but are the deliberate abuse of therapist power (not guilty). As I sit in my office with a client who suffered from acts of deliberate evil or from evil acts resulting from unconscious needs the abuser did not attempt to understand or control, I am aware of how I need to be alert at all times. Not necessarily to never err, but to always be willing to examine the meaning behind any of my actions that prove to be wrong and to be there with the client to feel and to discuss the impact of those actions.

How do I experience this? With trepidation and exhilaration. Sometimes I feel my creativity and resources are boundless and sometimes I want to shout out to my client: "What do you want from me? I'm only human!"* I try to find the balance between these two extremes. What helps me do this are my friends and my supervisors. I am lucky to have friends and supervisors who are not afraid to tell me I have erred and to do so without shaming me. I think that because of the sensitive, potentially explosive issues we deal with in working with CSA survivors, the possibility of the therapist feeling shamed is great. Norris and colleagues (2003) speak of the need for the field to find a way to help therapists overcome "the feeling of being unable to discuss the case with anyone because of guilt, shame, or the fear of having one's failings acknowledged." Writers such as Maroda (1999) help do just that. In researching for this chapter, I found the following passage in her book:

> I probably make the mistake of saying too much almost every day, just as I make the mistake of withholding too much. Sometimes I am silent when I should talk, or talk when I should be silent. What determines these lapses in empathy varies from fatigue, to misunderstanding, to a need to distance, to a need to dominate or be passive, etc. Every patient wants something different, which is sometimes dizzying. And some days I just do not have it in me. Other days I surprise myself with how 'on' I am, and thank God there are some of these really good days to make up for the bad ones. What makes the struggle easier is the knowledge that I will never "win"—will never achieve perfection. If I am lucky and work hard, I will be "good enough." (pp. 101-102)

As more and more expert therapists and teachers let their humanity show and courageously talk about their failures as well as their successes, it helps all of us overcome the tendency to hide our imperfections. I think that when we are better able to do this as individuals and

---

*One of my daughters once very emphatically reminded me that I should not be misguided—I am not human; I am a mother! She was over twenty-years-old at the time.

as a profession it will give greater confidence to our clients and model for them the importance of being able to forgive oneself.

As my skills improve and I gain more knowledge, I look back at my clinical work in years past. I feel gratified that I was able to help many clients in spite of not knowing then what I know now. However, I was not able to help other clients. Some left angry or hurt. Some left with part of the work left undone just because I did not know enough then to continue. I know that this reverberates for most therapists— the fantasy of calling back former clients and saying: "Now I know how to help you more. Come on back."

Parallel Processes

Among other processes, the vicious rectangle, the same roles we identify in the incestuous family (victim, abuser, unprotective parent, rescuer) sometimes find expression in therapy supervision groups. The group may be dismayed to feel overt or covert anger plaguing the discussion. Neglecting this phenomenon can sometimes lead the group to reach the point of actual scapegoating of one or more of its members. Looking at the interactions calmly, it is often quite evident that some members of the group take on the role of victim, others the abuser, and others the unprotective parent. When the supervisor helps members look at group dynamics it is possible to explore the nature of the roles and the tendency of certain participants to take on a given role. This helps the group understand the environment of the particular client (or client family or community) under discussion, and of the phenomenon of abuse in general.

I have found myself taking on one of these roles (permit me the privacy of not disclosing which) in a number of supervision groups in which I have participated. It is a distinctly unpleasant experience. In fact, it is excruciating. All members of the group suffer painfully when this process goes unchecked and the group becomes toxic. When the supervisor does not take the situation in hand, does not find a way to help the group examine itself at a metalevel, then the group is not a safe place for any of its members. The responsibility for this lies with the group supervisor.

When the group has a peer-supervision format, with no formal leader, care needs to be taken to ensure that all members of the group feel safe. In my experience this is easier when the group is homogeneous. It is too easy for the group to scapegoat (even without intending to or without malice) a member who has a different theoretical orientation, a great deal more or less experience than the others, or some other element that makes him or her too different from the other members for the group to easily accommodate. One might expect that different orientations and types of experience would stimulate and enrich discussion; however, that is not always how it plays out. If *all* members are different enough from one another, then possibly less difficulty will be had with issues of scapegoating.

CONCLUDING WORDS

I am writing and revising this book against the "background music" of natural disaster and terrorist acts. The tsunami tragedy hit Asia (December 26, 2004), and Katrina hit the southern United States (August 2005), and the news of the latter is like a broken record of the former—what devastation a few tens of meters of water are able to inflict. At the same time, the news is also filled with the psychological devastation wrought by UN peacekeepers in the Republic of the Congo who rape teenage girls in exchange for food or a couple of bucks and by the loss of innocent lives in bombings in Baghdad. These are only the bigger stories that make it to the headlines. It only takes a moment to shatter a life and then years of hard work to put it back together again. For each of the clients that I and many other dedicated professionals help to resolve issues of helplessness, guilt, shame, horror, and pain, so many more are created each day around the world.

It is so difficult to remain optimistic with the ongoing traumatization playing out in the background. It is hard on me and it is hard on my clients, some of whom wonder what right they have to feel so bad when "other people hit by natural disaster or war or terror have it worse."

What keeps me going is contact with other people, with the growing fellowship of sexual trauma therapists in my country in addition to my friends and family. The Internet has also been a great boon in this regard. Now professionals can keep in touch with peers from all corners of the globe to exchange ideas, support one another, and challenge one another. This adds an exciting element to interpersonal interaction beyond the bounds of our local intimate communities.

I woke up this morning, not thinking about tsunami or Katrina or bombs, and not about my clients either. I woke up this morning to a bright sunny day, and I took my coffee to the balcony that overlooks a view of the Mediterranean with a green valley in the foreground and bordered by hills dotted with white houses. Later I will call some friends and perhaps go for a walk with someone on the beach. My eldest daughter called and read me a paper she wrote for college, impressing me with her command of literary Hebrew, and I will speak later with my younger daughter who is having a great adventure building mud houses in a small community in the desert near Elat. Tomorrow I go back to work in the clinic.

Final Thoughts

Sheri

My goal in writing this book was to put together my clinical and training experience in a form that would be useful both for therapists and for clients. I hoped that, together with my former client, Sarah-Jane, we would produce a guide that would shed light on the subjective experiences of clients and clinicians struggling, as a team, to overcome the ravages of the clients' childhood sexual abuse (CSA) and the dysfunctional families in which they grew up.

Understanding the subjective therapy experience of the client can enhance the clinician's ability to appreciate the nature of the client's fear of therapy itself throughout the therapeutic process. When the fear of therapy is demystified and normalized, both survivor and therapist should find the painful and sometimes overwhelming work somewhat less threatening. Two concepts defined in this book, the World of Trauma and the Wall of Fear, form the backbone for understanding this fear.

Appreciating the subjective therapy experience of the clinician helps to demystify some aspects of the therapist's role for the client. I hope that what I have written here rings true for other therapists and that they, as well as survivors, find value in my sharing some of the dilemmas and difficulties I have encountered in my work.

In addition to presenting the subjective experiences of the two major players in the drama of the recovery journey, we decided to explore the impact on the second generation. Although parenting skills of survivor parents has been the subject of research, the subjective experiences of growing up with survivor parents has not. We hope that second-generation readers will find solace in seeing their experiences reflected in these pages.

Overcoming Childhood Sexual Trauma
Published by The Haworth Press, Inc., 2006, All rights reserved.
doi:10.1300/5668_10

It is not common for a therapist and former client to embark upon a conjoint enterprise such as this one. In fact, in my search for similar co-author teams around the world, I found only eight pairs that produced ten books. Interestingly, five of these eight clients were CSA survivors and three of the survivors suffered from dissociative identity disorder (DID). I wonder what this means in terms of boundary issues in therapy and countertransference. Is something unique about clinical work with CSA survivors? I explored this question in Chapter 9 on the therapist's subjective experience of working with this population.

Our work with all clients is poignant, but our work with CSA survivors is especially demanding and agonizing. The degrees of rage and guilt and shame break the sound barrier. I wish, instead of CSA being a "dirty little secret," hiding within the bounds of our clinics protecting abusers and their apologists, that all that anguish would echo around the world in every nook and every cranny until no denial is left. I wish that the world would take as much interest in the children terrorized *in their own homes* as they did in the victims in New York after September 11, 2001, or in Southeast Asia after the tsunami. The numbers are staggering, after all.

Just when I'm feeling most discouraged, just when I wonder what difference I really make in this vicious, unfeeling world that can create monsters who sodomize little girls and boys, just then, I get a phone call. A small miracle has happened. A client calls in pain, afraid he or she won't last the night. But I notice that she's angry for the first time, or that he's crying for the first time, or that she understands for the first time why she feels this way or acts that way, that it makes sense for the first time in her forty years of life. Then a former client sends an e-mail to tell me about another little triumph. She tells me because she feels some of the credit for her triumph belongs to me. I feel my heart swell (it really does, you know) with pride. I am proud of her and so honored that I was invited to play a part in that miracle. I am amazed at how much pain our hearts can bear and how huge they can swell and not burst. And I think that this joy and pride is something the unrepentant abuser and the nonprotective adults will never ever know or experience. I guess that has to be enough. For now. Perhaps sadly, perhaps angrily, one of my clients remarked how unfortunate it is that "you cannot put your soul in a wheelchair." I leave you, the reader, to ponder on this cryptic statement as I do.

Sarah-Jane

Writing this book was not easy. Using the diaries I have written for more than twenty years, I have documented a desolate adolescence, and I have recorded my struggle to break the chain of abuse and be the kind of mother to my children that I would have wanted for myself. My diary entries describe the journey I made into my past when I was in therapy with Sheri. They describe the journey I am making now, into myself, as I write this book.

Although my primary goal was to help others in their healing process, writing this book has been part of my healing process too. It has given me the courage to go back into therapy for the next lap of my journey, by reminding me that the last time I went on a journey I ended it as a person I liked better.

When I turned my diary entries into a narrative I saw the pattern of my life, how many of my past choices—career, relationship, or otherwise—were made from the standpoint of a survivor of childhood sexual abuse. Life choices based on the trauma of the past are shaky, to say the least, but let's not forget that they are also choices of a "survivor," which is no small achievement. Getting through my childhood sane and in one piece proves that I am a survivor. Recognizing the pain and loss of that childhood, and realizing that the rest of my life is in my hands, has made it possible for me to make choices based on a love of life, not just a need to survive. Even though life is by no means easy, even this far along the path of healing, I am excited about what lies ahead.

If I could give one piece of advice to the human race, apart from take care of your health, be nice to one another, and don't lose your sense of humor, it would be: keep a diary. It doesn't matter what it says, or how it says it, as long as it's honest. Nobody has to see it but you. My diary entries recorded in this book have been crucial to me in telling my story. Their most significant contribution has been to enrich my relationship with myself, and their greatest value has been as milestones, enabling me to see what was, compare it with what is, and imagine what could be.

Appendix A

Beginning Therapy

Sheri Oz

Some child sex abuse (CSA) survivors do not necessarily know what it is that they want from therapy, or, knowing, do not know how to put it into words. They are sometimes ashamed that they feel needy and are asking for help, and may be afraid of the therapeutic process into which they are venturing. Because of this many drop out between the phone call initiating therapy and the first scheduled session, and their arriving to the first session does not necessarily mean that they are committed to therapy. Because survivors find it difficult to verbalize what they are thinking and/or feeling, I help them organize their thoughts and feelings by using drawing or semi-projective tasks in the session. I will describe here two such tasks.

BEFORE-AND-AFTER DRAWING

The client is asked to fold a sheet of paper (legal size) in half and open it up so that it has a crease down the middle. He or she is asked to think about how life is now, how he or she feels and functions, and how life will be when he or she successfully completes therapy. (I always say "when you successfully complete therapy" because I don't want the client to be concerned with the question of whether or not therapy will be successful, but rather with what he or she would like his or her life to look like.)

I then say, "I would like you to draw on half the paper 'how life is now,' and on the other half 'how life will be when you successfully complete therapy.' You can draw figures or objects, something abstract, or just a play of colors."

Some examples are presented in Figures A.1, A.2, and A.3.

Overcoming Childhood Sexual Trauma
Published by The Haworth Press, Inc., 2006, All rights reserved.
doi:10.1300/5668_11

FIGURE A.1. Before-and-after drawing (female, age thirty-three). *Before:* "I am in a bubble and at the same time I feel so small and tired." *After:* "I will be near the sea, with someone I love, feeling calm."

The client (age thirty-three) who drew Figure A.1 explained that she felt unable to communicate with people and would withdraw from all kinds of interactions except those that were absolutely necessary, such as at work. She felt small and tired most of the time. She had no joy in life. Her hope for therapy was that she would eventually be able to interact with people freely and would have an inner sense of calm. She did not really believe that this was actually possible. However, in being able to discuss her current feelings and her hopes for the future, she already showed some of the people skills that she did not attribute to herself.

Figure A.2 represents the feelings of entrapment and confusion endured by the client (age twenty-six). She anticipated that working through her traumas would open her up and allow her to achieve a sense of stability and strength. She talked about having roots and at the same time being able to anticipate a future that would have meaning. She wanted to be able to marry and have children, to be productive and someone others could depend upon. The knot in the tree shows that she will never forget what happened to her. At the start of therapy, she felt that she had trapped herself in a cage as a result of the workings of her own mind. Yet she recognized the strength

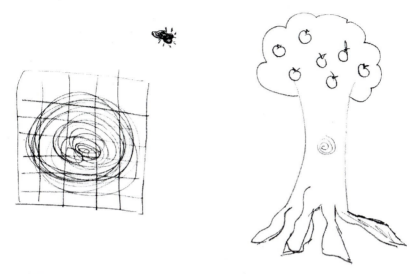

FIGURE A.2. Before-and-after drawing (female, age twenty-six). *Before:* "I am confused, everything is a muddle, and I am trapped in a cage of my own making. But there is hope, even though the sun is covered with clouds, at least I knew how to come and ask for help." *After:* "I will be strong, able to stand on my own feet, I will be able to have a family and have other people rely on me."

involved in having sought professional help and this is represented by the sun hidden by clouds in the top right corner of her drawing.

In Figure A.3, the client (age fifty) reveals her experience of herself as a shattered vase. The broken window may represent her inability to view the world clearly. Inside and out, everything is disjointed and in pieces. Because she was so emotionally overwhelmed at the beginning of therapy, we did this exercise after she had been in therapy for some time and she was able to be more introspective. She hoped that therapy would bring a sense of calm and connection, that she would feel herself to be a part of the world and that she would be order in her life. The old man climbing the hill still faces challenges but of a very different kind than she faces in her life at present. The presence of the clouds, means that her traumatic memories will not just go away, but they will no longer overwhelm her.

TWO-PHOTO COLLAGE

The client folds a sheet of paper (legal size) in half and opens it, so that it has a crease down the middle. He or she examines a journal or magazine

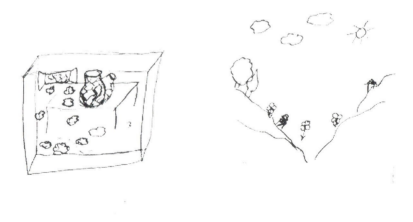

FIGURE A.3. Before-and-after drawing (female, age fifty). *Before:* "The vase fell and shattered into pieces and the window is broken also." *After:* "This is in nature, peaceful and quiet. There are hills and an old man is climbing to the top but he still has a way to go."

(I use *National Geographic*), therapeutic cards, or a collection of photos that the therapist has assembled. First, the client selects a picture that attracts his or her attention or sparks his or her interest, then he or she is asked to select a second picture that conveys a feeling very different from that aroused by the first picture. These are placed on the paper and the client is asked to write down all of his or her associations to each of the two pictures. Collages completed by the clients described in the previous section are presented in Figures A.4, A.5, and A.6.

In Figure A.4, the client (age thirty-three) showed preoccupation with the idea of peacefulness. For her, peace seemed possible only if she died. Highly dissociative, this client would sense herself disappearing in what felt like a kind of death and she yearned for true death from which she would not return. She had never experienced a "rest," a temporary respite from the pressures of daily life. Note that her picture of death has no people and her picture of rest does, similar to the "after" part of her before-and-after drawing. It seems, therefore, that for this client one major theme is being with people versus being alone.

In one of the photos of the collage in Figure A.5 the client (age twenty-six) returns to the theme of feeling trapped that she showed in her before-and-after drawing. In contrast, the other photo illustrates a sense of freedom

FIGURE A.4. Two-photo collage (Female, age thirty-three). *Left:* "To disappear, loneliness, death, peacefulness, end." *Right:* "Peacefulness, together but separate, rest."

FIGURE A.5. Two-photo collage (Female, age twenty-six). *Left:* "Darkness, trapped, suffocating, alone, secrets." *Right:* "Freedom, clean, air, light, calm, holding, infinity."

FIGURE A.6. Two-photo collage (Female, age fifty). *Left:* "Nowhere, unfeeling, wandering around aimlessly, alone, nobody there, don't owe anyone anything, from nowhere to nowhere, freedom, emptiness." *Right:* "Do feel, sadness, being with you and in your room in a corner, greyness, clouds, quiet, calm, tears."

and space. When asked how, in her life, these two different feelings find expression, she talked about the seeming permanence of the trapped feeling and how even if she goes to the beach to calm herself, the feeling of freedom is temporary, illusory, and fleeting. In spite of that, the exercise shows that this client has found on her own a safe-place tool that we introduce to many clients who do not know how to calm themselves to any degree.

The collage in Figure A.6 depicts the difference between feeling and not feeling. The client (age fifty) did this collage after having seen me for some time. She had not anticipated staying in therapy with me as she came only because a social worker insisted that she do so. Having been in therapy many times during her life, she did not think it would make much difference. However, she found that allowing me to help her connect with her feelings, gave her a sense of calm. Although she still felt a great deal of pain, she felt stronger and better able to cope with the rest of the week after having experienced and expressed her pain in session, with me to contain her. The client was surprised when I pointed out how her picture of loneliness and aimlessness had so many people in it and her picture of calm and togetherness with me had none. This opened another window for exploration of her experience of herself.

Other themes that emerge from clients' collages are control versus helplessness, safety versus danger, inside versus outside, trust versus mistrust. Some clients have trouble selecting pictures, and perhaps are unwilling to commit themselves to any particular picture, or there may be many that "speak" to them. In the former situation, the significance of declaring a choice can be an important avenue for discussion. In the latter case, all the pictures can be looked at and their associations elicited.

TIMING OF THE EXERCISES

If the client is unsure about starting therapy, I will usually do the Two-Photo Collage first. If clients are clearly motivated from the start to engage in therapy, demonstrated by discussion of their goals, their understanding of the therapy process, and/or having been in therapy before, then I begin with the Before-and-After Drawing. The Two-Photo Collage can be done at any point later in therapy.

I repeat the Two-Photo Collage at various times during therapy as it usually brings out whatever theme the client is currently preoccupied with, and it is interesting and beneficial to both of us to trace the development of his or her themes of interest.

Appendix B

Interview Questions

Sheri Oz and Sarah-Jane Ogiers invite you to participate in an ongoing study of child sex abuse (CSA) survivors and their families that may be used in future revisions of this work or in other publications. We would like to contribute to the growing understanding of what it is like to live in the shadow of the World of Trauma—for survivors, their partners, siblings, and children. We ask you to join us in this project.

Read the questions in the following pages and answer those that interest you. You do not have to answer every question. The questionnaire can also be found on Sheri Oz's Web site. You can send your answers to Sheri Oz either by e-mail or by regular mail to the addresses below. This is anonymous. Please do not sign the questionnaire.

Sheri Oz
HaRav Kook 13
26361 Kiryat Motzkin
ISRAEL
E-mail: ozsheri@netvision.net.il
Web site: www.machoneitan.org.il

THE QUESTIONNAIRE

General Information

1. Male or female?
2. What is your age?
3. Where where you born?
4. In which country do you currently reside?
5. What is your religion? Are you observant?
6. Number of siblings?
7. Years of education?
8. Average income of parents while you were growing up?

Overcoming Childhood Sexual Trauma
Published by The Haworth Press, Inc., 2006, All rights reserved.
doi:10.1300/5668_12

9. Your marital status/number of children?
10. Your current family income?
11. Are you or have you ever been in therapy? When?

For Survivors

12. Who abused you? At what age(s) were you abused?
13. Who else, if anyone, knew about the abuse at the time it happened?
14. Was the abuse reported? If so, what happened as a result?
15. Did you grow up your entire childhood in your parental home? If not, explain.
16. Were you raped or sexually harassed in adulthood? How did you function academically from elementary to high school?
17. Did you have friends growing up? If so, were you outgoing, with a lot of friends, or did you tend toward having one or two friends only?
18. Were you close to your friends or did you generally put on "an act"? Were you satisfied with your social interactions? Explain.
19. At what age did you begin puberty: First menstruation/wet dream? Appearance of pubic hair? Beginning of breast development?
20. How did you feel about the changes in your body?
21. What is your sexual orientation? At what age did you know?
22. When did you start dating?
23. Did you want to date or was it a result of pressure of some kind?
24. How did your family relate to you dating?
25. Did you ever have a steady boyfriend/girlfriend? If so, at what age?
26. At what age did you first begin consensual sexual relations: Your first kiss? First petting? First intercourse?
27. Did you feel comfortable engaging in these behaviors?
28. Can you describe your experience of your first consensual sexual intercourse?
29. Did you ever have an unplanned pregnancy? At what age? What was the outcome?
30. Did you ever contract a sexually transmitted disease? How did you deal with it?
31. Was there a period of time during which you engaged in indiscriminate sex with numerous partners? When?
32. Was there a period of time during which you abstained from sex totally? When?
33. Were you ever troubled by sexual fantasies involving children/violence/other? If so, when?
34. Are you or have you ever been married/cohabiting with a steady partner? For how long?

35. What is it about your partner that attracted you to him or her?
36. What do you think attracted your partner to you?
37. Describe your experience of emotional intimacy within the relationship.
38. What, if any, sexual problems are/were there in your relationship(s)?
39. Is your experience of sex in a committed relationship different from casual sex?
40. If you are no longer together, explain the reasons for the separation.
41. If you are together, can you explain what has maintained the relationship?
42. How many children do you have?
43. Are you raising/did you raise your children or were they raised by someone else?
44. For mothers: Describe your experiences of pregnancy, birth, and nursing.
45. For fathers: Describe how you experienced your partner's pregnancy, birth, and nursing.
46. What were your expectations of yourself as a parent before the birth of your firstborn?
47. Did the reality fit those expectations? Explain.
48. Was your experience of raising your firstborn different to that of raising later-born children? In what way(s)?
49. How do/did you experience the intimate hygienic care of your infants and toddlers?
50. What is/was the hardest thing about being a parent?
51. What is/was the easiest thing about being a parent?
52. How do/did you handle your children's sex education?
53. Do your children know you were abused? How old were they when they found out about it? How has it affected them? Your relationship with them? Their relationship with your family of origin?

If Your Parent Was Abused

If you are under eighteen, please check first with a parent, guardian, or therapist before responding to these questions.

54. Were you also a victim of sexual trauma? Childhood sexual abuse? (Did you answer the questions in the survivor section?) Acquaintance rape? Workplace harrassment?
55. How did you find out your parent was abused? How did you react to finding out?
56. Did knowing about the abuse confuse you or clarify things that previously confused you about your parent?

57. Did knowing about the abuse change what you thought about your childhood?
58. As a child, did you think your family or parent(s) were different from your friends' families? Explain.
59. Now looking back, do you think your family was or parent(s) were different from those of your childhood friends?
60. Do you feel your parent broke the "chain of abuse" that is transferred from one generation to the next?
61. Was your parent overprotective, too permissive, or just right regarding decision making, trusting others, dating, dress, responsibilities, other? Explain.
62. Was your parent demonstrative or more restrained in showing affection? Did he or she tell you he or she loves you? Did he or she show it in other ways?
63. Did your parent allow you privacy or did he or she walk into your room without knocking, read your diaries or letters, or invade your privacy in other ways?
64. Was your parent able to talk to/educate you about dating and sexual matters?
65. How open was/is your parent about what happened to him or her?
66. What is your relationship with your parent like today?
67. How do you feel about the person who abused your parent? What kind of relationship do you have with that person?
68. How do you feel about your parent's parent(s) who didn't protect your mother/father? What kind of relationship do you have today with your grandparent(s)?
69. Was your parent in therapy? What was he or she like while going through therapy? How was that period of time for you? Did your parent change as a result of therapy?
70. Were there other things in your parent's life aside from therapy that helped him or her?
71. Do you think your parent has successfully overcome the effects of having been abused as a child? What makes you say so?
72. Do you think parents should tell their children they were abused? If so, at what age do you think it is appropriate? Explain.
73. How do you think it affected your childhood/adulthood having a parent who was sexually abused in their childhood?

If Your Partner Was Abused

74. Were you also a victim of sexual trauma? Childhood sexual abuse? (Did you answer the questions in the survivor section?) Acquaintance rape? Workplace harrassment?

75. How did you find out your partner was abused? How did you react to finding out?
76. Did knowing about the abuse confuse you or clarify things that previously confused you about your partner?
77. Do you feel your partner broke the "chain of abuse" that is transferred from one generation to the next?
78. How open was/is your partner about what happened to him or her?
79. How open are you with your partner about your problems/feelings?
80. Is your partner demonstrative or more restrained in showing affection? Is he or she overly clingy? Does he or she tell you he or she loves you? Does he or she show it in other ways? How would you answer these questions regarding yourself?
81. Are there sexual problems? Can he or she discuss these openly? Can you?
82. Does your partner respect your privacy? Do you respect his or hers?
83. What is your relationship with your partner like today?
84. Is/was your partner in therapy? What is/was he or she like while going through therapy? How was/is this period of time for you? Is there a difference in your partner as a result of therapy?
85. Were there other things in your partner's life aside from therapy that helped him or her?
86. What sources of support do you have?
87. How do you feel about the person who abused your partner? What kind of relationship do you have with that person?
88. How do you feel about the nonprotective parent and other adults in your partner's family? What kind of relationships do you have with them?

If Your Sibling Was Abused

89. Were you also a victim of sexual trauma? Childhood sexual abuse? (Did you answer the questions in the survivor section?) Acquaintance rape? Workplace harassment?
90. How did you find out your sibling was abused? How did you react to finding out?
91. Did knowing about the abuse confuse you or clarify things that previously confused you about your sibling?
92. Did it explain things to you about yourself that you did not understand before?
93. Do you feel your sibling broke the "chain of abuse" that is transferred from one generation to the next? Did you?
94. What is your relationship with your sibling like today?

95. Is/was your sibling in therapy? What is/was he or she like while going through therapy? How was that period of time for you? Is there a difference in your sibling as a result of therapy?

96. Were there other things in your sibling's life aside from therapy that helped him or her?

97. Have you been in therapy? Describe how you have worked on the abuse/vicarious traumatization issues in your therapy.

98. How do you feel about the person who abused your sibling? What kind of relationship do you have with that person?

99. How do you feel about your nonprotective parent(s) and other adults in your family? What kind of relationships do you have with them?

Glossary

a priori countertransference: Attitudes of the therapist regarding a client or a type of therapy before actually beginning therapy.

a priori transference: Expectations on the part of a client regarding a therapist or type of therapeutic process based on hearsay or readings prior to beginning therapy.

borderline: Borderline personality disorder (BPD) is one in which sharp extremes exist in behavior and/or feelings. The person suffering from BPD may suddenly flip from rage to sadness or from idealizing the therapist to devaluing the therapist. Now thought to be mainly trauma based, it is important to distinguish between borderline traits and dissociative phenomena.

burnout: The therapist's experience of being worn down emotionally by the hard work of helping those who have been traumatized. In order to prevent burnout, which may lead the therapist to leave the field, the therapist should maintain a support network and engage in pleasurable activities outside of work hours.

codependence: A term that originated in the field of alcoholism and referred to spouses or children of alcoholics who denied their own personal needs to attend to the needs of the alcoholic and attempt to "cure" him or her. Today, the term refers to anyone in a relationship who denies his or her own needs or wants, feeling his or her self-esteem depends on "saving" the other person.

cognitive-behavioral therapy: Generally a brief approach to therapy which seeks to change the thought patterns that lead to problematic behaviors using specific tasks and homework assignments. Often used to help with depression and phobias.

countertransference: Refers to the feelings that the therapist has toward the client. They may be based on the therapist's early relation-

Overcoming Childhood Sexual Trauma
Published by The Haworth Press, Inc., 2006, All rights reserved.
doi:10.1300/5668_13

ships (see TRANSFERENCE), in which case the therapist needs to learn to prevent such feelings from interfering with the therapeutic work with the client. In other instances, the countertransference feelings may be in response to the work with the client and, as such, may provide more material for the therapeutic process.

DDNOS: Dissociative disorder not otherwise specified. For lack of a better term, this is a classification used to describe the great multitude of childhood sexual abuse survivors who have dissociated to a degree of having inner parts but not to the extent of DID. The experience of DDNOS is one of having thoughts or feelings that seem inconsistent with how one knows oneself, or being compelled from within to behave in ways inconsistent with how one feels. This is not a mental illness. Although no amnesia exists for present events, some childhood memories may not be accessible. This condition is sometimes confused with DID, and it is important to make an accurate diagnosis.

depersonalization: Form of dissociation in which the individual feels detached from himself or herself. This is not a mental illness. The person may feel like an observer of his or her own behaviors, thought processes, or feelings, as if watching a movie or standing behind himself or herself.

depression: It is important to distinguish between clinical depression and feeling depressed. In both cases, problems with sleep (too much or too little), low appetite, low energy levels, low self-esteem, apathy, and/or suicidal thoughts can exist. A certain degree of depression is to be expected over the course of therapy for child sexual abuse. More serious levels of depression are associated with chemical imbalances in the brain. A psychiatrist can determine whether the level of depression would be best treated with medication in addition to psychotherapy.

derealization: Form of dissociation in which the individual feels detached from his or her surroundings. This is not a mental illness. The world does not feel real. The individual may feel as if the world is a dream or movie, or as if he or she is observing it through a glass wall or fog.

DID: Dissociative identity disorder. People with DID have dissociated parts of self to the degree that many of these parts do not feel like parts of the self, but as if they are other people. This is not a mental illness. Amnesia, exists not only for childhood memories but also for present events. In the past century a great amount of fascination with DID and consequently a great amount of controversy has surrounded this diagnosis. However, the experience of DID to the sufferer includes much fear and confusion. It is important to accurately diagnose this condition, because confusion between DDNOS and DID can have serious implications on therapy. According to a previous classification system, DID was called MPD (multiple personality disorder).

dissociation: Dissociation is the experience of being disconnected either from oneself or from one's surroundings, or both. Different levels of dissociation exists, and each is defined separately in this glossary: depersonalization, derealization, DDNOS, DID. Dissociation alone is not a mental illness, but is commonly regarded as a form of psychological defense against overwhelming trauma when the individual cannot fight back or escape.

dual relationship: Therapists are not supposed to engage in any relationship with the client outside of the therapy hour. Any additional relationship during therapy is considered a dual relationship. Examples include (but are not restricted to) therapy with friends, having sexual relations with a client, consulting on business matters with a client who is expert in this area, etc. Given the possibility for exploitation of the client, the issue of dual relationships is controversial and complex and is subject to an ongoing debate in the professional literature. It is discussed in detail in Chapter 9.

dynamic psychotherapy: Also called psychodynamic therapy. A form of therapy in which the relationship between the therapist and the client is the most significant tool for change. Dynamic therapy works with transference and countertransference and projections.

EMDR: Eye movement desensitization and reprocessing (Shapiro, 1995). A technique developed for the resolution of traumatic memories, phobias, and some other psychological problems. The basic approach works well for simple one-time traumas when childhood was essentially healthy. For more chronic complicated traumas associated with childhood sexual abuse, EMDR may be a useful tool when used within a well-defined treatment plan. A helpful Web site for further information is www.emdrportal.com.

emotional numbness: The individual does not experience feelings in response to people or situations. Whereas others may be sad, angry, happy, loving, etc., the numb individual feels flat and unable to connect with any emotions.

empathic failure: Empathy is the ability to identify and understand what another person feels without taking on that feeling oneself. An empathic failure is the failure, on the part of the clinician, to understand the needs of the client at a particular time. This leaves the client feeling abandoned.

entrance ritual: Somewhat similar to an induction into a hypnotic state. The abuser somehow signals to the victim—by a phrase or a gesture—that the abuse is about to begin. The victim is triggered into a state of mind in which he or she does not feel able to resist.

exit ritual: A signal that the abuse is over. By word or gesture, the abuser signals to the victim that the abuse event is over and it is time to reenter the Shared World.

false self: A false self is the mask people present to others in order to get along in the world. As people get to know one another better, it is expected that they will be able to let their masks down to incrementally greater degrees, letting one another know their true selves more and more. For some the mask may be quite substantial and the individual may be overly compliant, afraid to speak his or her true mind out of fear he or she will not be liked. The childhood sexual abuse survivor may be so overwhelmed by feelings of guilt and shame that they are terrified to let anyone see them without their mask.

flashback: The experience of reliving an event of the past as if it is happening in the present time. Flashbacks can include any sensory modality. Some flashbacks are pictures of the event, and others consist of smells, sounds, or touch sensations. Flashback implies a negative emotional response to the experience and is usually associated with a high level of anxiety. The term *flashback* also refers to reexperiencing previous drug states, usually with hallucinogens such as LSD.

grooming: Process by which the abuser initiates the victim into the abuse. This occurs gradually and by progressively more sexual behaviors. At first, the abuser spends time with the targeted child, paying attention to him or her. When trust exists, the abuser no longer hides his or her sexual feelings. Although sensing that something has changed, the naive child does not recognize the feelings as sexual and therefore does not run away or tell anyone. Gradually, the sexual feelings turn into sexualized behavior, but by this time the child feels guilty for not having said no earlier and therefore does not feel he or she can say no to the more overt sexual acts.

group therapy: This is to be distinguished from a support group. In group therapy the participants deal with personal issues by working on relationships with one another and with the group leaders. Transference, countertransference, and projective identification are the major instruments for change.

guided imagery: Also called guided fantasy. This is a form of relaxation that allows for increased concentration and ability to notice feelings or sensations that are otherwise not attended to. It is related to hypnosis, but without the formal hypnotic induction process, and it can be used for resolution of traumatic memories or correction of cognitive errors. The most common guided imagery in trauma therapy is the safe-place imagery. Although an abundance of self-help books giving instruction to the professional and layman alike are available, this is a powerful tool and should not be attempted without attending a course with a qualified instructor.

hypervigilance: An exaggerated sensitivity to sounds or other triggers in the environment. The individual is constantly alert, expecting danger at any moment.

in vivo cognitive-behavioral therapy: In the treatment of phobias, the therapist may help the client face the feared stimulus outside of the office. Such phobias may include fear of elevators, fear of flying, fear of walking in open spaces, etc.

Kinetic HTP: (Burns, 1987). This is an adaptation of the common house-tree-person test used by psychologists in personality tests. Usually the house, tree, and person are drawn on separate pieces of paper. In kinetic HTP the three elements are drawn on the same piece of paper with the instruction that some kind of movement must be included in the drawing. Usually the person is drawn doing something, but the movement can include trees moving in the wind. Some individuals add other elements that depict movement, such as birds or a river.

Mind/body approaches: Since Wilhelm Reich began exploring the relationship between mind and body, more specifically, the impact of trauma on the mind and its expression in the body, a wide range of body-oriented approaches have emerged. These include, and are not limited to, somatic experiencing (www.traumahealing.com), sensorimotor psychotherapy (www.sensorimotorpsychotherapy.org), and movement therapy (which originated as dance therapy). Before you agree to a particular form of therapy suggested either by an acquaintance or a therapist, research it to find out if it is a bona fide therapy technique.

obsessive-compulsive disorder (OCD): A person is plagued by repetitive thoughts, urges, or behaviors over which they feel they have no control. These can include hand washing, checking that doors are locked, counting things, seeing a bizarre or disturbing image in one's mind, etc. This is a severe disturbance that is diagnosed by a psychiatrist. Treatment usually includes medication.

obsessive-compulsive symptoms: Repetitive thoughts, urges, or behaviors as noted for OCD that do not reach the level of disturbance that would be labeled as a disorder.

parallel process: Sometimes relationships or processes that occur between the therapist and client are mirrored in relationships and processes that emerge when the therapist seeks supervision, whether this is in individual or group supervision.

parentified child: When a parent is, for some reason, unable to function adequately as a parent, one or more of the offspring may take on parental roles. In such cases, children may clean the house, care for younger siblings, make meals, sober a drunk parent, console the parent, etc.

polarity rule: Refers to the state in which an individual is fixated and consistently displays behavior at one pole of a gradient regardless of the specific nature of the situation. For instance, one would hope to have the flexibility to act appropriately to a situation by taking into account one's wants and needs, the specific nature of the situation, and the kind of relationships with the people involved. Thus, one would likely find oneself moving along a gradient between extremes of behavior, sometimes behaving one way and sometimes another (such as expressing rage or apathy, laughing or crying, agreeing with others versus disagreeing with others). According to the polarity rule, no such flexibility exist, and behaviors would be consistently either one way or the other.

post-traumatic stress disorder (PTSD): A condition resulting from exposure to a traumatic event in which the individual was either personally injured or threatened with injury or was witness to the injury or threat of injury of another. About 85 percent of people exposed to serious single-event trauma recover spontaneously over a period of six months to one year. The remaining 15 percent may develop PTSD. Chronic childhood trauma leads to a greater likelihood of PTSD.

primary therapeutic relationship: The relationship between the client and his or her individual therapist. Adjunct therapy relationships may include leaders of therapy groups, a family or couples therapist, etc.

projection: A psychological process whereby thoughts or feelings of which the individual is unaware are displaced onto another person. The other person may find himself or herself acting in accordance with the projected thoughts or feelings without realizing he or she is doing so. In other cases, the person onto whom the thoughts or feelings are projected may be accused by the projector of behaving in accordance with the projection even when this is not so.

projective identification: The process by which an individual responds to the projections of others by feeling or behaving in ways consistent with the projection, and not necessarily consistent with his or her own spontaneous feelings. The term originated with respect to therapist response to clients, but it has been expanded to include all interpersonal interactions.

safe-place imagery: Using guided imagery, the therapist helps the client find an image that represents safety. The "safe place" can be a room, beach, forest, etc. It can be a place the client has actually been to or someplace the client would like to visit. Alternatively, it can be a totally imaginary place. Using the safe place, the client learns to calm the body and reduce anxiety. This is an important skill to attain before beginning any work on traumatic memories.

self-disclosure: Sharing of personal information, such as personal data (age, marital status, etc.) or feelings one has toward the other person. In therapy, the client is expected to self-disclose and the therapist is not. The use of self-disclosure on the part of the therapist is still controversial and undergoing review in the professional literature.

self-harm/self-mutilation: The practice of hurting oneself by cutting the skin with a knife, piece of glass, fingernails, etc.; extinguishing cigarettes on one's arms or legs; hitting oneself; pulling out hairs; etc. Some professionals classify eating disorders as a form of self-harm. Self-harm can have several motivations. It can calm the individual by diverting attention from anxiety and emotional distress to physical pain. Due to the release of certain hormones in the brain, it can result in a temporary sense of euphoria. It can be an expression of self-hate and punishment. Some dissociative individuals may not feel the pain of the cutting or burning, so the resulting wound may prove to them that they are alive.

semiprojective task: Exercise in which the client responds to a given stimulus in order to understand something about himself or herself. For example, the client may be asked to write down all thoughts that come to mind when viewing a picture (see Appendix A).

sexual harassment: Sexual harassment includes unwanted attention of a sexual nature that continues even after being asked to stop. This includes comments about physical appearance and romantic invitations or sexual propositions. Whether or not the comments are complimentary or derisive, they make the receiver feel uncomfortable. In many countries, sexual harassment in the workplace is against the law.

Shared World: The world of sanity. The "real" world. The victim of sexual abuse feels that two dimensions exist—the World of Trauma, in which the abuse takes place, and the Shared World, the dimension everyone else occupies all the time.

splitting: A separation into parts. Just like the world splits into two (Shared World and World of Trauma), the victim feels as if he or she splits into two or more parts—the victimized child part and a part of self that does not feel as if it experiences the abuse. The abuser likewise splits into the good loving or attentive part and the bad abusive part.

support group: This is to be distinguished from group therapy. In support groups participants share current dilemmas with the group members and help one another find new ways of coping. The benefits of participation are accrued from the social support as opposed to the deeper psychological change sought in group therapy.

support system: The individuals that can be relied upon to provide emotional or technical support as needed. Emotional support can be provided by talking, listening, or offering a safe place to rest. Technical support might include keeping the house clean, making meals, looking after children, etc.

therapy frame: The boundaries that define a relationship as therapeutic. These boundaries are determined by time and space—the place in which the therapy takes place and the length and frequency of sessions.

TIR: Traumatic incident reduction (French and Harris, 1999). A form of exposure therapy that consists of having the client repeatedly review the traumatic event that he or she is interested in resolving. Sessions are not time limited and proceed until the client reaches a point of resolution marked by three criteria: (1) the event is experienced as having happened in the past, (2) the client is obviously relaxed and relieved of the negative emotional charge previously associated with the memory, and (3) the client has reached a new cognitive understanding of the event or its context. The therapist, who provides a safe milieu within which to process the trauma, offers no interpretation and all insights originate from within the client. A helpful Web site for more information is www.tirtraining.com.

transference: The way people relate to others according to patterns that were laid down in their relationships with their earliest caretakers (usually their parents). In other words, they "transfer" feelings from those early relationships to later ones, sometimes even in contradiction to the personalities and behaviors of those with whom they interact. In the therapy relationship the word *transference* refers to the process by which the client relates to the therapist in accordance with the patterns that were established in early childhood. When transference feelings are recognized they can be reworked, if necessary, so that the client can establish new interpersonal patterns that may be more appropriate for current life.

trauma resolution: This involves reducing the negative emotional charge associated with traumatic memories such that recall of traumatic events does not result in flashbacks. The individual feels the trauma is in his or her past and that decisions in the present time are based on current needs and no longer driven by patterns that resulted from the traumatic events.

traumatic transference: A transference reaction in which the client behaves toward the therapist as if the therapist was the abuser.

trigger: A stimulus that, while the abuse is still going on, serves as an induction into the World of Trauma. In other situations, triggers are stimuli that, in some way, remind the victim of the abuse, and result in a flashback.

vicarious traumatization: When a person feels traumatized, not by having experienced a trauma firsthand but as a result of close association with someone else who has. It is not clear if this form of trauma results from unconscious "projection" of the trauma or from the inability to anticipate the survivor's reactions. Because the survivor's reactions are sometimes disproportional to the situation, those close to the survivor are in a constant state of alert. Therapists, children, and partners of individuals with PTSD can be vicariously traumatized.

Wall of Fear: A stage of therapy during which the client feels overwhelmed by fear and/or anxiety. An urge exists to continue forward and face the fear, but the client feels as if he or she must break through a wall or jump off a cliff into an unknown state.

World of Trauma: Term denoting the experience of the victim during the sexual abuse event. The abuse appears to take place in a different dimension from the rest of the world, something like a twilight zone in which time does not seem to exist.

References

Abraham, G. (2002). The psychodynamics of orgasm. *International Journal of Psychoanalysis 83:* 325-338.

Abraham, S. (1997). Revenge: A dish best served cold. A personal story. Available at: www.menweb.org/scottrev.htm.

Adelman, A. (1995). Traumatic memory and the intergenerational transmission of Holocaust narratives. *Psychoanalytic Study of the Child 50:* 343-367.

Ahrens, C.E. and R. Campbell. (2000). Assisting rape victims as they recover from rape: The impact on friends. *Journal of Interpersonal Violence 15:* 959-986.

Akhtar, S. (2002). Forgiveness: Origins, dynamics, psychopathology, and technical relevance. *Psychoanalytic Quarterly 71:* 175-212.

Alexander, P.C., Teti, L., and C.L. Anderson. (2000). Childhood sexual abuse history and role reversal in parenting. *Child Abuse and Neglect 24:* 829-838.

American Psychological Association. (2002). Ethical principles of psychologists and code of conduct. APA online. Available at: www.apa.org/ethics/code2002 .html.

Appelbaum, P.S. and R. Zoltek-Jick. (1996). Psychotherapists' duties to third parties: Ramona and beyond. *American Journal of Psychiatry 153:* 457-465.

Aron, L. (2000). Ethical considerations in the writing of psychoanalytic case histories. *Psychoanalytic Dialogues 10:* 231-245.

Auerbach, Y. (2004). The role of forgiveness in reconciliation. In: Bar-Siman-Tov, Y. (Ed.), *From conflict resolution to reconciliation* (pp. 149-175). New York: Oxford University Press.

Auerhahn, N.C. and D. Laub. (1998). Intergenerational memory of the Holocaust. In Danieli, Y. (Ed.), *International handbook of multigenerational legacies of trauma* (pp. 21-41). New York: Plenum Press.

Axelsen, E. and S. Bakke. (1991). *Travel back in time.* Oslo, Norway: Pax. [In Norwegian.]

Bacon, B. and L. Lein. (1996). Living with a female sexual abuse survivor: Male partners' perspectives. *Journal of Child Sexual Abuse 5:* 1-16.

Baider, L., Peretz, T., Hadani, P.E., Perry, S., Avramov, R., and A. Kaplan De-Nour. (2000). Transmission of response to trauma? Second-generation Holocaust survivors' reaction to cancer. *American Journal of Psychiatry 157:* 904-910.

Banyard, V.L. (1997). The impact of childhood sexual abuse and family functioning on four dimensions of women's later parenting. *Child Abuse & Neglect 21:* 1095-1107.

Overcoming Childhood Sexual Trauma
Published by The Haworth Press, Inc., 2006, All rights reserved.
doi:10.1300/5668_14

Banyard, V.L., Williams, L.M., and J.A. Siegel. (2003). The impact of complex trauma and depression on parenting: An exploration of mediating risk and protective factors. *Child Maltreatment* 8: 334-349.

Barcus, R. (1997). Partners of survivors of abuse: A men's therapy group. *Psychotherapy* 34: 316-323.

Barnes, M. and J. Berke. (2002). *Mary Barnes: Two accounts of a journey through madness*. New York: Other Press.

Bar-On, D., Eland, J., Kleber, R.J., Krell, R., Moore, Y., Sagi, A., Soriano, E., Suedfeld, P., van der Velden, P.G. and M.H. van Ijendoorn. (1998). Multigenerational perspectives on coping with the Holocaust experience: An attachment perspective for understanding the developmental sequelae of trauma across generations. *International Journal of Behavioral Development* 22: 315-338.

Barrett, M.J. (2003). Constructing the third reality. *Psychotherapy Networker* 27: 45-49, 61.

Barrett, M.S. and J.S. Berman. (2001). Is psychotherapy more effective when therapists disclose information about themselves? *Journal of Consulting and Clinical Psychology* 69: 597-603.

Barton, C.K.B. (1999). *Getting even: Revenge as a form of justice*. Chicago, IL: Open Court Publishers.

Bass, E. and L. Davis. (1988). *The courage to heal*. New York: HarperPerennial.

Benatar, M. (2000). A qualitative study of the effect of a history of childhood sexual abuse on therapists who treat survivors of sexual abuse. *Journal of Trauma & Dissociation* 1: 9-28.

Benjamin, L.R., Benjamin, R., and B. Rind. (1996). Dissociative mothers' subjective experience of parenting. *Child Abuse & Neglect* 20: 933-942.

Bennett-Levy, J. (2006). Therapist skills: A cognitive model of their acquisition and refinement. *Behavioural and Cognitive Psychotherapy* 34: 57-78.

Bergman, Z. and Sarah. (1998). *Love is not a knife*. Tel Aviv: Yedioth Ahronot Press. [In Hebrew.]

Birnbaum, L. and Birnbaum, A. (2005). The technique of guided mindfulness meditation in suicide. In Merrick, J. and G. Zalsman (Eds.), *Suicidal Behavior in Adolescence* (pp. 331-348). London: Freund.

Blatt, S.J. (2001). Commentary: The therapeutic process and professional boundary guidelines. *Journal of the American Academy of Psychiatry Law* 29: 290-293.

Blume, E.S. (1990). *Secret survivors: Uncovering incest and its aftereffects in women*. New York: John Wiley & Sons.

Boszormenyi-Nagy, I. and G.M. Spark. (1984). *Invisible loyalties: Reciprocity in intergenerational family therapy*. New York: Brunner/Mazel.

Brady, J.L., Guy, J.D., Peolstra, P.L., and B.F. Brokaw. (1999). Vicarious traumatization, spirituality, and the treatment of sexual abuse survivors: A national survey of women psychotherapists. *Professional Psychology: Research and Practice* 30: 386-393.

Bramblett, J.R. and C.A. Darling. (1997). Sexual contacts: Experiences, thoughts, and fantasies of adult male survivors of child sexual abuse. *Journal of Sex & Marital Therapy 23:* 305-316.

Breckenridge, K. (2000). Physical touch in psychoanalysis: A closet phenomenon? *Psychoanalytic Inquiry 20:* 2-20.

Briere, J. (2002). Treating adult survivors of severe childhood abuse and neglect: Further development of an integrative model. In Myers, J.E.B., Berliner, L., Briere, J., Hendrix, C.T. Reid, T. and J. Jenny (Eds.), *The APSAC handbook on child maltreatment,* Second Edition (pp. 175-202). Newbury Park, CA: Sage Publications. Available at: http://www.johnbriere.com/STM.pdf.

Briere, J. and D.M. Elliot. (2003). Prevalence and psychological sequelae of self-reported childhood physical and sexual abuse in a general population sample of men and women. *Child Abuse & Neglect 27:* 1205-1222.

Briere, J. and E. Gil. (1998). Self-mutilation in clinical and general population samples: Prevalence, correlates, and functions. *American Journal of Orthopsychiatry 68:* 609-620.

Bross, D.C. (2005). Minimizing risks to children when they access the World Wide Web. *Child Abuse & Neglect 29:* 749-752.

Brown, J., Cohen, P., Chen, H., Smailes, E., and J.G. Johnson. (2004). Sexual trajectories of abused and neglected youths. *Journal of Developmental & Behavioral Pediatrics 25:* 77-82.

Brown, J., Cohen, P., Johnson, J.G., and E.M. Smailes. (1999). Childhood abuse and neglect: Specificity of effects on adolescent and young adult depression and suicidality. *Journal of the American Academy of Child & Adolescent Psychiatry 38:* 1490-1496.

Brown, L.S. (1994). Boundaries in feminist therapy: A conceptual formulation. *Women & Therapy 15:* 29-38.

Bryant, D. and J. Kessler. (1996). *Beyond integration: One multiple's journey.* New York: W.W. Norton & Co.

Buchanan, A. (1998). Intergenerational child maltreatment. In Danieli, Y. (Ed.), *International handbook of multigenerational legacies of trauma* (pp. 535-552). New York: Plenum Press.

Buist, A. (1998). Childhood abuse, parenting and postpartum depression. *Australian and New Zealand Journal of Psychiatry 32:* 479-487.

Burkett, L.P. (1991). Parenting behaviors of women who were sexually abused as children in their families of origin. *Family Process 30:* 421-434.

Burns, R.C. (1987). *Kinetic-house-tree-person drawings (K-H-T-P): An interpretive manual.* New York: Brunner/Mazel.

Buttenheim, M. and A. Levendosky. (1994). Couples treatment for incest survivors *Psychotherapy 34:* 316-323.

Button, B. and A. Dietz. (1995). Strengthening the heartline: Working with adult survivors of childhood sexual abuse and their partners. In Hunter, M. (Ed.), *Adult survivors of sexual abuse: Treatment innovations* (pp. 136-153). Thousand Oaks, CA: Sage Publications.

Cameron, C. (1994). Women survivors confronting their abusers: Issues, decision, and outcomes. *Journal of Child Sexual Abuse 3:* 7-35.

Carbonnell, J.L. and C. Figley. (1999). Promising PTSD approaches: A systematic clinical demonstration of promising PTSD treatment approaches. *Traumatology 5.* Available at: www.fsu.edu/~trauma/promising.html. Accessed September 3, 2005.

Casement, P. (1995). *On learning from the patient.* London: Routledge.

Caspar, F., Grossmann, C., Unmüssig, C. and E. Schramm. (2005). Complementary therapeutic relationship: Therapist behavior, interpersonal patterns, and therapeutic effects. *Psychotherapy Research 15:* 91-102.

Cavanaugh-Johnson, T. (1988). Child perpetrators: Children who molest children. *Child Abuse & Neglect 12:* 219-230.

Celenza, A. and G.O. Gabbard. (2003). Analysts who commit sexual boundary violations: A lost cause? *Journal of the American Psychoanalytic Association 51:* 617-636.

Chambless, D.L., Baker, M.J., Baucom, D.H., Beutler, L.E., Calhoun, K.S., Critz-Christoph, P., Daiuto, A., DeRubeis, R., Detweiler, J., Haaga, D.A.F. et al., (1998). Update on empirically validated therapies, II. *The Clinical Psychologist 51:* 3-16.

Chauncey, S. (1994). Emotional concerns and treatment of male partners of female sexual abuse survivors. *Social Work 39:* 669-676.

Clarkson, P. (1987). The bystander role. *Transactional Analysis Journal 17:* 82-87.

Cleese, J. and R. Skynner. (1996). *Life and how to survive it.* New York: W.W. Norton & Co.

Cohen, E. (2003). *Playing hard at life: A relational approach to treating multiply traumatized adolescents.* Hillsdale, NJ: The Analytic Press.

Cohen, T. (1995). Motherhood among incest survivors. *Child Abuse & Neglect 19:* 1423-1429.

Cole, P.M., Woolger, C., Power, T.G., and K.D. Smith. (1992). Parenting difficulties among adult survivors of father-daughter incest. *Child Abuse & Neglect 16:* 239-249.

Coleman, P.W. (1998). The process of forgiveness in marriage and the family. In Enright, R.D. and J. North (Eds.), *Exploring forgiveness* (pp. 75-94). Madison, WI: The University of Wisconsin Press.

Collin-Vezina, D. and M. Cyr. (2003). La transmission de la violence sexuelle: description du phenomene et pistes de comprehension. *Child Abuse & Neglect 27:* 489-507.

Courtois, C.A. (1988). *Healing the incest wound: Adult survivors in therapy.* New York: W.W. Norton & Co.

Courtois, C.A. (1999). *Recollections of sexual abuse. Treatment principles and guidelines.* New York: W.W. Norton & Co.

Coyle, C. T. and R.D. Enright. (1997). Forgiveness intervention with post-abortion men. *Journal of Consulting and Clinical Psychology 65:* 1042-1046.

Cunningham, M. (1999). The impact of sexual abuse treatment on the social work clinician. *Child and Adolescent Social Work Journal 16:* 277-290.

Curnoe, S. and R. Langevin. (2002). Personality and deviant sexual fantasies: An examination of the MMPIs of sex offenders. *Journal of Clinical Psychology 58:* 803-815.

Curtis, J.M. (1981). Indications and contraindications in the use of therapist's self-disclosure. *Psychological Reports 49:* 499-507.

Dalenberg, C.J. (2000). *Countertransference and the treatment of trauma.* Washington DC: American Psychological Association.

Danieli, Y. (1998). Conclusions and future directions. In Danieli, Y. (Ed.), *International handbook of multigenerational legacies of trauma* (pp. 669-689). New York: Plenum Press.

Davies, J.M. (1994). Love in the afternoon: A relational reconsideration of desire and dread in the countertransference. *Psychoanalytic Dialogues 4:* 153-170.

Davies, J.M. (1998). Between the disclosure and foreclosure of erotic transference-countertransference: Can psychoanalysis find a place for adult sexuality? *Psychoanalytic Dialogues 8:* 747-766.

Davies, J.M. and M.G. Frawley. (1994). *Treating the adult survivor of childhood sexual abuse: A psychoanalytic perspective.* New York: Basic Books.

Davis, L. (1991). *Allies in healing: When the person you love was sexually abused as a child.* New York: HarperPerennial.

Davis. L. (2002). *I thought we'd never speak again: The road from estrangement to reconciliation.* New York: HarperCollins.

Davis, L. (2003). Four types of reconciliation. *Psychotherapy Networker 27:* 41.

Dicks, H. (1967). *Marital tensions.* New York: Basic Books.

DiLillo, D. (2001). Interpersonal functioning among women reporting a history of childhood sexual abuse: Empirical findings and methodological issues. *Clinical Psychology Review 21:* 553-576.

DiLillo, D. and A. Damashek. (2003). Parenting characteristics of women reporting a history of childhood sexual abuse. *Child Maltreatment 8:* 319-333.

DiLillo, D. and P.J. Long. (1999). Perceptions of couples functioning among female survivors of child sexual abuse. *Journal of Child Sexual Abuse 7:* 59-76.

DiLillo, D., Tremblay, G.C. and L. Peterson. (2000). Linking childhood sexual abuse and abusive parenting: The mediating role of maternal anger. *Child Abuse & Neglect 24:* 767-779.

Dolan, Y.M. (1991). *Resolving sexual abuse: Solution-focused therapy and Ericksonian hypnosis for adult survivors.* New York: W.W. Norton & Co.

Douglas, A.R. (2000). Reported anxieties concerning intimate parenting in women sexualy abused as children. *Child Abuse & Neglect 24:* 425-434.

Dubowitz, H., Black, M.M., Kerr, M.A., Hussey, J.M., Morrel, T.M., Everson, M.D., and R.H. Starr Jr. (2001). Type and timing of mothers' victimization: Effects on mothers and children. *Pediatrics 107:* 728-735.

Duhl, L. (1999). Confessions of a psychotherapist. *Bulletin of the Menninger Clinic 63:* 538-546.

Edmond, T. and A. Rubin. (2004). Assessing the long-term effects of EMDR: Results from an 18-month follow-up study with adult female survivors of CSA. *Journal of Child Sexual Abuse 13:* 69-86.

Elliott, D.M. and J. Briere. (1995). Transference and countertransference. In Classen, C. (Ed.), *Treating women molested in childhood* (pp. 187-226). San Francisco: Jossey-Bass.

Enright, R.D. and C.T. Coyle. (1998). Researching the process model of forgiveness within psychological interventions. In Worthington, E.L., Jr. (Ed.), *Dimensions of forgiveness: Psychological research and theological perspectives* (pp. 139-161). Philadelphia: Templeton Foundation Press.

Erez, E. (1991). *Victim impact statements.* Canberra, Australia: Australia Institute of Criminology.

Exline, J.J., Baumeister, R.F., Bushman, B.J., Campbell, W.K., and E.J. Finkel. (2004). Too proud to let go: Narcissistic entitlement as a barrier to forgiveness. *Journal of Personality and Social Psychology 87:* 894-912.

Exline, J.J., Ciarocco, N. and R.F. Baumeister. (2001). *Forgive and Regret? Misgivings in the Wake of Forgiveness and Apology.* Poster session presented at a meeting of the Society for Personality and Social Psychology, February 3, San Antonio, TX.

Exline, J.J., Worthington, E.L., Hill, P. and M.E. McCullough. (2003). Forgiveness and justice: A research agenda for social and personality psychology. *Personality and Social Psychology Review 7:* 337-348.

Fagan, M. (1995). *Adult male survivors of childhood sexual abuse: Was confronting your perpetrator beneficial?* Unpublished master's thesis, State University of New York at Stony Brook, Stony Brook, NY.

Feldman-Summers, S. and K.S. Pope. (1994). The experience of "forgetting" childhood abuse: A national survey of psychologists. *Journal of Consulting and Clinical Psychology 62:* 636-639.

Felsen, I. (1998). Transgenerational transmission of effects of the Holocaust: The North American research perspective. In Danieli, Y. (Ed.), *International handbook of multigenerational legacies of trauma* (pp. 43-68). New York: Plenum Press.

Fine, M. and J.E. Norris. (1989). Intergenerational relations and family therapy research: What we can learn from other disciplines. *Family Process 28:* 301-315.

Finkelhor, D. (1984). *Child sexual abuse: New theory and research.* New York: Free Press.

Finkelhor, D., Hotaling, G., Lewish, I.A., and C. Smith. (1990). Sexual abuse in a national survey of adult men and women: Prevalence, characteristics, and risk factors. *Child Abuse & Neglect 14:* 19-28.

Fitzgerald, M.M., Shipman, K.L., Jackson, J.L., McMahon, R.J., and H.M. Hanley. (2005). Perceptions of parenting versus parent-child interactions among incest survivors. *Child Abuse & Neglect 29:* 661-681.

Flanigan, B. (1998). Forgivers and the unforgivable. In Enright, R.D. and J. North (Eds.), *Exploring forgiveness* (pp. 95-105). Madison, WI: The University of Wisconsin Press.

Fleming, J.M. (1997). Prevalence of childhood sexual abuse in a community sample of Australian women. *The Medical Journal of Australia 166:* 65-68.

Follette, V.M. and J. Pistorello. (1995). Couples therapy. In Classen, C. (Eds.), *Treating Women Molested in Childhood* (pp. 129-161). San Francisco: Jossey-Bass.

Follette, V.M., Polusny, M.M. and K. Milbeck. (1994). Mental health and law enforcement professionals: Trauma history, psychological symptoms, and impact of providing services to child sexual abuse survivors. *Professional Psychology, Research and Practice 25:* 275-282.

Fonagy, P. and M. Target. (2004). Playing with the reality of analytic love. Commentary on paper by Jody Messler Davies "Falling in love with love." *Psychoanalytic Dialogues 14:* 503-515.

Fosshage, J.L. (2000). The meanings of touch in psychoanalysis: A time for reassessment. *Psychoanalytic Inquiry 20:* 21-43.

Fraiberg, S. (1959). *The magic years.* New York: Charles Scribner's Sons.

Frawley-O'Dea, M.G. (2004). Selecting a therapist. Available at: www.snapnetwork .org/links_homepage/finding_therapist.htm. Accessed September 2, 2005.

Freedman, S. (1999). A voice of forgiveness: One incest survivor's experience forgiving her father. *Journal of Family Psychotherapy 10:* 37-60.

Freedman, S.R. and R.D. Enright. (1996). Forgiveness as an intervention goal with incest survivors. *Journal of Consulting and Clinical Psychology 64:* 983-992.

French, G.D. and C.J. Harris. (1999). *Traumatic incident reduction (TIR).* Boca Raton, FL: CRC Press.

Freshwater, K., Aiscough, C., and K. Toon. (2002). Confronting abuser: The opinions of clinicians and survivors. *Journal of Child Sexual Abuse 11:* 35-52.

Freyd, J.J. (1996). *Beyond betrayal: The logic of forgetting childhood abuse.* Cambridge, MA: Harvard University Press.

Furniss, T. (1991). *The multiprofessional handbook of child sexual abuse: Integrated management, therapy, and legal intervention.* London: Routledge.

Gabbard, G.O. (2001). Commentary: Boundaries, culture, and psychotherapy. *Journal of the American Academy of Psychiatry Law 29:* 284-286.

Gampel, Y. (1992). Thoughts about the transmission of conscious and unconscious knowledge to the generation born after the Shoah. *Journal of Social Work and Policy in Israel 5-6:* 43-50.

Gavish, R. (2006). Selection of a therapist: The client's perspective. Manuscript in preparation.

Geert, A.C., Vervaeke, H., and G.S. Vertommen. (1997). Client and therapist values in relation to drop-out. *Clinical Psychology & Psychotherapy 4:* 1-6.

Getzler-Yosef, R. (2005). *Dialogues of mothers who were sexually abused during childhood with the children: The correlation with trauma resolution.* Unpublished master's thesis. University of Haifa. Haifa, Israel.

Gottlieb, M.C. (1993). Avoiding exploitive dual relationships: A decision-making model. *Psychotherapy 30:* 41-48.

Gold, S.M., Lucenko, B.A. Elhai, J.D., Swingle, J.M., and A.H. Sellers. (1999). A comparison of psychological/psychiatric symptomology of women and men sexually abused as children. *Child Abuse & Neglect 23:* 683-692.

Grocke, M., Smith, M., and P. Graham. (1995). Sexually abused and nonabused mothers' discussions about sex and their children's sexual knowledge. *Child Abuse & Neglect 19:* 985-996.

Group for the Advancement of Psychiatry. (2001). Reexamination of therapist self-disclosure. *Psychiatric Services 52:* 1489-1493.

Grubrich-Simitis, I. (1981). Extreme traumatization as cumulative trauma: Psychoanalytic investigation of the effects of concentration camp experiences on survivors and their children. *The Psychoanalytic Study of the Child 36:* 415-450.

Grubrich-Simitis, I. (1984). From concretism to metaphor: Thoughts on some theoretical and technical aspects of the psychoanalytic work with children of Holocaust survivors. *The Psychoanalytic Study of the Child 39:* 301-319.

Gutheil, T.G. and G.O. Gabbard. (1993). The concept of boundaries in clinical practice: Theoretical and risk-management directions. *American Journal of Psychiatry 150:* 188-196.

Gutheil, T.G. and G.O. Gabbard. (2003). Misuses and misunderstandings of boundary theory in clinical and regulatory settings. *Focus 1:* 415-421.

Haaken, J. and A. Schlaps. (1991). Incest resolution therapy and the objectification of sexual abuse. *Psychotherapy 28:* 39-47.

Haines, J. and C.L. Williams. (1997). Coping and problem solving of self-mutilators. *Journal of Clinical Psychology 53:* 177-186.

Halperin, D.S., Bouvier, P., Jaffe, P.D., Mounoud, R.L., Pawlak, C.H., Laederach, J., Wicky, H.R., and F. Astie. (1996). Prevalence of child sexual abuse among adolescents in Geneva: Results of a cross sectional survey. *British Medical Journal 312:* 1326-1329.

Hansen, P.A. (1991). *Survivors and Partners-Healing Relationships After Sexual Abuse.* Longmont, CO: Heron Hill Publishing Co.

Harper, K. and J. Steadman. (2003). Therapeutic boundary issues in working with childhood sexual-abuse survivors. *American Journal of Psychotherapy 57:* 64-79.

Haugaard, J.J. (2000). The challenge of defining child sexual abuse. *American Psychologist 55:* 1036-1039.

Hayez, J.Y. (2002). La confrontation des enfants et des adolescents à la porno-graphie *Archives de pediatrie 9:* 1183-1188.

Henry, W.P. (1998). Science, politics, and the politics of science: The use and misuse of empirically validated treatment research. *Psychotherapy Research 8:* 126-140.

Herman, J.L. (1981). *Father-daughter incest.* Cambridge, MA: Harvard University Press.

Herman, J.L. (1992). *Trauma and recovery. The aftermath of violence—from domestic abuse to political terror.* New York: Basic Books.

Herman-Giddens, M.E., Sandler, A.D., and N.E. Friedman. (1988). Sexual precocity in girls: An association with sexual abuse? *Archives of Pediatrics & Adolescent Medicine 142:* 431-433

Hersoug, A.G., Høglend, P., Monsen, J.T., and Havik, O.E. (2001). Quality of working alliance in psychotherapy: Therapist variables and patient/therapist siilarity as predictors. *Journal of Psychothery Practice and Research 10:* 205-216.

Herzog, J.M. (1981). The aging survivor of the Holocaust. Father Hurt and Father Hunger: The effect of a survivor father's waning years on his son. *Journal of Geriatric Psychiatry 14:* 211-223.

Hiebert-Murphy, D. (1998). Emotional distress among mothers whose children have been sexually abused: The role of a history of child sexual abuse, social support, and coping. *Child Abuse & Neglect 22:* 423-435.

Hogman, F. (1998). Trauma and identity through two generations of the Holocaust. *Psychoanalytic Review 84:* 551-578.

Hooper, C. (1992). *Mothers surviving child sexual abuse.* London: Tavistock/ Routledge.

Howell, E.F. (2002). "Good girls," sexy "bad girls," and warriors: The role of trauma and dissociation in the creation and reproduction of gender. *Journal of Trauma & Dissociation 3:* 5-32.

Howitt, D. (2004). What is the role of fantasy in sex offending? *Criminal Behaviour in Mental Health 14:* 182-188.

Johnson, P. (2001). In their own voices: Report of a study on the later effects of child sexual abuse. *Journal of Sexual Aggression 7:* 41-56.

Johnson, S.M. and L. Williams-Keeler. (1998). Creating healing relationships for couples dealing with trauma: The use of emotionally focused marital therapy. *Journal of Marital and Family Therapy 24:* 25-40.

Joyce, A.S. and W.E. Piper. (1998). Expectancy, the therapeutic alliance, and treatment outcome in short-term individual psychotherapy. *Journal of Psychotherapy Practice and Research 7:* 236-248.

Karpman, S. (1968). Fairy tales and script drama analysis. *Transactional Analysis Bulletin 7:* 39-43.

Katsavdakis, K.A., Gabbard, G.O., and G.I. Athey Jr. (2004). Profiles of impaired health professionals. *Bulletin of the Menninger Clinic 68:* 60-72.

Katz, J., Street, A., and I. Arias. (1997). Individual differences in self-appraisals and responses to dating violence scenarios. *Violence and Victims 12:* 265-276.

Kearns, J.N. and F.D. Fincham. (2004). A prototype analysis of forgiveness. *Personality and Social Psychology Bulletin 30:* 838-855.

Keating, J. and R. Over. (1990). Sexual fantasies of heterosexual and homosexual men. *Archives of Sexual Behavior 19:* 461-475.

Kellerman, N.P.F. (2001a). Psychopathology in children of Holocaust survivors: A review of the research literature. *Israel Journal of Psychiatry & Related Sciences 38:* 36-46.

Kellerman, N.P.F. (2001b). Transmission of Holocaust trauma—An integrative view. *Psychiatry 64:* 256-267.

Kendall-Tackett, K. (1998). Breastfeeding and the sexual abuse survivor. *Breastfeeding Abstracts 17:* 27-28. Available at: www.lalecheleague.org/ba/May98 .html. Retrieved August 2005.

Kirschner, S. and D.A. Kirschner. (1996). Relational components of the incest survivor syndrome. In Kaslow, F.W. (Ed.), *Handbook of relational diagnosis and dysfunctional family patterns* (pp. 407-419). New York: John Wiley & Sons.

Kiselica, M.S. (2003). Transforming psychotherapy in order to succeed with adolescent boys: Male-friendly practices. *Journal of Clinical Psychology 59:* 1225-1236.

Kluft, R.P. (1987). The parental fitness of mothers with multiples personality disorder: A preliminary study. *Child Abuse & Neglect 11:* 273-280.

Knight, C. (1997). The use of self-disclosure by the therapist in the treatment of adult survivors of child sexual abuse. *Journal of Child Sexual Abuse 6:* 65-82.

Kogan, I. (1992). Discussion of "the impact of the Holocaust on the second generation" by Dinora Pines. *Journal of Social Work and Policy in Israel 5-6:* 115-121.

Koren-Karie, N., Oppenheim, D., and R. Getzler-Yosef. (2004). Mothers who were severely abused during childhood and their children talk about emotions: Co-construction of narratives in light of maternal trauma. *Infant Mental Health Journal 24:* 300-317.

Kroll, J. (2001). Boundary violations: A culture-bound syndrome. *Journal of the American Academy of Psychiatry & Law 29:* 274-283.

Lamb, S. and M. Coakley. (1993). "Normal" childhood sexual play and games: Differentiating play from abuse. *Child Abuse & Neglect 17:* 515-526.

Lambert, M.J. and D.E. Barley. (2001). Research summary on the therapeutic relationship and psychotherapy outcome. *Psychotherapy, 38:* 357-361.

Lampropoulos, G.K. (2000). Evolving psychotherapy integration: Eclectic selection and prescriptive applications of common factors in therapy. *Psychotherapy 37:* 285-297.

Leifer, M., Kilbane, T., and S. Kalllick. (2004). Vulnerability or resilience to intergenerational sexual abuse: The role of maternal factors. *Child Maltreatment 9:* 78-91.

Levine, D.P. (1999). The problem of character and the capacity for ethical conduct. Originally published as "The capacity for ethical conduct" in *Psychoanalytic Studies 1:* 1. Available at: www.du.edu/~dlevine/Ethical%20Conduct.doc. Retrieved January 2005.

Lew, M. (1988). *Victims no longer: Men recovering from incest and other childhood sexual abuse.* New York: Nevraumont Publishing Co.

Liotti, G. (1992). Disorganized/disoriented attachment in the etiology of the dissociative disorders. *Dissociation 4:* 196-204.

Little, L. and S.L. Hamby. (1996). Impact of a clinician's sexual abuse history, gender, and theoretical orientation on treatment issues related to childhood sexual abuse. *Professional Psychology: Research and Practice 27:* 617-625.

Mallow, A.J. (1998). Self-disclosure: Reconciling psychoanalytic psychotherapy and alcoholics anonymous philosophy. *Journal of Substance Abuse Treatment 15:* 493-498.

Malone, S.B., Reed, M.R., Norbeck, J., Hindsman, R.L., and F.E. Knowles III. (2004). Development of a training module on therapeutic boundaries for mental health clinicians and case managers. *Lippincott's Case Management 9:* 197-202.

Maltas, C. and J. Shay. (1995). Trauma contagion in partners of survivors of childhood sexual abuse. *American Journal of Orthopsychiatry 65:* 529-539.

Maltz, W. (2001). *The sexual healing journey: A guide for survivors of sexual abuse,* Revised edition. New York: Perennial Currents.

Marazziti, D. and D. Canale. (2004). Hormonal changes when falling in love. *Psychoneuroendocrinology 29:* 931-936.

Maroda, K.J. (1999). *Seduction, surrender, and transformation. Emotional engagement in the analytic process.* Hillsdale, NJ: The Analytic Press.

Mather, C.L. and K.E. Debye. (1994). *How long does it hurt? A guide to recovering from incest and sexual abuse for teenagers, their friends, and their families.* San Francisco: Jossey-Bass.

Mazhar, U. (2005). Rape and incest: Islamic perspective. Available at: http://www.crescentlife.com/articles/islamic%20psych/rape_and_incest_islamic_perspective.htm. Retrieved April 24, 2005.

McCann, L. and L. Pearlman. (1990a). *Psychological trauma and the adult survivor: Theory, therapy, and transformation.* New York: Brunner/Mazel.

McCann, L. and L. Pearlman. (1990b). Vicarious traumatization: A framework for understanding the psychological effects of working with victims. *Journal of Traumatic Stress 3:* 131-149.

McCollum, E.E. (1993). The effects of recovery from childhood sexual abuse on marital relationships: A multiple case report. *Journal of Family Psychotherapy 4:* 35-46.

McCullough, M.E., Gincham, F.D., and J. Tsang. (2003). Forgiveness, forbearance, and time: The temporal unfolding of transgression-related interpersonal motivations. *Journal of Personality and Social Psychology 84:* 540-557.

McCullough, M.E., Pargament, K.I., and C.E. Thoresen. (1999). The psychology of forgiveness. History, conceptual issues, and overview. In McCullough, M.E., Pargament, K.I., and C.E. Thoresen (Eds.), *Forgiveness: Theory, research, and practice* (pp. 1-14). New York: The Guilford Press.

McKinzie, S. (2000). *Standing in the truth: A phenomenological investigation of women's experience of confronting a childhood sexual abuse perpetrator.* Unpublished doctoral dissertation, Union Institute and University, Cincinnati, Ohio.

Miller, A. (1994). *The drama of the gifted child: The search for the true self,* Revised edition. New York: Basic Books.

Miller, S., Wachman, D., Nunnally, E., and P. Miller. (1988). *Connecting with self and other.* Littleton, CO: Interpersonal Communication Programs.

Moleski, S.M. and M.S. Kiselica. (2005). Dual relationships: A continuum ranging from the destructive to the therapeutic. *Journal of Counseling & Development 83:* 3-11.

Mook, J., Schreuder, B.J.N., van der Ploeg, H., Bramsen, I. van Tiel-Kadiks, G.W., and W. Feenstra. (1997). Psychological complaints and characteristics in postwar children of Dutch World War II victims: those seeking treatment as compared with their siblings. *Psychotherapy and Psychosomatics 66:* 268-275.

Morris, M. (2004). Healing and forgiveness. Available at: http://www.lovetakestime .com/art-healingandforgiveness.html. Retrieved March 15, 2005.

Morrison, D.P. (1991). Integrating consumerism into clinical care delivery: The role of the therapist. *Administration and Policy in Mental Health 19:* 103-119.

Muller, R.T., Goh, H.H., Lemieux, K.E., and S. Fish. (2000). The social supports of high-risk, formerly maltreated adults. *Canadian Journal of Behavioural Science 32:* 1-5.

Murphy, W.D., DiLillo, D., Haynes, M.R., and E. Steere. (2001). An exploration of factors related to deviant sexual arousal among juvenile sex offenders. *Sexual Abuse: A Journal of Research and Treatment 13:* 91-103.

Nader, K.O. (1998). Violence: Effects of parent's previous trauma on currently traumatized children. In Danieli, Y. (Ed.), *International handbook of multigenerational legacies of trauma* (pp. 571-587). New York: Plenum Press.

Nelson, B.S. and K.S. Wampler. (2000). Systemic effects of trauma in clnic couples: An exploratory study of secondary trauma resulting from childhood abuse. *Journal of Marital and Family Therapy 26:* 171-184.

Nelson, B.S. and D.W. Wright. (1996). Understanding and treating post-traumatic stress disorder symptoms in female partners of veterans with PTSD. *Journal of Marital and Family Therapy 22:* 455-467.

Nelson, E.C., Heath, A.C., Madden, P.A.F., Cooper, M.L., Dinwiddie, S.H., Bucholz, K.K., Glowinski, A., McLaughlin, T., Dunne, M.P., Statham, D.J., and N.G. Martin. (2000). Association between self-reported childhood sexual abuse and adverse psychosocial outcomes: Results from a twin study. *Archives of General Psychiatry 59:* 139-145.

Neumann, D.A. and S.J. Gamble. (1995). Issues in the professional development of psychotherapists: Countertransference and vicarious traumatization in the new trauma therapist. *Psychotherapy 32:* 341-347.

Newcomb, M.D. and T.F. Locke. (2001). Intergenerational cycle of maltreatment: A popular concept obscured by methodological limitations. *Child Abuse & Neglect 25:* 1219-1240.

Noll, J.G., Trickett, P.K., and F.W. Putnam. (2003). A prospective investigation of the impact of childhood sexual abuse on the development of sexuality. *Journal of Consulting and Clinical Psychology 71:* 575-586.

Norcross, J.C. (2000). Toward the delineation of empirically based principles in psychotherapy: Commentary on Beutler (2000). *Prevention & Treatment 3,* Article 28. Available at: www.journals.apa.org/pt/prevention/volume3/pre0030028c.html. Retrieved September 3, 2005.

Norcross, J.C., Strausser, D.J., and F.J. Faltus. (1988). The therapist's therapist. *American Journal of Psychotherapy 72:* 53-66.

Norris, D.M., Gutheil, T.G., and L.H. Strasburger. (2003). This couldn't happen to me: Boundary problems and sexual misconduct in the psychotherapy relationship. *Psychiatric Services 54:* 517-522.

Nuttall, R. and H. Jackson. (1994). Personal history of childhood abuse among clinicians. *Child Abuse and Neglect 18:* 455-472.

Nutter, D.E. and M.K. Condron. (1983). Sexual fantasy and activity patterns of females with inhibited sexual desire versus normal controls. *Journal of Sex & Marital Therapy 9:* 277-282.

Oates, R.K., Tebbutt, J., Swanston, H., Lynch, D.L., and B.I. O'Toole. (1998). Prior childhood sexual abuse in mothers of sexually abused children. *Child Abuse & Neglect 22:* 1113-1118.

Olarte, S.W. (2003). Personal disclosure revisited. *Journal of the American Academy of Psychoanalysis and Dynamic Psychiatry 31:* 599-607.

Oliver, J.E. (1993). Intergenerational transmission of child abuse: Rates, research, and clinical implications. *American Journal of Psychiatry 150:* 1315-1324.

Omaha, J. (2004). *Psychotherapeutic interventions for emotion regulation.* New York: W.W. Norton & Co.

Orchin, I. (2004). In consultation: The advantages of conducting therapy in the great outdoors. *Psychotherapy Networker 28:* 27-28.

Osvath, P., Vörös, V., and S. Fekete. (2004). Life events and psychopathology in a group of suicide attempters. *Psychopathology 37:* 36-40.

Oz, S. (2001). When the wife was sexually abused as a child: Marital relations before and during her therapy for abuse. *Sexual and Relationship Therapy 16:* 287-298.

Oz, S. (2002). Working with mothers and daughters when the daughter was sexually abused during her childhood. Lecture at workshop organized by the Tel Aviv and Jerusalem Rape Crisis Centers, November. Available at: http://www.machoneitan.org.il/mother.asp.

Oz, S. (2005). Gender and culture issues in helping survivors of child sexual abuse and violence. In Rabin, C.L. (Ed.), *Understanding gender and culture in the helping process: Practitioners' narratives from global perspectives* (pp. 84-97). Belmont CA: Thomson Wadsworth.

Oz, S. and M. Fine. (1988). A comparison of childhood backgrounds of teenage mothers and their nonmother peers: A new formulation. *Journal of Adolescence 11:* 251-261.

Oz, S. and R. Yahav. (2002). Therapy for clients sexually abused by a previous therapist. *Sichot 16:* 173-185. [In Hebrew.]

Packman, W.L., Marlitt, R.E., Bongar, B., and T. O'Connor Pennuto. (2004). A comprehensive and concise assessment of suicide risk. *Behavioral Sciences and the Law 22:* 667-680.

Paulus, L.A. (1997). *An investigation of "counterdissociation" phenomena in therapists treating sexual abuse survivors.* Unpublished doctoral dissertation. Antioch University, New England Graduate School, Keene, New Hampshire.

Pearlman, L.A. and K.W. Saakvitne. (1995). *Trauma and the therapist: Countertransference and vicarious traumatization in psychotherapy with incest survivors.* New York: W.W. Norton & Co.

Perry, B., Rollard, R.A., Blakley, T.L., Baker, W.L., and D. Vigilante. (1996). Childhood trauma, the neurobiology of adaptation and use-dependent developments of the brain: How states become traits. *Infant Mental Health Journal 16:* 271-291.

Pines, D. (1992). The impact of the Holocaust on the second generation. *Journal of Social Work and Policy in Israel 5-6:* 85-105.

Pinson, B. (2002). Touch in therapy: An effort to make the unknown known. *Journal of Contemporary Psychotherapy 32:* 179-196.

Pistorello, J. and V.M. Follette. (1998). Childhood sexual abuse and couples' relationship: Female survivors' reports in therapy groups. *Journal of Marital and Family Therapy 24:* 473-485.

Pope, K.S. (2003). Developing and practicing ethics. In Prinstein, M.J. and M. Patterson (Eds.), *The portable mentor: Expert guide to a successful career in psychology.* New York: Plenum Press.

Pope, K.S. and T.R. Bajt. (1988). When laws and values conflict: A dilemma for psychologists. *American Psychologist 43:* 828.

Pope, K.S. and V.A. Vetter. (1991). Prior therapist-patient sexual involvement among patients seen by psychologists. *Psychotherapy 28:* 429-438.

Prince, R.M. (1975). *The legacy of the Holocaust: Psychological themes in the second generation.* Ann Arbor, MI: Univerity of Michigan Research Press.

Prochaska, J.O. and J.C. Norcross. (2001). Stages of change. *Psychotherapy 38:* 443-448.

Quinn, J. (2003). Acknowledgement: The road to forgiveness. *Working Paper Series.* McMaster University Institute on Globalisation and the Human Condition. Available at: www.humanities.mcmaster.co/~global/wps/Quinn.pdf. Retrieved March 2005.

Reconciliation Australia. (2004). Australian declaration towards reconciliation. Available at: www.austlii.edu.au/au/other/IndigLRes/car/2000/12/pg3.htm. Retrieved April 2005.

Regehr, C. and S. Cadell. (1999). Secondary trauma in sexual assault crisis work: Implications for therapists and therapy. *Canadian Social Work 1:* 56-63.

Regehr, C. and T. Gutheil. (2002). Apology, justice, and trauma recovery. *Journal of the American Academy of Psychiatry & Law 30:* 425-430.

Reid, K.S., Wampler, R.S., and D.K. Taylor. (1996). The "alienated" partner: Responses to traditional therapies for adult sex abuse survivors. *Journal of Marital and Family Therapy 22:* 443-453.

Roberts, R., O'Connor, T., Dunn, J., Golding, J., and The ALSPAC Study Team. (2004). The effects of child sexual abuse in later family life: Mental health, parenting and adjustment of offspring. *Child Abuse & Neglect 28:* 525-545.

Rogala C, and T. Tyden. (2003). Does pornography influence young women's sexual behavior? *Women's Health Issues 13:* 39-43.

Rogers, B. (2005). The trap of forgiveness. Available at: www.alice-miller.com/sujet/art46a.htm. Retrieved March 2005.

Romans, S.E., Martin, J.M., Gendall, K., and G.P. Herbison. (2003). Age of menarche: The role of some psychosocial factors. *Psychological Medicine 33:* 933-939.

Roush, D.J. (1999). *A qualitative study of sex abuse survivors' experience of confronting the perpetrator.* Unpublished doctoral dissertation, Texas Tech University, Lubbock, Texas.

Rowland-Klein, D. and R. Dunlop. (1998). The transmission of trauma across generations: Identification with parental trauma in children of Holocaust survivors. *Australian and New Zealand Journal of Psychiatry 32:* 358-369.

Rubin, S.S. (2000). Differentiating multiple relationships from multiple dimensions of involvement: Therapeutic space at the interface of client, therapist, and society. *Psychotherapy 37:* 315-324.

Rubin, S.S. (2002). The multiple roles and relationships of ethical psychotherapy: Revisiting the ideal, the real, and the unethical. In Lazarus, A.A. and O. Zur (Eds.), *Dual relationships and psychotherapy* (pp. 98-112). New York: Springer.

Ruedenberg -Wright, L. (1997). The second and third generations: Where do we go from here? Presentation at the 29th Annual Conference of the Association for Jewish Studies, December 21-23, 1997, Boston, MA. Available at: http://lrw.net/percent7/Elucia/pub/ajs/. Retrieved March 30, 2005.

Ruscio, A.M. (2001). Predicting the child-rearing practies of mothers sexually abused in childhood. *Child Abuse & Neglect 25:* 369-387.

Rye, M.S., Pargament, K.I., Ali, M.A., Beck, G.L., Dorff, E.N., Hallisey, C., Narayanan, V., and J.G. Williams. (1999). Religious perspectives on forgiveness. In McCullough, M.E., Pargament, K.I., and C.E. Thoresen (Eds.), *Forgiveness, theory, research, and practice* (pp. 17-40). New York: The Guilford Press.

Saakvitne, K.W. (1991). Countertransference in psychotherapy with incest survivors: When the therapist is a survivor of child abuse. Paper presented at the APA Annual Convention, August 16-20, 1991, San Francisco CA.

Saakvitne, K.W. and Gamble, S.J. (2002). Risking connection with our clients: Implications for the current state of the therapeutic relationship. *Clinical Psychology: Science and Practice 9:* 439-443.

Safran, J.D., Muran, J.C., Samstag, L.W., and Stevens, C. (2001). Repairing alliance ruptures. *Psychotherapy 38:* 406-412.

Sagi-Schwartz, A., van Ijzendoorn, M.H., Joels, T., Grossmann, K., Scharf, M., Koren-Karie, N., and S. Alkalay. (2003). Attachment and traumatic stress in female Holocaust child survivors and their daughters. *American Journal of Psychiatry 160:* 1086-1092.

Salter, A. C. (1995). *Transforming trauma: A guide for understanding and treating adult survivors of child sexual abuse.* Thousand Oakes, CA: Sage Publications.

Saulny, S. (2005). Goodbye, therapist. Hello, anxiety? *The New York Times, January 9.* Available at: www.nytimes.com/2005/09/01/fashion/thursdaystyles/01THERAPY.html?ei=5070&en=86993043ff7a021&ex=1143435600&adxnnl=1&adxnnlx=1143303854-LBKvTHwrax985d6WiBXvjw. Retrieved September 2, 2005.

Scharff, J.S. and D.E. Scharff. (1994). *Object relations therapy of physical and sexual trauma.* Northvale, NJ: Jason Aronson Inc.

Schauben, L.J. and P.A. Frazier. (1995). Vicarious trauma: The effects on female counselors of working with sexual violence survivors. *Psychology of Women Quarterly 19:* 49-64.

Scheidt, C.E., Burger, T., Strukely, S., Hartmann, A., Fritzsche, K., and M. Wirsching. (2003). Treatment selection in private practice psychodynamic psychotherapy: A naturalistic prospective longitudinal study. *Psychotherapy Research 13:* 292-305.

Schmidt, U., Evena, K., Tiller, J., and J. Treasure. (1995). Puberty, sexual milestones and abuse: How are they related in eating disorder patients? *Psychological Medicine 25:* 413-417.

Schore, A.N. (2002). Dysregulation of the right brain: A fundamental mechanism of traumatic attachment and the psychopathogenesis of posttraumatic stress disorder. *Australian and New Zealand Journal of Psychiatry 36:* 9-30.

Schuetze, P. and R.D. Eiden. (2005). The relationship between sexual abuse during childhood and parenting outcomes: Modeling direct and indirect pathways. *Child Abuse & Neglect 29:* 645-659.

Seligman, M.E.P. (1995). The effectiveness of psychotherapy: The Consumer Reports study. *American Psychologist 50:* 965-974.

Seligman, Z. (2004). The witnessing process in incest trauma therapy: Reenactment and trauma resolution within transference and countertransference relationships.

In Seligman, Z. and Z. Solomon (Eds.), *Critical and clinical perspectives on incest* (pp. 240-256). Tel Aviv: Hakibbutz Hameuchad Publishing House Ltd. [In Hebrew.]

Serafin, J.M. (1996). Treating disrupted relationships: Couples therapy for female child sexual abuse survivors and their partners. *NCP Clinical Quarterly 6:* 42-45.

Sgroi, S.M., Blick, L.C., and F.S. Porter. (1982). A conceptual framework for child sexual abuse. In Sgroi, S.M. (Ed.), *Handbook of clinical intervention in child sexual abuse* (pp. 9-37). Lexington, MA: Lexington Books.

Shapiro, F. (1995). *Eye movement desensitization and reprocessing: Basic principles, protocols, and procedures.* New York: The Guilford Press.

Sholty, M.J., Ephorss, P.H., Plaut, M., Fischman, S.H., Charnas, J.F., and C.A. Cody. (1984). Female orgasmic experience: A subjective study. *Archives of Sexual Behavior 13:* 155-164.

Simon, R.I. (2001). Commentary: Treatment boundaries—flexible guidelines, not rigid standards. *Journal of the American Academy of Psychoatry & Law 29:* 287-289.

Simon, R.I. and I.C. Williams. (1999). Maintaining treatment boundaries in small communities and rural areas. *Psychiatric Services 50:* 1440-1446.

Simpson, P.E. and A. Fothergill. (2004). Challenging gender stereotypes in the counselling of adult survivors of childhood sexual abuse. *Journal of Psychiatric and Mental Health Nursing 11:* 589-594.

Somer, E. (2003). Mutual attempts to expand the therapy relationship: The wish for normalization or the slippery slope to exploitation? Lecture given to Psychiatric Department of the Sourasky Hospital (Ichilov), December 12, 2003, Tel Aviv, Israel. Available at: http://www.maytal.co.il/heb_articles/article_15.html. Retrieved March 2005. [In Hebrew.]

Sorscher, N. and L.J. Cohen. (1997). Trauma in children of Holocaust survivors: Transgenerational effects. *American Journal of Orthopsychiatry 67:* 493-500.

Stevens, M. and D.J. Higgins. (2002). The influence of risk and protective factors on burnout experienced by those who work with maltreated children. *Child Abuse Review 11:* 313-331.

Stoller, R.J. (1976). Sexual excitement. *Archives of General Psychiatry 33:* 899-909.

Strasburger, V.C. (1989). Adolescent sexuality and the media. *Pediatric Clinics of North America 36:* 747-773.

Sutton, J. (1999). *Healing the hurt within: Understand and relieve the suffering behind self-destructive behaviour.* Oxford, UK: How To Books.

Swanston, H.W., Tebbutt, J.S., O'Toole, B.I., and R.K. Oates. (1997). Sexually abused children 5 years after presentation: A case-control study. *Pediatrics 100:* 600-608.

Tauber, Y. (1998). *In the other chair: Holocaust survivors and the second generation as therapists and clients.* Jerusalem, Israel: Gefen Publishing House.

Trickett, P.K. and C. McBride-Chang. (1995). The developmental impact of different forms of child abuse and neglect. *Developmental Review 15:* 311-337.

Trudel, G. (2002). Sexuality and marital life: Results of a survey. *Journal of Sex & Marital Therapy 28:* 229-249.

Tutu, D. (1999). *No future without forgiveness.* New York: Doubleday.

van der Kolk, B. (1989). The compulsion to repeat the trauma: Re-enactment, revictimization, and masochism. *Psychiatric Clinics of North America 12:* 389-411.

van der Kolk, B. (1994). The body keeps the score: Memory and the evolving psychobiology of post traumatic stress. *Harvard Review of Psychiatry 1:* 253-265. Available at: http://www.trauma-pages.com/vanderk4.htm. Retrieved March 30, 2005.

Walker, R. and J.J. Clark. (1999). Heading off boundary problems: Clinical supervision as risk management. *Psychiatric Services 50:* 1435-1439.

Wardi, D. (1992). *Memorial candles: Children of the holocaust.* London: Routledge.

Warner, S. (1996). Constructing feminity: Models of child sexual abuse and the production of "woman." In Burman, E., Alldred, P., Bewley, C., Goldberg, B., Heenan, C., Marks, C., Marshall, J., Taylor, K., Ullah, R., and S. Warner (Eds.), *Challenging women: Psychology's exclusions, feminist possibilities* (pp. 36-53). Buckingham: Open University Press.

Watkins, J.G. and R.J. Johnson. (1982). *We, the divided self.* New York: Irvington Publications.

Way, I., VanDeusen, A.M., Martin, G., Applegate, B., and D. Jandle. (2004). Vicarious trauma: A comparison of clinicians who treat survivors of sexual abuse and sexual offenders. *Journal of Interpersonal Violence 19:* 49-71.

Weiss, M. and S. Weiss. (2000). Second generation to Holocaust survivors: Enhanced differentiation of trauma transmission. *American Journal of Psychotherapy 54:* 372-384.

Westerlund, E. (1992). *Women's sexuality after childhood incest.* New York: W.W. Norton & Co.

Williams, M.H. (1997). Boundary violations: Do some contended standards of care fail to encompass commonplace procedures of humanistic, behavioral and eclectic psychotherapies? *Psychotherapy 34:* 239-249.

Winnicott, D.W. (1960). Ego distortions in terms of true and false self. In Winnicott, D.W. (Ed.), *The maturational processes and the facilitating environment* (pp. 140-152). London: Hogarth Press.

Witvliet, C.V.O., Ludwig, T.E., and K.L. van der Laan. (2001). Granting forgiveness or harboring grudges: Implications for emotion, physiology, and health. *Psychological Science 121:* 117-123.

Wood, C., Welman, M., and L. Netto. (2000). A profile of young sex offenders in South Africa. *Journal of Child and Adolescent Mental Health 12:* 45-58.

Wyatt, G.E. and S.D. Peters. (1986). Issues in the definition of child sexual abuse in prevalence research. *Child Abuse & Neglect 10:* 231-240.

Yahav, R. and S. Oz. (2005). The relevance of psychodynamic psychotherapy to understanding therapist-patient sexual abuse and treatment of survivors. *Journal of the American Academy of Psychoanalysis & Dynamic Psychiatry 34:* in press.

Yalom, I.D. and G. Elkin. (1990). *Every day gets a little closer: A twice told therapy.* New York: Basic Books.

Yang, B. and G.A. Clum. (1996). Effects of early negative life experiences on cognitive functioning and risk for suicide: A review. *Clinical Psychology Review 16:* 177-195.

Yehuda, R., Bierer, L.M., Schmeidler, J., Aferiat, D.H., Breslau, I. and S. Dolan. (2001). Low cortisol and risk for PTSD in adult offspring of Holocaust survivors. *American Journal of Psychiatry 157:* 1252-1259.

Yehuda, R., Schmeidler, J., Wainber, M., Binder-Brynes, K., and T. Duvdevani. (1998). Vulnerability to posttraumatic stress disorder in adult offspring of Holocaust survivors. *American Journal of Psychiatry 155:* 1163-1171.

Younggren, J.N. (2002). Ethical decision-making and dual relationships. Available at: www.kspope.com/dual/younggren.php#contentarea. Retrieved February 2005.

Zechmeister, J.S. and C. Romero. (2002). Victim and offender accounts of interpersonal conflict: Autobiographical narratives of forgiveness and unforgiveness. *Journal of Personality and Social Psychology 82:* 675-686.

Zur, O. (2001). Out-of-office experience: When crossing office boundaries and engaging in dual relationships are clinically beneficial and ethically sound. *Independent Practitioner 21:* 96-100.

Zur, O. (2002). How consensus regarding the prohibition of dual relationships has been contrived. In Lazarus, A.A. and O. Zur (Eds.), *Dual relationships and psychotherapy* (pp. 449-462). New York: Springer.

Zur, O. and N. Nordmarken. (2004). To touch or not to touch: Rethinking the prohibition on touch in psychotherapy and counseling. Clinical, ethical and legal considerations. Available at: http://www.drozur.com/touchintherapy.html. Retrieved April 2005.

Zuravin, S.J. and C. Fontanella. (1999). Parenting behaviors and perceived parenting competence of child sex abuse survivors. *Child Abuse & Neglect 23:* 623-632.

Index

Overcoming Childhood Sexual Trauma
Published by The Haworth Press, Inc., 2006, All rights reserved.
doi:10.1300/5668_15

Order a copy of this book with this form or online at:

http://www.haworthpress.com/store/product.asp?sku=5668

OVERCOMING CHILDHOOD SEXUAL TRAUMA
A Guide to Breaking Through the Wall of Fear
for Practitioners and Survivors

_____in hardbound at $59.95 (ISBN-13: 978-0-7890-2979-9; ISBN-10: 0-7890-2979-0)

_____in softbound at $34.95 (ISBN-13: 978-0-7890-2980-5; ISBN-10: 0-7890-2980-4)

296 pages plus index • Includes illustrations

Or order online and use special offer code HEC25 in the shopping cart.

COST OF BOOKS_____	☐ **BILL ME LATER:** (Bill-me option is good on US/Canada/Mexico orders only; not good to jobbers, wholesalers, or subscription agencies.)
	☐ Check here if billing address is different from
POSTAGE & HANDLING_____	shipping address and attach purchase order and
(US: $4.00 for first book & $1.50	billing address information.
for each additional book)	
(Outside US: $5.00 for first book	Signature_____
& $2.00 for each additional book)	
SUBTOTAL_____	☐ **PAYMENT ENCLOSED: $**_____
IN CANADA: ADD 6% GST_____	☐ **PLEASE CHARGE TO MY CREDIT CARD.**
STATE TAX_____	☐ Visa ☐ MasterCard ☐ AmEx ☐ Discover
(NJ, NY, OH, MN, CA, IL, IN, PA, & SD	☐ Diner's Club ☐ Eurocard ☐ JCB
residents, add appropriate local sales tax)	Account # _____
FINAL TOTAL_____	
(If paying in Canadian funds,	Exp. Date_____
convert using the current	
exchange rate, UNESCO	Signature_____
coupons welcome)	

Prices in US dollars and subject to change without notice.

NAME_____

INSTITUTION_____

ADDRESS_____

CITY_____

STATE/ZIP_____

COUNTRY_____ COUNTY (NY residents only)_____

TEL_____ FAX_____

E-MAIL_____

May we use your e-mail address for confirmations and other types of information? ☐ Yes ☐ No
We appreciate receiving your e-mail address and fax number. Haworth would like to e-mail or fax special
discount offers to you, as a preferred customer. **We will never share, rent, or exchange your e-mail address
or fax number.** We regard such actions as an invasion of your privacy.

Order From Your Local Bookstore or Directly From

The Haworth Press, Inc.

10 Alice Street, Binghamton, New York 13904-1580 • USA
TELEPHONE: 1-800-HAWORTH (1-800-429-6784) / Outside US/Canada: (607) 722-5857
FAX: 1-800-895-0582 / Outside US/Canada: (607) 771-0012
E-mail to: orders@haworthpress.com

For orders outside US and Canada, you may wish to order through your local
sales representative, distributor, or bookseller.
For information, see http://haworthpress.com/distributors

(Discounts are available for individual orders in US and Canada only, not booksellers/distributors.)

PLEASE PHOTOCOPY THIS FORM FOR YOUR PERSONAL USE.

http://www.HaworthPress.com